Twenty Years of Hippocampus Press

Twenty Years of Hippocampus Press

2000–2020

Derrick Hussey, S. T. Joshi, and David E. Schultz

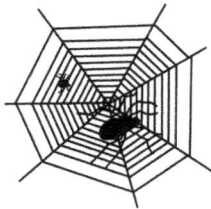

Hippocampus Press

New York

Published by Hippocampus Press
P.O. Box 641, New York, NY 10156
www.hippocampuspress.com

Cover illustration and design by Daniel V. Sauer, dansauerdesign.com
Hippocampus Press logo designed by Anastasia Damianakos.

ISBN 978-1-61498-319-4 paperback
ISBN 978-1-61498-321-7 ebook

Foreword

Derrick Hussey

Ten years ago, as Hippocampus Press entered its second decade, I remarked that one measure of our success was the ability to continue our activities and to increase both the size and number of our projects. Now, at twenty years of Hippocampus Press, it is gratifying to look back and acknowledge that we have fulfilled these criteria. Although our rate of publication has mercifully leveled off at around 25 publications per year, the page counts of the books themselves seem to be growing apace, so that the heft of a 500 page tome is barely remarkable nowadays. Additionally, we have largely stayed true to our vision, which was to publish editions of surpassing interest and utility to Lovecraftians the world over, without undue concern over the appeal of these titles to the greater book-buying public. We are Lovecraft specialists who publish books with our fellow enthusiasts in mind. H. P. Lovecraft's legacy is, of course, immutable; we are proud to have contributed thereto. From modest beginnings, we have released under our own imprint in very accurate editions an array of titles which, astoundingly, includes all the canonical fiction, nonfiction, and verse written by H. P. Lovecraft, together with a growing number of annotated editions of his letters, as well as a wide range of other material. For our efforts, we have earned the Horror Writers Association's Specialty Press Award, and the Robert E. Howard Foundation's Black River–Special Achievement Award. In 2014, *Publishers Weekly* proclaimed us "the world's leading publisher of books related to horror writer H. P. Lovecraft."

In 2017 we first welcomed Dan Sauer onboard; often providing his own phantasmagorical artwork as well as design, Dan's skill and inspiration have led him to become a star at Hippocampus. The rest of our core team, happily, is still intact. Barbara Silbert, Anastasia, and I are still in New York; David E. Schultz is in Milwaukee; and S. T. Joshi is in Seattle. A few words about these last two. Mr. Schultz, in addition to his almost fathomless knowledge and insight into Lovecraft, is a meticulous and creative designer, without whom we would be lost at sea. It has been a thrill to shepherd some of his long anticipated projects into print, including a critical edition of *The Book of Jade*, the annotated edition of *Fungi from Yuggoth*, and in 2020 the Leah Bodine Drake omnibus, *The Song of the Sun*. Mr. Joshi, of course, remains an unflagging engine of productivity and brilliance. His energies propel, not only Hippocampus Press, but the entire world of Lovecraft. It is truly a prize beyond price to work so closely with these gentlemen, and to count them as friends.

One very welcome byproduct of longevity as a press is the opportunity to see the field develop, as new stars ignite and burn brightly. The past five years has witnessed our publication of original fiction by Michael Cisco, John Langan, Jeffrey Thomas, and Stephen Woodworth, among others. Here I must also mention a succession of talented young men: the Hippocampus interns. To date the roster comprises Dejan Ognjanovic, who has gone on to edit an edition of Lovecraft's tales in his native Serbia, and other books; Michael J. Abolafia, now coeditor (with Alex Houstoun) of *Dead Reckonings* and (with David E. Schultz) of item 157 below; and Alex Lugo, now an occasional contributor to *Dead Reckonings*. In addition, several proofreaders deserve mention for their meticulous work: Martin Andersson, Torin Mizenko, and Jesse Clark Tucker. Jordan Smith is in a category by himself; starting as an intern, he has advanced to the role of editorial assistant, superbly accomplishing a variety of duties including publicity and research. Although we continue to use established Lovecraftian artists for our book covers, including Jason C. Eckhardt, David Verba, and Jason Van Hollander, we have also engaged newer talents, such as Aeron Alfrey, Samuel Araya, and Kim Bo Yung, seeking to develop a new visual vocabulary for cosmic horror beyond the traditional (perhaps somewhat overfamiliar) iconography associated with Lovecraft. It is not much of a stretch to draw a parallel between the upswing of modern Lovecraftian art and that resurgence in quality of modern Lovecraftian literary productions that impelled S. T. Joshi to revise and retitle his overview of the Cthulhu Mythos (item 165).

Hippocampus Press does not operate in a vacuum, but rather as part of a larger biocosm of readers, writers, artists, and editors, from which a community is formed. A word about our periodicals line is in order. At present we publish five periodicals, with some of them appearing twice per year. Let us set aside the challenges of issuing print journals in the digital age. With submissions arriving from around the world, these publications often occupy a liminal space between "real books" and mere magazines, and are the most kinetic of our offerings.

Finally, it has been of real satisfaction to aid in the development of scholarly resources at institutions around the country to benefit Lovecraftians now and in the future. Hippocampus Press has been significantly involved in the establishment of three endowed research fellowships: the S. T. Joshi Endowed Research Fellowship for H. P. Lovecraft at the John Hay Library, Brown University; the Donald Sidney-Fryer Research Fellowship for Clark Ashton Smith, George Sterling, Ambrose Bierce, and their Literary Circle at the Bancroft Library, UC–Berkeley; and the Hippocampus Press Endowed Robert E. Howard Fellowship at the Harry Ransom Center, UT–Austin. The long-overdue cataloguing and conservation of the C. W. "Tryout" Smith archive of amateur journals at the New York Public Library was completed at our behest; we were also involved in erecting a headstone for Tryout Smith himself in

Haverhill, MA. In 2018, we assisted in organizing the R. H. Barlow Centennial Celebration at the John Hay Library. Doubtless more such projects will emerge in due course of time.

I remain grateful to have been afforded the opportunity to work with all the fine people and agencies mentioned above, together with many other authors and editors; artists, printers, and booksellers; agencies and estates; for the benefit of our readers worldwide. In a blind cosmos, if such we truly inhabit, such a convergence of talent, inspiration, and enthusiasm is fortuitous indeed.

My Years with Hippocampus Press

S. T. Joshi

I t must have been sometime in 1999 when, at a dinner of the "New Kalem Club"—an informal group of Lovecraft devotees who gathered at O'Reilly's Irish Pub on 31st Street in Manhattan once a month or so to shoot the bull and down a pint of Guinness (some of the more faint-hearted members settled for Bass Ale)—that I leaned over to Derrick Hussey and said, "How'd you like to start a new small press?"

I will be frank: my purpose was in some sense self-serving. Marc Michaud's Necronomicon Press was undergoing a certain turmoil because of Marc's personal difficulties, and I felt the need for another small press to take up the slack. By that time, my horizons had expanded from the narrow world of Lovecraft scholarship to the broader study of weird fiction, and I felt that a press that could take advantage of the burgeoning interest in Lovecraft and other weird writers, both "classic" and modern, could serve an important purpose.

Back in 1999, a number of needs in the study of Lovecraft were still unmet. His collected poetry had not been issued (I had prepared such an edition, initially scheduled for publication by Arkham House, then by Necronomicon Press, and finally released by Night Shade Books in 2001), his collected essays had not been assembled, his immense body of letters remained largely unpublished; and, of course, there was the ongoing need to advance Lovecraft scholarship—a task that was being hindered by the virtual cessation of the flagship journal in the field, *Lovecraft Studies*. (Over the next several years, a few more issues of *Lovecraft Studies* did appear—one published by Hippocampus Press—but the journal finally collapsed in 2004.)

In addition, there remained many significant works of weird fiction—both novels and collections of stories—whose intrinsic merit, and whose influence upon Lovecraft's own work, demanded their reprinting. Although such publishers as Ash-Tree Press and Tartarus Press were then engaging in a course of reprinting many weird classics, these were for the most part in the tradition of the Victorian ghost story, which did not influence Lovecraft significantly and therefore would not have any direct appeal to Lovecraftians. (Tartarus Press began as an imprint for restoring the work of Arthur Machen into print.) So the outlook for a new press seemed bright.

In fact, I recall mentioning to Derrick, "If you begin a press, I can guarantee that I myself can supply you with enough titles to keep it operating indefinitely." This was not spoken out of arrogance, or for the purpose of making

9

Hippocampus Press a private imprint of my own; it was simply a recognition that the press could fill a niche in the realm of small-press publishing that was currently not being met by other imprints, and that, after twenty or more years of research, I was in a position to prepare editions of Lovecraft and other writers that could keep a small press busy for years. Whether such a press could actually keep afloat financially by issuing such editions was a question for another day.

Derrick, who had recently left a position at the New York office of Routledge and seemed to be looking for something to fill up his time, readily assented. I was aware that he had a certain modicum of capital behind him—an essential requirement for a small press, since it was unlikely that our first several titles would be blockbusters. As our first title, I offered my extensively annotated edition of *Supernatural Horror in Literature*—an edition that had actually been assembled all the way back in 1981 (based on an initial expression of interest by Greenwood Press that was subsequently withdrawn). My friend and colleague David E. Schultz had done a preliminary layout of the book, for the purpose of estimating how big it might be, and Derrick felt satisfied that the result was a book worth publishing. So the first Hippocampus Press title slipped unobtrusively into print in the year 2000.

My recollection is that the book was fairly well received; I have no figures on how well it sold, but it did eventually get reprinted. It took us a full year to prepare another volume for the press, and this too was a book that had long been delayed—an annotated edition of the corrected text of Lovecraft's "The Shadow out of Time." The spectacular discovery of Lovecraft's original manuscript, among the effects of a woman in Hawaii, created a furore in 1994. I was the first scholar to be allowed access to the manuscript, and in February of 1994 I prepared a corrected text; but that text sat for years while legal and other difficulties were resolved.

Since then, Hippocampus Press has published books on a seemingly wide array of subjects, but I believe most or all of them can boil down to a few broad rubrics: 1) material by or about H. P. Lovecraft; 2) material by Lovecraft's friends and colleagues; 3) material that may have influenced Lovecraft; and 4) original work by leading authors of weird fiction or by promising newcomers.

It was not long after the publication of the first two Hippocampus titles that I broached the subject of publishing Lovecraft's collected essays. There still remained a few essays by Lovecraft that had not been published at all, while many others were scattered in a multitude of small-press volumes. The framework of what became the five-volume *Collected Essays* (2004–06) was suggested by my edition of Lovecraft's *Miscellaneous Writings* (Arkham House, 1995), where a topical or thematic division of the essays was presented, rather than a strictly chronological arrangement. And yet, this division itself was based upon a provisional arrangement of Lovecraft's complete works that I had devised as early as 1980, as I was working on the first edition of my bibliography of Lovecraft (1981). In that sense, the *Collected Essays* constitutes virtually the final instalment of what I had then envisioned as a 13-volume *Collected Works of H. P. Lovecraft*. More recently, the press's issuance of David E. Schultz's landmark annotated edition of *Fungi from Yuggoth* (2017), a project on which the editor had been working for decades, constituted both a signal advance in scholarship and a pinnacle in book production, with its distinctive green ink and illustrations of every single sonnet by veteran artist Jason C. Eckhardt.

Of course, the last frontier in the publication of Lovecraft's work is his letters. Necronomicon Press had made a start by issuing batches of letters to individual correspondents (Henry Kuttner, Richard F. Searight, Samuel Loveman and Vincent Starrett, Robert Bloch) in the early 1990s, and Hippocampus Press followed up that program by publishing the letters to Alfred Galpin (2003) and Rheinhart Kleiner (2005), edited by David E. Schultz and myself. At that point our horizons expanded, and we wondered whether the entirety of Lovecraft's letters could be issued in book form (as opposed to electronically), with exhaustive annotations. Our first venture in this regard was the massive two-volume edition of Lovecraft's letters to August Derleth (2008), followed—after years of legal and logistical difficulties—with the even more massive two-volume edition of Lovecraft's letters to Robert E. Howard (2009). These titles, in effect, constitute the first four volumes of what promise to be approximately 25 volumes of Lovecraft letters. We have now issued more than a dozen volumes, including an enormous compendium of the joint correspondence of Lovecraft and Clark Ashton Smith.

Mention of Smith brings to mind that we have engaged in substantial work in Smith studies. My edition of Smith's juvenile novel, *The Black Diamonds* (2002), was again based on work that had been done years ago: in 1979–81, Marc Michaud and I had catalogued Smith's papers and manuscripts for the John Hay Library of Brown University, and among those papers was *The Black Diamonds*. The manuscript was a fearful mess, and it took me some time to ascertain that it constituted a full version (minus a few pages) of the first draft and several short attempts at subsequent drafts (these drafts have not been published); it took still more time to decipher Smith's youthful chirography and transcribe the text. After the book was issued, Dr. W. C. Farmer, a late colleague of Smith's, announced that he had the two missing pages of the manuscript, along with another, somewhat shorter juvenile novel, *The Sword of Zagan*, as well as other material. These texts were issued in 2004. We also issued Smith's *The Last Oblivion* (2002), a selection of his best fantastic poetry, which set the stage for the three-volume edition of Smith's *Complete Poems and Translations* (2007–08), an edition that David E. Schultz had been working on since the 1980s. We also published a noteworthy collection of articles about Smith, *The Freedom of Fantastic Things* (2006), edited by Scott Connors, as well as the joint correspondence of Smith and August Derleth, and also Smith and Samuel Loveman. An exhaustive bibliography of Smith came out in 2020.

Lovecraft's other colleagues have fared well at Hippocampus Press, with editions of the writings of R. H. Barlow (2002), Samuel Loveman (2004), Donald Wandrei (*Sanctity and Sin* [2008], an expansion of Wandrei's *Collected Poems* [Necronomicon Press, 1988]), Edith Miniter (2008), and a number of others. Expanded editions of some of these volumes have appeared or will soon appear. Hippocampus publications of George Sterling, the California poet who was the early mentor of Clark Ashton Smith, are a result of my own devoted interest in this much-neglected writer. I was pleased to issue a volume of Sterling's weird verse, *The Thirst of Satan* (2003), which set the stage for the massive three-volume edition of Sterling's collected poetry and verse drama that appeared in 2013. Schultz and I also edited the joint correspondence of Sterling and Smith (*The Shadow of the Unattained*, 2005).

Scholarship on Lovecraft has been enhanced by the re-establishment of a journal devoted to his life and work, the *Lovecraft Annual* (2007f.), as well as volumes of critical essays by Robert H. Waugh, Donald R. Burleson, myself, and others. Hippocampus also reprinted *An Epicure in the Terrible: A Centennial Anthology of Essays in Honor of H. P. Lovecraft* (2011), a significant collection of essays that first appeared in 1991. Kenneth W. Faig, Jr.'s *The Unknown Lovecraft* (2009) will, I hope, finally bring recognition to this pioneering Lovecraft scholar for the invaluable work he has done over the past thirty years or more. Faig's *Lovecraftian Voyages*, a treatise he wrote in the 1970s, was issued in 2017 as an important historical document.

The NecronomiCon convention of 2013, which attracted an unprecedented 1200 devotees to the Biltmore Hotel in Providence, R.I., set the stage for a number of significant publications relating to Lovecraft, including those by David Goudsward and Steven J. Mariconda, and an extensively revised version of my edition of Lovecraft's collected poetry, *The Ancient Track*. Even some works of Lovecraftian fiction, from Kenneth W. Faig, Jr.'s *Lovecraft's Pillow* to my whimsical novel *The Assaults of Chaos*, graced the dealer's tables at the convention. Over the years, three volumes of papers from the Armitage Symposium of the NecronomiCon have been published, featuring cutting-edge scholarship on all aspects of Lovecraft's life and work.

The fostering of scholarship has been an important objective at Hippocampus Press. We are well aware that there are fewer and fewer outlets for the study of weird fiction, as many academic publishers that formerly published this material are now cutting back in the wake of budget cuts. Benjamin Szumskyj's admirable anthology of essays on Robert E. Howard (2006), along with several of my own volumes, culminating in *Lovecraft and a World in Transition: Collected Essays on H. P. Lovecraft* (2014), have been generally well received. I was pleased to lend some assistance to Rosemary Pardoe in a splendid volume of criticism of M. R. James, *Warnings to the Curious* (2007). Gary William Crawford, Jim Rockhill, and Brian J. Showers edited an exemplary collection of essays on J. Sheridan Le Fanu (2011); and a volume on Arthur Machen was published in 2019. William F. Nolan's *Nolan on Bradbury* (2013), a compilation of more than sixty years of the author's writings on the California author of fantasy and science fiction, won a Bram Stoker Award. Massimo Berruti and others assembled the first full-length volume of critical essays on William Hope Hodgson (2014).

In a somewhat related vein, our founding of *Dead Reckonings* (2007f.), a review journal devoted to weird fiction—based in large part upon the successful *Necrofile* (1991–99), issued by Necronomicon Press—has resulted in substantive analysis of contemporary work in the field. It has gone through several editors, and is currently in the capable hands of Alex Houstoun and Michael J. Abolafia.

The press has also done important work in another area of weird fiction that tends to be given short shrift—weird poetry. The volumes by Barlow, Loveman, and Wandrei, cited above, contain substantial amounts of poetry, and the publication of Nora May French's collected poetry (2009) connects with the press's interest in Smith and Sterling. *Dreams of Fear: Poetry of Terror and the Supernatural* (2013) is the most exhaustive historical anthology of weird poetry since August Derleth's *Dark of the Moon* (1947), and the long-awaited edition of Park Barnitz's *The Book of Jade* (2015) was augmented with much biographical and critical information on the little-known poet. The pinnacle of this trend is David E. Schultz's exhaustive edition of the writings of Leah Bodine Drake (2020).

The press's first work of original creative writing was R. Nemo Hill's *The Strange Music of Erich Zann* (2004), a poetic extrapolation from Lovecraft's "The Music of Erich Zann." The publication of Donald Sidney-Fryer's immense *Atlantis Fragments* (2008)—a compendium of his three volumes of *Songs and Sonnets Atlantean*, some of the finest weird poetry and prose-poetry written since the heyday of Clark Ashton Smith—represents the culmination of Sidney-Fryer's illustrious career as a creative artist. Volumes of original poetry by Ann K. Schwader, Wade German, K. A. Opperman, Michael Fantina, Ashley Dioses, Fred Phillips, and D. L. Myers have generated considerable interest among devotees of this genre.

In 2014 Hippocampus initiated the biennial journal *Spectral Realms* for the publication of original weird poetry along with selected "classic" reprints as well as articles and reviews on weird poetry; the journal has proven to be spectacularly popular (among poets, at any rate), in large part due to its exquisite production values.

The publication of my revised edition of *Lovecraft's Library: A Catalogue* (2002)—a third edition appeared in 2012, and a fourth edition in 2017—may have triggered the "Lovecraft's Library" series, in which novels and tales that inspired Lovecraft, or in some cases were simply appreciated by him, are reprinted. The series was initiated even before the publication of *Lovecraft's Library* by Stefan Dziemianowicz's edition of A. Merritt's *The Metal Monster* (2002), but got underway in earnest with the issuance of Herbert Gorman's *The Place Called Dagon* (2003). In 2007 we released the first Hippocampus Press "double," an imitation of the format of the old "Ace doubles," where two novels were printed in one book. In this way, several short novels could be issued together, since there still remain numerous titles that Lovecraftians will wish to read for their possible influence on Lovecraft's seminal tales.

In recent years, the press has branched out to cover the leading figures of weird fiction from the nineteenth and early twentieth centuries. Most impressive in this regard has been a three-volume edition of Arthur Machen's *Collected Fiction* (2019). A similar set of Ambrose Bierce's fiction appeared in 2020. The press has also begun to issue a series of volumes, Classics of Gothic Fiction, presenting the complete weird writings of such authors as Mary E. Wilkins Freeman, W. W. Jacobs, and several others. Lord Dunsany has been an important focus, with the issuance of a previously unpublished novel, *The Pleasures of a Futuroscope* (2007), along with a collection of uncollected and unpublished short fiction.

The most exciting development at Hippocampus Press—and one that we never envisioned when we first began the press—was the issuance of new creative work by leading contemporary writers and promising new voices. As mentioned, R. Nemo Hill's booklet was our first such venture, but the program gathered steam with the issuance of *The Fungal Stain and Other Dreams* (2006), by W. H. Pugmire, a writer whose Lovecraftian-related work I have long admired, and who has now sadly departed this life. We have subsequently published distinguished work by both veterans (Ramsey Campbell, Donald R. Burleson) and newcomers (Philip Haldeman, Jonathan Thomas, Joseph S. Pulver, Sr., Michael Aronovitz).

More recently, Hippocampus has issued important new volumes by Richard Gavin, John Langan, Jason V Brock, Simon Strantzas, Clint Smith, Rhys Hughes, Don Swaim, Sam Gafford, Matt Cardin, Michael Cisco, and Mark Samuels. We are thrilled that most of these volumes have been well received by critics and readers. Our promotion of noteworthy contributions to Lovecraft's "Cthulhu Mythos" began with Robert M. Price's edition of *Tales out of Dunwich* (2005) and continued through Franklyn Searight's *Lair of the Dreamer* (2007), a trio of novels by Adam Niswander, and collections by Don Webb, Cody Goodfellow, Lois H. Gresh, and John Shirley.

The second NecronomiCon convention, held in Providence, R.I., in the summer of 2015, triggered the publication of what might be the crowning jewel in the entire Hippocampus line: H. P. Lovecraft's *Collected Fiction: A Variorum*

Edition. This edition, whose initial work I had begun as a freshman at Brown University in the fall of 1976, was a fully collaborative venture between myself and the two other chief editorial figures at Hippocampus, Derrick Hussey (who meticulously checked the texts of Lovecraft's stories as well as my thousands of textual notes, catching many errors in the process) and David E. Schultz, who not only lent his exhaustive knowledge of Lovecraft to many phases of the venture but applied his formidable skills in design and layout to a work of particular difficulty in terms of formatting. With this edition, Hippocampus completes its publication of the definitive editions of Lovecraft's fiction, essays, and poetry—and with the ongoing publication of Lovecraft's complete surviving correspondence, there will come a day when every word of H. P. Lovecraft's work is available in accurate Hippocampus Press editions.

As Hippocampus Press continues its publications in its several different lines—ranging from my two-volume biography, *I Am Providence: The Life and Times of H. P. Lovecraft* (2010), to original fiction by Jonathan Thomas and others, verse by a multitude of poets old and new, continuing editions of Lovecraft's letters, and much other work—I think it can safely be said that the press has established itself as one of the most vital imprints in the field of weird fiction, and can look forward to many years of critical success. But it is the devotion of its many readers that will carry the press into the future, and we hope to continue earning that devotion by the publications we hope to issue in the coming years.

Publications of Hippocampus Press
2000–2020

1.   H. P. LOVECRAFT. *The Annotated Supernatural Horror in Literature*. Edited by S. T. Joshi. 2000 (rpt. 2004). 172 pp. tpb.

    Contents. Preface; Introduction; Supernatural Horror in Literature, by H. P. Lovecraft; Appendix: The Favorite Weird Stories of H P. Lovecraft; Notes; Bibliography of Authors and Works; Index.

    Notes. Cover illustration by Vrest Orton from the *Recluse* 1 (1927). First printing, 1000 copies plus unspecified overrun, Morris Publishing, Kearney, NE. Rpt November 2004 as a print-on-demand (POD) book. A work Joshi compiled as early as 1981 but for which he could not find a publisher. The text of Lovecraft's essay has been printed accurately here for the first time, as Joshi has collated all previous publications, including the original publication in the *Recluse* (1927) and the serialization in the *Fantasy Fan* (1933–35). Joshi has added extensive commentary and a substantial primary and secondary bibliography for all authors and works discussed in the treatise. A new and updated edition appeared in 2012 (see item 101).

2.   H. P. LOVECRAFT. *The Shadow out of Time.* Edited by S. T. Joshi and David E. Schultz. 2001 (rpt. 2003). 136 pp. tpb.

    Contents. Introduction; The Shadow out of Time, by H. P. Lovecraft; APPENDIX: Notes to "The Shadow out of Time"; Early draft; Notes; Textual Notes.

    Notes. Cover illustration by Howard V. Brown. First printing, 1000 copies plus unspecified overrun; Morris Publishing. Reprint issued simultaneously in 2003 with two competing POD companies, Booksurge and Lightning Source, to compare quality and service. Booksurge POD edition was taken out of print sometime later, and only a handful of this variant state were circulated. Booksurge edition distinguished by matte finish on cover; Lightning Source paperback has a glossy finish on cover. Lightning Source POD and Morris Publishing editions were available simultaneously for a time.

    A landmark publication of the original ms. of Lovecraft's story, which was believed lost until it surfaced in 1994. Joshi was the first scholar to be allowed to consult the text, which he did in February 1994;

but various logistical delays prevented the publication of the edition until 2001. The text, which contains at least 400 textual corrections from the minimally corrected edition in *The Dunwich Horror and Others* (Arkham House, 1984), is exhaustively annotated, with textual variants and a discussion of the finding of the ms. by John H. Stanley, a curator at the John Hay Library, Brown University.

3. *Studies in Weird Fiction* No. 25 (Summer 2001). EDITED BY S. T. JOSHI. 40 pp.

Contents. From Haunted Rose Gardens to Lurking Wendigos: Liminal and Wild Places in M. R. James and Algernon Blackwood, by Linda J. Holland-Toll; Hawthorne, Hitchcock, and the Fine Women of *Blithedale* and *Psycho*, by Marilyn Knight; Gesturing toward the Infinite: Clark Ashton Smith and Modernism, by Scott Connors; The Weird Verse of Christopher Brennan, by Phillip A. Ellis; Things from the Sea: The Early Weird Fiction of Frank Belknap Long, by S. T. Joshi; Correspondence.

Notes. Cover illustration by Robert H. Knox. Back cover photograph of Clark Ashton Smith in 1912 by Bianca Conti. Two hundred copies plus unspecified overrun. A long-delayed issue of a magazine first published (1986f.) by Necronomicon Press. Awkwardly, Necronomicon Press itself issued its own No. 25 (Summer 2003), followed by the final issue, No. 27 (Spring 2005).

4. *Lovecraft Studies* Nos. 42–43 (Autumn 2001). EDITED BY S. T. JOSHI. 76 pp.

Contents. Editorial; The Book, by H. P. Lovecraft; The Book of "The Book," by Michael Cisco; H. P. Lovecraft: Reluctant American Modernist, by Steven J. Mariconda; H. P. Lovecraft in Florida, by Stephen J. Jordan; Antique Dreams: Marblehead and Lovecraft's Kingsport, by Donovan K. Loucks; A Note on "The Book," by Donald R. Burleson; The Problem with Solving: Implications for Sherlock Holmes and Lovecraft Narrators, by Deborah D'Agati; The Lurker at the Threshold of Interpretation: Hoax *Necronomicons* and Paratextual Noise by Dan Clore; The Mirror in the House: Looking at the Horror of Looking at the Horror, by P. S. Owens; Review.

Notes. Cover illustration by Jason C. Eckhardt. Two hundred copies plus unspecified overrun. Another long-delayed issue of a journal first published (1979f.) by Necronomicon Press. The latter published two further issues, No. 44 (2004) and No. 45 (Spring 2005). The journal was succeeded by the *Lovecraft Annual* (items 44ff).

5.   CLARK ASHTON SMITH. *The Black Diamonds.* Edited by S. T. Joshi. 2002 (rpt. 2004). 181 pp. tpb.

Notes. Cover and interior illustrations by Jason C. Eckhardt. First printing, 1040 copies: Morris Publishing. A transcript of Smith's juvenile novel, probably written at the age of 14 (i.e., c. 1907). The ms. consists of nearly 246 pp. of foolscap sheets that had been sent to the John Hay Library of Brown University in 1979–80 by Smith's literary executor as part of the Clark Ashton Smith Papers there. Joshi began transcribing the text at that time but did not finish until years later. The ms. is missing two sheets; shortly after publication, Dr. W. C. Farmer (see item 17) located them in his effects, and they were made available for transcription. The new printing (184 pp.) incorporates the missing text.

6.   A. MERRITT. *The Metal Monster.* Edited by Stefan Dziemian-owicz. 2002. 237 pp. tpb.

Notes. Cover illustration by Virgil Finlay. First printing, 1050 copies: Morris Publishing. The first reprint of the 1920 *Argosy All-Story Weekly* serialization of the novel, one of three different texts of the work that appeared in Merritt's lifetime. This is the first title in the "Lovecraft's Library" series, which reprints texts that Lovecraft read and was influenced by. Lovecraft read the text in 1934, when it was lent to him by R. H. Barlow. A slow seller despite an abundance of merit, copies were eventually given away free with the purchase of item 21.

7.   S. T. JOSHI. *Lovecraft's Library: A Catalogue.* 2nd rev. ed. 2002. 175 pp. tpb.

Contents. Introduction; Explanatory Notes; Lovecraft's Library [981 titles]; Weird &c. Items in Library of H. P. Lovecraft; INDICES: A. Names; B. Titles; C. Works by Lovecraft; D. Publishers; E. Subjects.

Notes. Cover illustration by Jason C. Eckhardt. Our first POD title, printed by Lightning Source. Exhaustive revision of the catalogue first published by Necronomicon Press in 1980, with the addition of 60 more titles and listings of tables of contents of many important volumes, along with other additions to the notes. Since publication, dozens of additional titles have been identified; for the third edition, see item 102.

8.   CLARK ASHTON SMITH. *The Last Oblivion: Best Fantastic Poems of Clark Ashton Smith*. Edited by S. T. Joshi and David E. Schultz. 2002. 194 pp. tpb.

Contents. Introduction; A Note on the Text; Acknowledgments; *The Hashish-Eater; or, The Apocalypse of Evil*; I. THE STAR-TREADER: The Star-Treader; Ode to the Abyss; Nirvana; The Song of a Comet; Lament of the Stars; In Saturn; Triple Aspect; The Abyss Triumphant; The Motes; Desire of Vastness; Shadows; A Dream of the Abyss; After Armageddon; The Ancient Quest; A Dream of Oblivion; Ode to Light; Ode to Matter; II. MEDUSA AND OTHER HORRORS: Nero; Medusa; Averted Malefice; The Medusa of the Skies; Saturn; In Lemuria; Satan Unrepentant; The Ghoul and the Seraph; The Medusa of Despair; A Vision of Lucifer; The Witch in the Graveyard; The Flight of Azrael; The Mummy; Minatory; To the Chimera; The Whisper of the Worm; The Envoys; Nyctalops; Jungle Twilight; Necromancy; The Witch with Eyes of Amber; Cambion; The Saturnienne; Chance; Revenant; Song of the Necromancer; *Pour chercher du nouveau*; Witch-Dance; Not Theirs the Cypress-Arch; III. THE ELDRITCH DARK: A Song from Hell; The Titans in Tartarus; The Twilight Woods; Lethe; Atlantis; The Eldritch Dark; White Death; A Dead City; The Cloud-Islands; The City of the Titans; The City of Destruction; Beyond the Great Wall; Solution; *Rosa Mystica*; Symbols; The City in the Desert; The Melancholy Pool; Twilight on the Snow; The Land of Evil Stars; Memnon at Midnight; The Kingdom of Shadows; Moon-Dawn; Outlanders; Warning; The Nightmare Tarn; The Prophet Speaks; The Outer Land; In Thessaly; *Le Miroir des blanches fleurs*; The Moonlight Desert; Ougabalys; Desert Dweller; Amithaine; The Dark Chateau; Averoigne; Zothique; IV. SAID THE DREAMER: The Castle of Dreams; The Dream-God's Realm; Imagination; The Last Night; Shadow of Nightmare; A Song of Dreams; The Dream-Bridge; Said the Dreamer; Dolor of Dreams; *Luna Aeternalis*; Echo of Memnon; Nightmare; The Last Goddess; Love Malevolent; The Wingless Archangels; Enchanted Mirrors; Selenique; Maya; *Fantaisie d'Antan*; In Slumber; V. THE REFUGE OF BEAUTY: The Power of Eld; Strangeness; The Nereid; Exotique; Transcendence; The Tears of Lilith; Cleopatra; The Refuge of Beauty; Sandalwood; The Last Oblivion; Alienage; Adventure; Interrogation; Canticle; To Antares; Connaissance; Exorcism; Lamia; Farewell to Eros; Some Blind Eidolon; Bacchante; Resurrection; The Sorcerer to His Love; The Hill of Dionysus; Midnight Beach; Omniety; VI. TO THE DARKNESS: Ode on Imagination; Retrospect and Forecast; To the Darkness; A Dream of Beauty; The Pursuer; In the Desert; The Nameless Wraith; To the Daemon of Sublimity; Desolation; Inferno; Dissonance; Remembered

Light; The Incubus of Time; *Laus Mortis*; The Hope of the Infinite; Antepast; Forgotten Sorrow; Lunar Mystery; The Funeral Urn; Mors; September; Ennui; VII. THE SORCERER DEPARTS: To Omar Khayyam; To Nora May French; On Re-reading Baudelaire; To George Sterling: A Valediction; To Howard Phillips Lovecraft; H. P. L.; Soliloquy in an Ebon Tower; Cycles. Glossary. Bibliography. Index of Titles. Index of First Lines.

Notes. Cover and interior illustration by Clark Ashton Smith. First printing, 1650 copies, Vaughan Printing, Nashville TN. The first book to feature color reproductions of artwork by Clark Ashton Smith. A kind of stopgap volume while Smith's *Complete Poetry and Translations* (see items 37 and 50) were being prepared. The basic selection was done by Joshi, with additions by Schultz, who supplied the texts based on his years of work with Smith's poetry mss.

9.   R. H. BARLOW. *Eyes of the God: The Weird Fiction and Poetry of R. H. Barlow*. Edited by S. T. Joshi, Douglas A. Anderson, and David E. Schultz. 2002. 210 pp. tpb.

Contents. Introduction by S. T. Joshi and Douglas A. Anderson; FICTION: The Slaying of the Monster (with H. P. Lovecraft); Eyes of the God; *Annals of the Jinns:* I. The Black Tower; II. The Shadow from Above; III. The Flagon of Beauty; IV. The Sacred Bird; V. The Tomb of the God; VI. The Flower God; VII. The Little Box; VIII. The Fall of the Three Cities; IX. The Mirror; X. The Theft of the Hsothian Manuscripts; XI. An Episode in the Jungle; The Hoard of the Wizard-Beast (with H. P. Lovecraft); The Battle That Ended the Century (with H. P. Lovecraft); The Fidelity of Ghu; The Inhospitable Tavern; The Misfortunes of Butter-Churning; "Till A' the Seas" (with H. P. Lovecraft); The Temple; The Adventures of Garoth; The Experiment; Collapsing Cosmoses (with H. P. Lovecraft); The Bright Valley; The Priest and the Heretic; The Summons; A Dream; A Memory; Pursuit of the Moth; The Root-Gatherers; A Dim-Remembered Story; The Night Ocean (with H. P. Lovecraft); Origin Undetermined; The Swearing of an Oath; The Questioner; The Artizan's Reward; Return by Sunset; POETRY: I. Poems 1936–1939; [Untitled]; Sonnet V; Sonnet VI; Sonnet VII; Song; [Untitled]; Sonnet; [Untitled]; [Untitled]; R. E. H.; St. John's Churchyard; Dirge for the Artist; Alcestis; N. Y.; [Untitled]; [Untitled]; Altamira; Cycle from a Dead Year; H. P. L.; I. March 1937; II. March 1938; [Untitled]; [Untitled]; H. P. L.; H. P. L.; March; [Untitled]; The Unresisting; Shub-Ad; Who Will Not Know; To Bacchus; [Untitled]; [Untitled]; Winter Mood; Burlesque; Frustration; To a Companion;

Dawn Delayed; To a Wayfarer; [Untitled]; Fragments; To Alta, On Her Original American Sonnet; Sonnet; [Untitled]; [Untitled]; Fragments; [Untitled]; [Untitled]; [Untitled]; Quetzalcoatl; Quetzalcoatl; Out of the Dark; Prophecy; A Gull From a Cliff; [Untitled]; [Untitled]; [Untitled]; To Sleep; [Untitled]; Isolde; II. POEMS FOR A COMPETITION (1942): Date Uncertain; Nostalgia; For D.; Lines to Diana; The Gods in the Patio; The School Where Nobody Learns What; For Leon Trotzky and Huitzilopochtli; Sacre du Printemps; In Black and White; Explanation to M.; III. [STATEMENT ABOUT POETRY]; IV. VIEW FROM A HILL (1947): I. For D.; 1. From This Tree; 2. Air for Variations; 3. New Directions; 4. To a Friend on Sailing; 5. To One Rescued; II. Fresco of Priests and Beans; On a Feather Poncho; The Chichimecs; Stela of a Mayan Penitent; Tepuzteca, Tepehua; The Conquered; III. For Rosalie; blotted a beetle; Table Set for Sea-Slime; IV. Five Years; First Year: Sebastian; Second Year: Dream While Paris Was Threatened; Third Year: About a Mythical Factory-Area; Fourth Year: Letter to My Brother; Fifth Year: Viktoria; V. For E. and For W.; "¿Que Quieres? ¿Mis Costillas?" (For E.); Chili Sin Carne (For W.); VI: View from a Hill; To the Builders of a Dam; View from a Hill; Recantation; On the Lights of San Francisco; A Escoger; In Order to Clarify; We Kept on Reading "Tuesday"; VII: For Barbara Mayer; On Leaving Some Friends at an Early Hour; V. A STONE FOR SISIPHUS (1949): Sonnet to Siva; Anniversary; Invocation; Evening; The Coming Fructification by Night of Our Cyrus; Of the Names of the Zapotec Kings; Framed Portent; Orientation to the West; VI. MISCELLANEOUS POEMS: Mourning Song; Admittance; The City; A Tapestry; Warning to Snake Killers; [Untitled]; Mythological Episode; Rainy-Day Pastime; The Heart; Mozart's G. Minor; [Miscellaneous Lines]; Letter for Last Christmas; [Untitled]; Colors; [Untitled]; [Untitled]; [Untitled]; [Untitled]; Poema de Salida; Intimations of Mortality; Bibliography; Index of Poetry Titles; Index of First Lines.

Notes. Cover illustration by R. Saunders (from the *Californian*, Winter 1936, illustrating "The Night Ocean"), colored by Barbara Briggs Silbert. An exhaustive edition of Barlow's extant fiction and poetry, including a number of unpublished items derived from Barlow's papers. The fiction was largely edited by Joshi and Schultz, the poetry by Anderson, who also drafted the bibliography.

10.   H. P. LOVECRAFT. *From the Pest Zone: The New York Stories*. Edited by S. T. Joshi and David E. Schultz. 2003. 150 pp. tpb.

Contents. Abbreviations; Introduction; The Shunned House; The Horror at Red Hook; He; In the Vault; Cool Air; APPENDIX: Preface to "The Shunned House" by Frank Belknap Long, Jr.; Little Sketches About Town; Notes; Textual Notes.

Notes. Cover illustration by Sean Madden. Interior photographs by Ron Breznay, Donovan K. Loucks, and Steven Mariconda. An extensively annotated edition of the five stories Lovecraft wrote while in New York (1924–26), analogous to the Joshi–Schultz editions of *The Shadow over Innsmouth* (Necronomicon Press, 1994, 1997) and *The Shadow out of Time* (see item 2).

11.   HERBERT GORMAN. *The Place Called Dagon*. 2003 (rpt. 2008). 187 pp. tpb.

Contents. Introduction, by Larry Creasy; *The Place Called Dagon* by Herbert Gorman; Afterword: Gorman and Lovecraft, by S. T. Joshi.

Notes. Cover design by Barbara Briggs Silbert; interior illustrations by Allen Koszowski. Reprint edition replaced "merman" cover illustration with illustration by Allen Koszowski. Part of the Lovecraft's Library series. A reprint of Gorman's chilling horror novel of 1927. The Hippocampus staff fortuitously teamed up with Larry Creasy (proprietor of Charon House), who was planning his own reprint; Creasy contributed an extensive biographical introduction, and Joshi added an afterword discussing the novel's possible influence on Lovecraft.

12.   JACK MADISON HARINGA. *Drafts from the Moon Pool: The Influence of A. Merritt on H. P. Lovecraft*. 2003. 24 pp. tpb.

Notes. Cover photograph of A. Merritt from the collection of Sam Moskowitz. Printed in a numbered edition of 100 copies, the first thirty of which were included in the 30th Anniversary Mailing of the Esoteric Order of Dagon Amateur Press Association. A sensitive essay on Merritt's influence on Lovecraft. Haringa later became coeditor of *Dead Reckonings* (see items 40ff.).

13.   H. P. LOVECRAFT. *Letters to Alfred Galpin*. Edited by S. T. Joshi and David E. Schultz. 2003 (rpt. 2004). 287 pp. tpb.

Contents. Introduction; Letters to Alfred Galpin; WORKS OF ALFRED GALPIN: Mystery; Two Loves; Selenaio-Phantasma; Remarks to My Handwriting; Marsh-Mad; The Critic; Stars; Some Tendencies of

Modern Poetry; The Spoken Tongue; The World Situation; The United's Policy 1920–1921 (with H. P. Lovecraft); Form in Modern Poetry; Picture of a Modern Mood; Nietzsche as a Practical Prophet; To Sam Loveman; The Vivisector; *Four Translations from* Les Fleurs du mal *by Charles Pierre Baudelaire* (Au Lecteur; L'Ennemi; Remords Posthume; L'Ange Gardien); Scattered Remarks upon the Green Cheese Theory; Department of Public Criticism; Intuition in the Philosophy of Bergson; Ennui; A Critic of Poetry; From the French of Pierre de Ronsard ("Amours"—Livre II.): Aubade; Echoes from Beyond Space; Red; En Route (An American to Paris, 1931): I. New York Harbor; II. On Deck; November; A Partial Bibliography of Alfred Galpin; Index.

Notes. Cover design by Anastasia Damianakos. First edition, first printing issued as POD by Booksurge, taken out of print in 2004 and reissued 2004 as first edition, second printing with Lightning Source, our standard POD printer from then on. Booksurge edition lacked frontispiece (photo of Galpin). The interior paper stock was changed from cream to white in 2011, at which time slight changes were made to the cover. The first of what was planned as a series of volumes presenting unabridged and extensively annotated editions of Lovecraft's letters to important correspondents; in the event, only one other volume was published (see item 25). Nearly 50 pp. of Galpin's writings were included. Nominated for the 2003 International Horror Guild award for nonfiction.

14.   GEORGE STERLING. *The Thirst of Satan: Poems of Fantasy and Terror.* Edited by S. T. Joshi. 2003. 215 pp. tpb.

Contents. Introduction, by S. T. Joshi; I. THE TESTIMONY OF THE SUNS: The Testimony of the Suns; Mystery; Three Sonnets on Oblivion; Oblivion; The Dust Dethroned; The Night of Gods; Three Sonnets of the Night Skies (I—Aldebaran at Dusk; II—The Chariots of Dawn; III—The Huntress of Stars); The Evanescent; The Thirst of Satan; The Setting of Antares; Outward; The Face of the Skies; Ephemera; Disillusion; The Meteor; The Last Man. II. THE GARDENS OF THE SEA: The Nile; The Fog Siren; The Sea-Fog; Darkness; "Sad Sea-Horizons"; Sonnets by the Night Sea; The Gardens of the Sea; At the Grand Cañon; The Last of Sunset; Caucasus; The Caravan; III. THE MUSE OF THE INCOMMUNICABLE: Memory of the Dead; The Altar-Flame; Ultima Thule; The Directory; In Extremis; Romance; A Mood; The Moth of Time; The Muse of the Incommunicable; "Omnia Exeunt in Mysterium": To One Self-Slain; Three Sonnets on Sleep; Illusion; Essential Night; To Life; To Science; Waste; Amber;

The Dweller in Darkness; Here and Now; IV. THE BLACK VULTURE: The Black Vulture; The Sibyl of Dreams; The Last Monster; "That Walk in Darkness"; To the Mummy of the Lady Isis; Witch-Fire; Song; The Young Witch; Eidolon; The Sphinx; V. THE NAIAD'S SONG: The Haunting; The Naiad's Song; White Magic; The Golden Past; The Revenge; To a Girl Dancing; Flame; The Stranger; VI. A WINE OF WIZARDRY: The Summer of the Gods; Nightmare; A Wine of Wizardry; The Apothecary's; Under the Rainbow; The Shadow of Nirvana; The Wiser Prophet; The Oldest Book; Farm of Fools; VII. THE PASSING OF BIERCE: To Edgar Allan Poe; To Ambrose Bierce; The Ashes in the Sea; The Coming Singer; The Passing of Bierce; Shelley at Spezia. VIII. THE RACK: The Lords of Pain; A Dream of Fear; The Rack; Conspiracy; The Hidden Pool; The Death of Circe; To a Monk's Skull; To Pain; Epilogue: My Swan Song; George Sterling: An Appreciation, by Clark Ashton Smith; Commentary; Index of Titles; Index of First Lines.

Notes. Cover and interior illustrations by Virgil Finlay. A sampling of Sterling's weird verse—the first major reprinting of his poetry since 1969 and a foretaste of our edition of his complete poetry and verse drama (see items 117–19).

15.   LORD DUNSANY. *The Pleasures of a Futuroscope.* Edited by S. T. Joshi. 2003 hc (rpt. 2005 [tpb]). 200 pp.

Notes. Cover illustration by Jeff Remmer. Hardcover edition 1000 copies: Covington Group, St. Louis. The first Hippocampus Press hardcover edition, and the first publication of Dunsany's last novel, probably written in 1955 and unearthed by Joe Doyle, archivist at Dunsany Castle. A splendid fantasy/science fiction hybrid about a man who invents a "futuroscope" that allows him to see into the future—where he finds that a nuclear holocaust has reduced humanity to a primitive state.

16.   S. T. JOSHI. *Primal Sources: Essays on H. P. Lovecraft.* 2003. 208 pp. tpb.

Contents. Introduction; I. LOVECRAFT THE MAN: Lovecraft and the Munsey Magazines; Lovecraft and *Weird Tales*; A Look at Lovecraft's Letters; Lovecraft and the Films of His Day; Lovecraft's Library; II. LOVECRAFT THE WRITER AND THINKER: Autobiography in Lovecraft; "Reality" and Knowledge; *In Defence of Dagon* and Lovecraft's Philosophy; The Rationale of Lovecraft's Pseudonyms; The Dream World and the Real World in Lovecraft; Lovecraft's Alien Civilisations: A Political Interptetation; Topical References in

Lovecraft; III. STUDIES ON INDIVIDUAL WORKS: Lovecraft, Regner Lodbrog, and Olaus Wormius; On "Polaris"; What Happens in "Arthur Jermyn"; "The Tree" and Ancient History; The Sources for "From Beyond"; Lovecraft and the *Regnum Congo*; Lovecraft and Dunsany's *Chronicles of Rodriguez*; On "The Descendant"; Some Sources for "The Mound" and *At the Mountains of Madness*; On "The Book"; Lovecraft's Fantastic Poetry.

Notes. Cover illustration by Robert H. Knox ("Antarktos," 2003), colored by Barbara Briggs Silbert. *Primal Sources* bears the distinction of having been S. T. Joshi's 100th published book. A generous sampling of Joshi's critical essays on Lovecraft, most of them published in *Lovecraft Studies* and *Crypt of Cthulhu* from 1979 onward.

17.   CLARK ASHTON SMITH. *The Sword of Zagan and Other Writings.* Edited by Dr. W. C. Farmer. 2004. 181 pp. tpb.

Contents. Introduction, by S. T. Joshi; *The Sword of Zagan;* POEMS: The River of Life; The World; The Departed City; Bedouin Song; Zuleika: An Oriental Song; Benares; Rubaiyat of Saiyed; The Isle of Saturn; Temporality; Shapes in the Sunset; Epitaph for the Earth; Night; Rêve Parisien; Averiogne; SHORT STORIES: The Emir's Captive; Fakhreddin; Prince Alcorez and the Magician; The Haunted Gong; The Malay Creese; The Shah's Messenger; The Bronze Image; The Fulfilled Prophecy; The Haunted Chamber; FRAGMENTS: When the Earth Trembled; Oriental Tales: The Yogi's Ring; The Opal of Delhi [I]; The Opal of Delhi [II]; The Guardian of the Temple; The Emerald Eye; [Untitled]; [Fragment of an essay]; [Letter to Munsey's]; Lost Pages from *The Black Diamonds*; Clark Ashton Smith: A Memoir, by W. C. Farmer.

Notes. Cover and interior illustrations by Jason C. Eckhardt. A follow-up to *The Black Diamonds* (item 5), printing another previously unpublished juvenile novel along with other early stories and fragments. All these items derived from the collection of Dr. Farmer, who knew Smith in the latter's final years and was given these mss. over the course of years.

18.   H. P. LOVECRAFT. *Collected Essays, Volume 1: Amateur Journalism.* Edited by S. T. Joshi. 2004. 440 pp. hc.

Contents. Introduction by S. T. Joshi; A Task for Amateur Journalists; Department of Public Criticism (November 1914); Department of Public Criticism (January 1915); Department of Public Criticism (March 1915); What Is Amateur Journalism?; Consolidation's Autopsy; The Amateur Press; Editorial (April 1915); The Question of the Day; The Morris Faction; For President—Leo Fritter; Introducing Mr. Chester Pierce Munroe; [Untitled Notes on Amateur Journalism]; Department of Public Criticism (May 1915); Finale; New Department Proposed: Instruction for the Recruit; Our Candidate; Exchanges; For Historian—Ira A. Cole; Editorial (July 1915); The Conservative and His Critics (July 1915); Some Political Phases; Introducing Mr. John Russell; In a Major Key; Amateur Notes; The Dignity of Journalism; Department of Public Criticism (September 1915); Editorial (October 1915); The Conservative and His Critics (October 1915); The Youth of Today; An Impartial Spectator; [Untitled Notes on Amateur Journalism]; Little Journeys to the Homes of Prominent Amateurs: II. Andrew Francis Lockhart; Report of First Vice-President (November 1915); Department of Public Criticism (December 1915); Systematic Instruction in the United; United Amateur Press Association: Exponent of Amateur Journalism; Introducing Mr. James Pyke; Report of First Vice-President (January 1916); Editorial (February 1916); Department of Public Criticism (April 1916); Among the New-Comers; Department of Public Criticism (June 1916); Department of Public Criticism (August 1916); Department of Public Criticism (September 1916); Among the Amateurs; Concerning "Persia—in Europe"; Amateur Standards; A Request; Department of Public Criticism (March 1917); Department of Public Criticism (May 1917); A Reply to *The Lingerer*; The United's Problem; Editorially; The "Other United"; Department of Public Criticism (July 1917); Little Journeys to the Homes of Prominent Amateurs: V. Eleanor J. Barnhart; News Notes (July 1917); President's Message (September 1917); President's Message (November 1917); President's Message (January 1918); Department of Public Criticism (January 1918); President's Message (March 1918); Department of Public Criticism (March 1918); President's Message (May 1918); Department of Public Criticism (May 1918); Comment; President's Message (July 1918); Amateur Criticism; The United 1917–1918; The Amateur Press Club; *Les Mouches Fantastiques*; Department of Public Criticism (September 1918); Department of Public Criticism (November 1918); News Notes (November 1918); [Letter to the Bureau of Critics]; Department of Public Criticism (January 1919); Department of Public Criticism (March 1919); Winifred Virginia Jordan: Associate Editor; Helene Hoffman Cole—Litterateur; Department of Public Criticism (May 1919); Trimmings; For Official Editor—Anne Tillery Renshaw; Amateurdom; Looking Backward; For What Does the United Stand?; The Pseudo-United; The Conquest of the Hub Club; News Notes (September 1920); Amateur Journalism: Its Possible Needs and Betterment; Editorial (November 1920); News Notes (November 1920); News Notes (January 1921); The United's Policy 1920–1921 (with Alfred Galpin); What Amateurdom and I Have Done for Each Other; News Notes (March 1921); The Vivisector (March 1921); [Letter to John Milton Heins]; Lucubrations Lovecraftian; News Notes (May 1921); The Vivisector (June 1921); The Haverhill Convention; News Notes (July 1921); Within the Gates; The Convention Banquet; Editorial (September 1921); News Notes (September 1921); A Singer of Ethereal Moods and Fancies; News Notes (November 1921); [Letter to John Milton Heins]; Editorial (January 1922); News Notes (January 1922); *Rainbow* Called Best First Issue; News Notes (March 1922); The Vivisector (March 1922); News Notes (May 1922); [Letter to the N.A.P.A.]; President's Message (November 1922–January 1923); President's Message (March 1923); Bureau of Critics (March 1923); Rursus Adsumus; The Vivisector (Spring 1923); President's Message (May 1923); Lovecraft's Greeting; President's Message (July 1923); [Untitled Notes on Amateur Journalism]; The President's Annual Report; Trends and Objects; Editorial (May 1924); News Notes (May 1924); Editorial (July 1925); News Notes (July 1925); A Matter of Uniteds; The Convention; Bureau of Critics (December 1931); Critics Submit First Report; Verse Criticism; Report of Bureau of Critics; Bureau of Critics Comment on Verse, Typography, Prose; Bureau of Critics (June 1934); Chairman of the Bureau of Critics Reports on Poetry; Mrs. Miniter—Estimates and Recollections; Report of the Bureau of Critics (December 1934); Report of the Bureau of Critics (March 1935); Lovecraft Offers Verse Criticism; Dr. Eugene B. Kuntz; Some Current Amateur Verse; Report of the Executive Judges; Some Current Motives and Practices; [Letter to the N.A.P.A.]; [Literary Review]; Defining the "Ideal" Paper; APPENDIX: [Miscellaneous Notes in the *United Amateur*]; Official Organ Fund; [Untitled Note on Amateur Poetry]; [On *Notes High and Low* by Carrie Adams Berry]; [A Voice from the Grave]; Index.

Notes. Cover illustration (uniform for all five volumes of the series) by Virgil Finlay. Published simultaneously in hardcover and paperback. Hardcover 250 copies, Covington Group. One of the most ambitious projects undertaken by Hippocampus Press—the publication of Lovecraft's complete nonfiction writings, arranged thematically, with extensive annotations. Previously these writings had been scattered throughout many Arkham House volumes, including Joshi's edition of *Miscellaneous Writings* (Arkham House, 1995); but many items remained unreprinted.

19.   H. P. LOVECRAFT. *Collected Essays, Volume 2: Literary Criticism.* Edited by S. T. Joshi. 2004. 248 pp. hc.

Contents. Introduction, by S. T. Joshi; Metrical Regularity; The Allowable Rhyme; The Proposed Authors' Union; The Vers Libre Epidemic; Poesy; The Despised Pastoral; The Literature of Rome; The Simple Spelling Mania; The Case for Classicism; Literary Composition; Editor's Note to "A Scene for *Macbeth*" by Samuel Loveman; Winifred Virginia Jackson: A "Different" Poetess; The Poetry of Lilian Middleton; Lord Dunsany and His Work; Rudis Indigestaque Moles; Introduction [to *The Poetical Works of Jonathan E. Hoag*]; Ars Gratia Artis; In the Editor's Study; [Random Notes]; [Review of *Ebony and Crystal* by Clark Ashton Smith]; The Professional Incubus; The Omnipresent Philistine; The Work of Frank Belknap Long, Jr.; Supernatural Horror in Literature; Preface [to *White Fire* by John Ravenor Bullen]; Notes on "Alias Peter Marchall", by A. F. Lorenz; Foreword [to *Thoughts and Pictures* by Eugene B. Kuntz]; Notes on Verse Technique; Weird Story Plots; [Notes on Weird Fiction]; Notes on Writing Weird Fiction; Some Notes on Interplanetary Fiction; What Belongs in Verse; [Suggestions for a Reading Guide]; APPENDIX: The Poetry of John Ravenor Bullen; The Favourite Weird Stories of H. P. Lovecraft; Supernatural Horror in Literature [1936 condensation of sections 1 through 8]. Index.

Notes. Cover illustration by Virgil Finlay. Simultaneously published in hardcover and paperback. Hardcover 250 copies, Covington Group. The slimmest of the five volumes of *Collected Essays*.

20.   S. T. JOSHI AND DAVID E. SCHULTZ. *An H. P. Lovecraft Encyclopedia.* 2004. xx, 339 pp. tpb.

Notes. Cover design by Gaile Ivaska. Paperback reprint of the edition first published by Greenwood Press (2001), with a few additions and corrections.

21.   ALGERNON BLACKWOOD. *Incredible Adventures.* 2004. 224 pp. tpb.

Contents. Introduction by S. T. Joshi; The Regeneration of Lord Ernie; The Sacrifice; The Damned; A Descent into Egypt; Wayfarers.

Notes. Cover illustration by W. Graham Robertson (from the 1916 Macmillan edition of Blackwood's *The Centaur*). Part of the Lovecraft's Library series. A reprint of Blackwood's classic story collection of 1914, which Joshi regards as one of the greatest weird volumes of all time.

22.   S. T. JOSHI. *The Evolution of the Weird Tale.* 2004. 216 pp. tpb.

Contents. Introduction; I. SOME AMERICANS OF THE GOLDEN AGE: W. C. Morrow: Horror in San Francisco; Robert W. Chambers: The Bohemian Weird Tale; F. Marion Crawford: Blood-and-Thunder Horror; Edward Lucas White: Dream and Reality; II. SOME ENGLISH-MEN OF THE GOLDEN AGE: Sir Arthur Quiller-Couch: Ghosts and Scholars; Rudyard Kipling: The Horror of India; E. F. Benson: Spooks and More Spooks; L. P. Hartley: The Refined Ghost; III. H. P. LOVE-CRAFT AND HIS INFLUENCE: H. P. Lovecraft: The Fiction of Materialism; Frank Belknap Long: Things from the Sea; A Literary Tutelage: Robert Bloch and H. P. Lovecraft; Passing the Torch: H. P. Lovecraft and Fritz Leiber; IV. CONTEMPORARIES: Rod Serling: The Moral Supernatural; L. P. Davies: The Workings of the Mind; Les Daniels: The Horror of History; Dennis Etchison: Spanning the Genres; David J. Schow and Splatterpunk; Poppy Z. Brite: Sex, Horror, and Rock-&-Roll; Bibliography.

Notes. Cover illustration by Wallace Smith (from Ben Hecht's *Fantazius Mallare*, 1922). A loose follow-up of Joshi's previous treatises, *The Weird Tale* (Univ. of Texas Press, 1990) and *The Modern Weird Tale* (McFarland, 2001), covering authors from the mid-19th century to the present day, including three chapters (on Les Daniels, Dennis Etchison, and David J. Schow) that had been scheduled to appear in *The Modern Weird Tale* but were omitted for space reasons.

23.   SAMUEL LOVEMAN. *Out of the Immortal Night: Selected Works of Samuel Loveman.* Edited by S. T. Joshi and David E. Schultz. 2004. 244 pp. tpb.

Contents. Introduction, by S. T. Joshi; I. POETRY: *Poems* (1911): In Pierrot's Garden; Ode to Ceres; Fra Angelico; Song; To P. G.; Lines; A Twenty-second Birthday; *The Hermaphrodite and Other Poems* (1936): The Hermaphrodite; River Pattern; Will o' the Wisp; Steener Haakonson Dances; Dream Song; Heckscher Building; Euphorion; Agathon; Arcesilaus; Lineage; For a Book of Poems; Ascension; Thomas Holley Chivers; The Ramapos; Oscar Wilde; John Clare in a Madhouse; The Minstrel; The Chopin-Player; A Dedication; Vice; Transience; Dolore; Bacchanale; To Simone's; Ad Fratrem; Isolation; Remonstrance; Proteus; A Voyage; Legend; The Return; Memoralia; Forest of Rhododendron; Understanding; Ecce Homo; Ariel; Visitor; Inarticulate; Madison Square; Contrast; Invocation; Song; Harbour; Admonition; Foes; Limbo; Interlude; Gates Mills; Wasteland; Amy Levy; Forest Hill; Andenkung; Dream of Spring; Finis; A Georgia Garden; Palingenesis; Belated Love; Nostalgia; Becalmed; Mutation;

Dirge; To Dionysus; To Apollo; Quatrains (Poppies; Forgotten Poets; Space; Music; Simeon Solomon; Aftermath); A Chinese Pavilion; Ben De Casseres in Camden; Terminus; UNCOLLECTED POEMS: A Poet; A Sonnet: Lethe; The Birth of Fear; Pierced; A Lily; Lost Youth; Avalon; Hope; The Old Cobbler; Shadow-Land; The Song Unsung; Ship of Dreams; The Birth of Poesy; On Lost Friendship; Peccavi; The Plaint of Bygone Loves; Eventide (I. Sunset; II. Twilight; III. Night); David Gray; An Epitaph; Quatrains; To Alfred Noyes, Oversea; Michael Scott's Wooing; Thomas Dermody; Resurgam; Shadow-Love; Euthanasia; A Burden; A Song of Chamisso's; A Departure; W. E.; On the Passing of Youth; A Triumph in Eternity; Talent; [Untitled]; Adventure; In Sepulcretis; Saturday Evening; A Letter to G—— K——; Ernest Nelson; Heldenleben; Winter; To Satan; Christmas—1923; Genesis; Night Piece (Forest Hill); Mono-lith; Oscar Redivivus; Unfulfilled; To Mr. Theobald; To George Kirk on His 27th Birthday; Music; Vigil; To a Child; The Dead King; Kin; Episode; Rescue; Transit; An Admonition to the Ladies; Debs in Pris-on; For the Chelsea Book Shop [I]; For the Chelsea Book Shop [II]; Nepenthe; Quatrain; Reliquiae; Spring at El Retiro; Versailles; [Un-titled]; The Goal; John Clare in 1864; II. DRAMA: Oedipus at Colo-nus; Belshazzar; Nero; Narcisse; Arcady; A Scene for *King Lear*; A Scene for *Macbeth*; The Sphinx: A Conversation; III. TRANSLATIONS: Twenty-four Translations from Heine; Catullus; Translations from Baudelaire: La Musique; Parfum Exotique; Horreur Sympathique; De Profundis Clamavi; La Beauté; Causerie; Chant d'Automne; Le Couvercle; Le Chat; La Fontaine de Sang; Sonnet d'Automne; Ciel Brouillé; Les Chats; Translations from Verlaine: Sagesse; Bruxelles; Romances sans Paroles; Il Bacio; La Bonne Chanson; Vert; Sappho; Sonnet: After Leconte de Lisle; God's Work; IV. FICTION: Antenor; The Faun; The Dog; An Impression; The One Who Found Pity; Christmas-Eve with Sherlock Holmes; V. ESSAYS: Mr. Sterling and Minor Poets; A Keats Discovery; Modern Poetry (An Exorcism); A Note [to *Twenty-one Letters of Ambrose Bierce*]; A Convention Ad-dress; The Book of Life; Foreword to *Poppies and Mandragora*; Preface to *The Man from Genoa*; Hubert Crackanthorpe: A Realist of the Nineties; Marcel Proust; Literature and Dry-rot; A Letter on Hart Crane; Howard Phillips Lovecraft; Lovecraft as Conversationalist; Bibliography; Index of Poetry Titles; Index of First Lines.

Notes. Cover illustration by William Sommer (from the 1944 W. Paul Cook edition of Loveman's *The Sphinx*). The product of many years' work by the editors in gathering Loveman's writings (chiefly his poet-ry) from amateur journals and unpublished manuscripts. All Loveman's known poetry was included, but only selections of his essays, reviews, and amateur journalism. The interior paper stock was changed from cream to white in 2011, at which time slight changes were made to the cover.

24.   R. NEMO HILL. *The Strange Music of Erich Zann.* 2004. 51 pp. tpb.

Notes. Cover illustration by Joe Werhle, Jr. With audio CD of the author reading his work. Booklet was issued in late 2004, but the CD was not produced until early the following year, hence it bears a 2005 copyright date. A long poem based on H. P. Lovecraft's tale "The Music of Erich Zann" (1921). The first original creative writing published by Hippocampus Press, commissioned by Derrick Hussey following a live reading by the poet in New York City.

25.   H. P. LOVECRAFT. *Letters to Rheinhart Kleiner.* Edited by S. T. Joshi and David E. Schultz. 2005. 298 pp. tpb.

Contents. Introduction; Letters to Rheinhart Kleiner; WORKS: A. POEMS BY RHEINHART KLEINER: Alas!; Dream Days, or, Metrical Musings; Another Endless Day; Motes; At Providence in 1918; Brooklyn, My Brooklyn; Epistle to Mr. and Mrs. Lovecraft; The Four of Us!; After a Decade; H. P. L.; B. ESSAYS BY RHEINHART KLEINER: A Note on Howard P. Lovecraft's Verse; The Kleicomolo; After a Decade and the Kalem Club; Howard Phillips Lovecraft; Lovecraft in Brooklyn; Some Lovecraft Memories; C. RHEINHART KLEINER VS. H. P. LOVECRAFT: To Mary of the Movies [Kleiner]; To Charlie of the Comics [Lovecraft]; To a Movie Star [Kleiner]; To Mistress Sophia Simple, Queen of the Cinema [Lovecraft]; Ruth [Kleiner]; Grace [Lovecraft]; John Oldham: 1653–1683 [Kleiner]; John Oldham: A Defence [Lovecraft]; Ethel: Cashier in a Broad Street Buffet [Kleiner]; Cindy: Scrub-Lady in a State Street Skyscraper [Lovecraft]; On Collaboration; D. POEMS BY H. P. LOVECRAFT ADDRESSED TO RHEINHART KLEINER: The Bookstall; Content; To Mr. Kleiner, on Receiving from Him the Poetical Works of Addison, Gay, and Somerville; R. Kleiner, Laureatus, in Heliconem; To Rheinhart Kleiner, Esq., Upon His Town Fables and Elegies; [On Rheinhart Kleiner Being Hit by an Automobile]; A Partial Bibliography of Rheinhart Kleiner; Index.

Notes. Cover design by Anastasia Damianakos (uniform with item 13). Complete publication of Lovecraft's letters to Kleiner, including lengthy letters to the Kleicomolo correspondence circle. Includes a generous selection of Kleiner's writings, including his poetry and essays, as well as poems by Lovecraft addressed to Kleiner. This nascent letters series (begun with item 13) was supplanted by the more sub-stantial *Collected Letters* series with the publication of item 54.

26.   M. P. SHIEL. *The House of Sounds and Others.* Edited by S. T. Joshi. 2005. 299 pp. tpb.

Contents. Introduction, by S. T. Joshi; Xélucha; The Pale Ape; The Case of Euphemia Raphash; Huguenin's Wife; The House of Sounds; The Great King; The Bride; *The Purple Cloud;* APPENDIX: Vaila.

Notes. Cover illustration by J. T. Lindroos. A small number of copies were printed bearing an erroneous price of $15.00. Some made their way into circulation before the error was caught and corrected. Part of the Lovecraft's Library series. An extensive selection of those works by Shiel that Lovecraft read and might have been influenced by, in-cluding the 1901 edition of *The Purple Cloud* (substantially different from the revised edition of 1929).

27.   ROBERT M. PRICE, EDITOR. *Tales out of Dunwich.* 2005. 302 pp. tpb.

Contents. Dunwich Homecoming, by Robert M. Price; *The Thing in the Woods,* by Harper Williams; The Mark of the Monster, by Jack Wil-liamson; The Thing from Lover's Lane, by Nancy A. Collins; Acute Spiritual Fear, by Robert M. Price; Black Brat of Dunwich, by Stanley C. Sargent; The Dunwich Lodger, by Brian McNaughton; The Doom That Came to Dunwich, by Richard A. Lupoff; The Dunwich Gate, by Don D'Ammassa; The N-Scale Horror, by Gerard E. Giannattasio; Dunwich Dreams, Dunwich Screams, by Eddy C. Bertin.

Notes. Cover illustration by Philip Fuller. The illustration has been said to bear a more than passing resemblance to Anastasia Dami-anakos. A large anthology featuring tales about Dunwich, including the first reprint of Harper Williams's short novel *The Thing in the Woods* (1924), which clearly influenced some elements of Lovecraft's "The Dunwich Horror" (1928).

28.   GEORGE STERLING AND CLARK ASHTON SMITH. *The Shadow of the Unattained: The Letters of George Sterling and Clark Ashton Smith.* Edited by David E. Schultz and S. T. Joshi. 2005. 342 pp. tpb.

Contents. Introduction; The Shadow of the Unattained [letters]; APPENDIX: To George Sterling, by Clark Ashton Smith; To George Sterling, by Clark Ashton Smith; To George Sterling, by Clark Ashton Smith; To the Editor of *Town Talk,* by Ambrose Bierce; The

Coming Singer, by George Sterling; Preface to *Odes and Sonnets*, by George Sterling; Preface to *Ebony and Crystal*, by George Sterling; Recent Books of Fact and Fiction, by George Sterling; Poetry of the Pacific Coast—California, by George Sterling; To George Sterling: A Valediction, by Clark Ashton Smith; George Sterling: An Appreciation, by Clark Ashton Smith; George Sterling: Poet and Friend, by Clark Ashton Smith; To George Sterling, by Clark Ashton Smith. Glossary of Names; List of Extant Enclosures; Bibliography; Index.

Notes. Cover illustration by Philip Fuller (based on photographs of Sterling and Smith). Fifteen interior illustrations from drawings by Smith from his letters to Sterling. Unabridged and annotated edition of the complete extant correspondence of the two writers, who wrote extensively to each other from 1911 until Sterling's death in 1926. Also included are writings by each author about the other.

29. H. P. LOVECRAFT. *Collected Essays, Volume 3: Science.* Edited by S. T. Joshi. 2005. 357 pp. hc.

Contents. Introduction, by S. T Joshi; My Opinion as to the Lunar Canals; No Transit of Mars; Trans-Neptunian Planets; The Moon; The Earth Not Hollow; ASTRONOMY ARTICLES FOR THE *Pawtuxet Valley Gleaner:* The Heavens for August; The Skies of September; Is Mars an Inhabited World?; Is There Life on the Moon?; An Interesting Phenomenon; October Heavens; Are There Undiscovered Planets?; Can the Moon Be Reached by Man?; The Moon; [Untitled]; The Sun; The Leonids; Comets; December Skies; The Fixed Stars; Clusters—Nebulae; January Heavens; ASTRONOMY ARTICLES FOR THE PROVIDENCE *Tribune:* In the August Sky; The September Heavens; Astronomy in October; The Skies of November; The Heavens for December; The Heavens in January; The Heavens in February; The Heavens in March; April Skies; The Heavens in May; The Heavens in June; Astronomy in August; The Heavens for September; The Skies of October; The Heavens in November; Heavens for December; The Heavens in January; February Skies; The Heavens in Month of March; Solar Eclipse Feature of June Heavens; Third Annual Report of the Prov. Meteorological Station; Celestial Objects for All; Venus and the Public Eye; ASTRONOMY ARTICLES FOR THE PROVIDENCE *Evening News:* The January Sky; The February Sky; The March Sky; The April Sky; May Sky; The June Sky; The July Sky; The August Sky; The September Sky; The October Sky; The November Sky; The December Sky; The January Sky; The February Sky; The March Sky; April Skies; The May Sky; The June Skies; The July Skies; The August Skies; September Skies; October Skies; November Skies; December Skies; January Skies; February Skies; March Skies; April Skies; May Skies; June Skies; July Skies; August Skies; September Skies; October Skies; November Skies; December Skies; January Skies; February Skies; March Skies; April Skies; May Skies; June Skies; July Skies; August Skies; September Skies; October Skies; November Skies; December Skies; January Skies; February Skies; March Skies; April Skies; May Skies; SCIENCE VERSUS CHARLATANRY: Science versus Charlatanry; The Falsity of Astrology; Astrology and the Future; Delavan's Comet and Astrology; The Fall of Astrology; [Isaac Bickerstaffe's Reply]; MYSTERIES OF THE HEAVENS REVEALED BY ASTRONOMY: I. The Sky and Its Contents; [II.] The Solar System; III. The Sun; IV. The Inferior Planets; V. Eclipses; VI. The Earth and Its Moon; VII. Mars and the Asteroids; VIII. The Outer Planets; [The Outer Planets, Part II]; IX. Comets and Meteors; Comets and Meteors [Part II]; X. The Stars; [The Stars, Part II]; XI. Clusters and Nebulae; [Clusters and Nebulae, Part II]; XII. The Constellations; [The Constellations, Part II]; XIII. Telescopes and Observatories; [Telescopes and Observatories, Part II]; Editor's Note to "The Irish and the Fairies" by Peter J. MacManus; Brumalia; The Truth about Mars; The Cancer of Superstition; [Some Backgrounds of Fairyland]; APPENDIX: Does "Vulcan" Exist?; Astronomical Notebook; [Astrology Articles by J. F. Hartmann]: Astrology and the European War; [Letter to the Editor]; The Science of Astrology; A Defense of Astrology; Lovecraft's Juvenile Scientific Manuscripts; Index.

Notes. Cover illustration by Virgil Finlay. Interior illustrations by Lovecraft. Hardcover 250 copies, Covington Group. Simultaneously published in hardcover and paperback. Complete publication of Lovecraft's scientific writings, including the first unabridged reprint of his dozens of astronomy columns for Providence newspapers (1906–18).

30.   H. P. LOVECRAFT. *Collected Essays, Volume 4: Travel.* Edited by S. T. Joshi. 2005. 300 pp. hc.

Contents. Introduction, by S. T. Joshi; The Trip of Theobald; Vermont—A First Impression; Observations on Several Parts of America; Travels in the Provinces of America; An Account of a Trip to the Antient Fairbanks House, in Dedham, and to the Red Horse Tavern in Sudbury, in the Province of the Massachusetts-Bay; Account of a Visit to Charleston, S.C.; An Account of *Charleston,* in His Maj^{ty's} Province of *South-Carolina*; A Description of the Town of Quebeck in New-France, Lately Added to His Britannick Majesty's Dominions; European Glimpses; Some Dutch Footprints in New

England; Homes and Shrines of Poe; The Unknown City in the Ocean; Charleston; APPENDIX: A Descent to Avernus; Sleepy Hollow To-day; Index.

Notes. Cover illustration by Virgil Finlay, interior illustrations by Lovecraft. Hardcover 250 copies, Covington Group. Simultaneously published in hardcover and paperback. First complete edition of Lovecraft's travel writings, including the first publication of two brief travelogues.

31.   ROBERT H. WAUGH. *The Monster in the Mirror: Looking for H. P. Lovecraft.* 2006. 302 pp. tpb.

Contents. Introduction; PART I: FIRST PRINCIPLES: Lovecraft's Hands; Documents, Creatures, and History; PART II: SORTIES: "The Picture in the House": Images of Complicity; *At the Mountains of Madness:* The Subway and the Shoggoth; PART III: MEDITATIONS ON "THE OUTSIDER": "The Outsider," the Terminal Climax, and Other Conclusions; Lovecraft and Keats Confront the "Awful Rainbow"; The Outsider, the Autodidact, and Other Professions; PART IV: MATERIALISM, THEOLOGY, AND IMAGINATION: Lovecraft and Leopardi: Sunsets and Moonsets; Lovecraft Born Again: An Essay in Apologetic Criticism; Works Cited; Index.

Notes. Cover illustration by Philip Fuller. An extensive selection of Waugh's critical essays on Lovecraft, most of them published in *Lovecraft Studies.*

32.   MARA KIRK HART AND S. T. JOSHI, EDITORS. *Lovecraft's New York Circle: The Kalem Club, 1924–1927.* 2006. 240 pp. tpb.

Contents. Preface, by Peter Cannon; Introduction, by Mara Kirk Hart; THE KALEM LETTERS OF GEORGE KIRK: Introduction, by Mara Kirk Hart; 1924; 1925; 1926; 1927; WRITINGS BY THE KALEMS: GEORGE KIRK: Book Collecting: The Prince of Hobbies; RHEINHART KLEINER: A Glee; At Providence in 1918; Epistle to Mr. and Mrs. Lovecraft; The Four of Us (Rondeau); Brooklyn, My Brooklyn; Columbia Heights, Brooklyn; [Prisky]; On a Favorite Cat: Killed by an Automobile; To George W. Kirk, Upon His 26th Birthday; To His Peculiar Friend, G. Kirk, Esq.; Your Street; Blue Pencil Anniversary Song; What My Ancestors Were Like; The Great Adventure; If I Had Lived a Hundred Years Ago; H. P. L.; ARTHUR LEEDS: He Had to Pay the Nine-Tailed Cat; FRANK BELKNAP LONG: A Man from Genoa; Come, Let Us Make; The Man Who Died Twice; H. P. LOVECRAFT: Plaster-All; To Endymion; Providence; Waste Paper; Primavera; To an Infant; To George Kirk, Esq.; To George Willard Kirk, Gent., of Chelsea Village in New York, upon His Birthday, Novr. 25, 1925; Two Christmas Poems to G. W. K.; A Year Off; In Memoriam Oscar Incoul Verelst of Manhattan 1920–1926; SAMUEL LOVEMAN: A Letter to G—— K——; To George Kirk on His 27th Birthday; For the Chelsea Book Shop [1]; For the Chelsea Book Shop [2]; For a Cat; For a Book of Poems; Admonition; Limbo; To H. P. L.; Genesis; Spring at El Retiro; Arcesilaus; John Clare in 1864; EVERETT MCNEIL: From *Tonty of the Iron Hand*; JAMES FERDINAND MORTON: To G. W. K. on His 27th Birthday; From *The Curse of Race Prejudice*; APPENDIX: After a Decade and the Kalem Club, by Rheinhart Kleiner; Bards and Bibliophiles, by Rheinhart Kleiner; Sources and Works Consulted; Index.

Notes. Cover illustration by Barbara Briggs Silbert. An innovative volume conceived and largely executed by Mara Kirk Hart (daughter of George Kirk), in which selections of the writings by the major members of the Kalem Club (George Kirk, Rheinhart Kleiner, Arthur Leeds, Frank Belknap Long, H. P. Lovecraft, Samuel Loveman, Everett McNeil, and James Ferdinand Morton) are reprinted; a few items are previously unpublished. The selections are preceded by an invaluable selection of letters written by Kirk (1924–27) to his fiancée Lucile Dvorak, shedding much light on the Kalems' activities in New York during and just after the period of Lovecraft's residence there.

33.   SCOTT CONNORS, EDITOR. *The Freedom of Fantastic Things: Selected Criticism on Clark Ashton Smith.* 2006. 376 pp. hc.

Contents. Introduction, by Scott Connors; The Centaur, by Clark Ashton Smith; Klarkash-Ton and "Greek," by Donald Sidney-Fryer; Contemporary Reviews of Clark Ashton Smith; Eblis in Bakelite, by James Blish; James Blish versus Clark Ashton Smith, to Wit, the Young Turk Syndrome, by Donald Sidney-Fryer; The Last Romantic, by S. J. Sackett; Communicable Mysteries: The Last True Symbolist, by Fred Chappell; What Happens in *The Hashish-Eater?*, by S. T. Joshi; The Babel of Visions: The Structuration of Clark Ashton Smith's *The Hashish-Eater*, by Dan Clore; Clark Ashton Smith's "Nero," by Carl Jay Buchanan; Satan Speaks: A Reading of "Satan Unrepentant," by Phillip A. Ellis; Lands Forgotten or Unfound: The Prose Poetry of Clark Ashton Smith, by S. T. Joshi; Outside the Human Aquarium: The Fantastic Imagination of Clark Ashton Smith, by Brian Stableford; Clark Ashton Smith: Master of the Macabre; John Kipling Hitz; Gesturing Toward the Infinite: Clark Ashton Smith and Modernism, by Scott Connors; Clark Ashton Smith: A Note on the

Aesthetics of Fantasy, by Charles K. Wolfe; Fantasy and Decadence in the Work of Clark Ashton Smith, by Lauric Guillaud; Humor in Hyperspace: Smith's Uses of Satire, by John Kipling Hitz; Song of the Necromancer: "Loss" in Clark Ashton Smith's Fiction, by Steve Behrends; Brave World Old and New: The Atlantis Theme in the Poetry and Fiction of Clark Ashton Smith, by Donald Sidney-Fryer; Coming In from the Cold: Incursions of "Outsideness" in Hyperborea, by Steven Tompkins; As Shadows Wait upon the Sun: Clark Ashton Smith's Zothique, by Jim Rockhill; Into the Woods: The Human Geography of Averoigne, by Stefan Dziemianowicz; Sorcerous Style: Clark Ashton Smith's *The Double Shadow and Other Fantasies*, by Peter H. Goodrich; Loss and Recuperation: A Model for Reading Clark Ashton Smith's "Xeethra," by Dan Clore; "Life, Love, and the Clemency of Death": A Reexamination of Clark Ashton Smith's "The Isle of the Torturers," by Scott Connors; Regarding the Providence Point of View, by Ronald S. Hilger; An Annotated Chronology of the Fiction of Clark Ashton Smith, by Steve Behrends; Bibliography; Contributors; Acknowledgments; Index.

Notes. Cover illustration by Frank Kupka ("Resistance, or the Black Idol," 1903). Simultaneously published in hardcover and paperback. The most extensive selection ever published of criticism of Clark Ashton Smith, including both reprinted and previously unpublished essays.

34. BENJAMIN SZUMSKYJ, EDITOR. *Two-Gun Bob: A Centennial Study of Robert E. Howard.* 2006. 233 pp. tpb.

Contents. Robert E. Howard: A Texan Master, by Michael Moorcock; Robert E. Howard: A Look at "Two-Gun Bob" 100 Years On, by Benjamin Szumskyj; *The Junto*: Being a Brief Look at the Amateur Press Association Robert E. Howard Partook In as a Youth, by Glenn Lord; . . . From Acorns Grow: Robert E. Howard Revealed in *Post Oaks and Sand Roughs*, by John Goodrich; Sleuths, Secrets, and Grisly Mysteries: The Detective Fiction of Robert E. Howard, by Fred Blosser; Words from the Outer Dark: The Poetical Works of Robert E. Howard, by Michele Tetro; Texas Talespinner: Robert E. Howard's Ways with Words, by Frank Coffman; Robert E. Howard: A Behavioral Perspective, by Charles Gramlich, Ph.D.; The Persistence of the Familiar: The Hyborian World and the Geographies of Fantastic Literature, by Lorenzo DiTommaso, Ph.D.; Bran Mak Morn and History, by S. T. Joshi; "Bitter Pleasures and Swinish Stupidity": Howard's Take on Human Character, by Charles Hoffman; El Borak, the Swift, by Scott Sheaffer; Stars and Strong Men: The Science and Cosmic Fiction of Robert E. Howard, by Martin Andersson; Laudator Temporis Acti: History and

Myth in the Works of Robert E. Howard, by Pietro Guarriello; Cimmerian Gloves: Studying Robert E. Howard's Ace Jessel from the Ringside, by Benjamin Szumskyj; About the Contributors; Acknowledgments; Index.

Notes. Cover illustration by Frank Coffman. A generous sampling of criticism of Howard to commemorate the centennial of his birth.

35.   W. H. PUGMIRE. *The Fungal Stain and Other Dreams.* 2006. 179 pp. tpb.

Contents. An Eidolon of Nothing; Hour of Their Appetite; The Sign That Sets the Darkness Free; Jigsaw Boy; The Fungal Stain; Balm of Nepenthe; Some Darker Star; The Saprophytic Fungi; A Phantom of Beguilement; Stupor Mundi; Past the Gate of Deepest Slumber; His Splintered Kiss; Oh, Baleful Theophany; The Strange Dark Folk; Your Metamorphic Moan.

Notes. Cover and interior illustrations by Robert H. Knox. A volume of Pugmire's recent weird writings, many of them in the Lovecraftian vein. The first Hippocampus Press publication of original fiction by a contemporary writer.

36.   H. P. LOVECRAFT. *Collected Essays, Volume 5: Philosophy; Autobiography and Miscellany.* Edited by S. T. Joshi. 2006. 382 pp. hc.

Contents. Introduction, by S. T. Joshi; PHILOSOPHY: The Crime of the Century; The Renaissance of Manhood; Liquor and Its Friends; More *Chain Lightning*; Symphony and Stress; Old England and the "Hyphen"; Revolutionary Mythology; The Symphonic Ideal; "Editor's Note" to "The Genesis of the Revolutionary War" by Henry Clapham McGavack; A Remarkable Document; At the Root; Time and Space; Merlinus Redivivus; Anglo-Saxondom; Amer-icanism; The League; Bolshevism; Idealism and Materialism–A Reflection; Life for Humanity's Sake; [*In Defence of Dagon*]; Nietzscheism and Realism; East and West Harvard Conservatism; The Materialist Today; Some Causes of Self-Immolation; Some Repetitions on the Times; A Layman Looks at the Government; The *Journal* and the New Deal; A Living Heritage: Roman Architecture in Today's America; Objections to Orthodox Communism; AUTOBIOGRAPHY AND MISCELLANY: The Brief Autobiography of an Inconsequential Scribbler; A Confession of Unfaith; [Diary: 1925]; [Commercial Blurbs]; Cats and Dogs; Notes on Hudson Valley History; Autobiography of Howard Phillips Lovecraft; In Memoriam: Henry St. Clair Whitehead; Some Notes on a Nonentity; Correspondence between R. H. Barlow and Wilson

Shepherd of Oakman, Alabama—Sept.–Nov. 1932; In Memoriam: Robert Ervin Howard; Commonplace Book; Instructions in Case of Decease; [Diary—1937]; NOTES FOR STORIES: [Notes to "Medusa's Coil"]; [Notes to *At the Mountains of Madness*]; [Notes to "The Shadow over Innsmouth"]; [The Round Tower]; [The Rose Window]; Of Evill Sorceries Done in New-England, of Daemons in No Humane Shape; [Notes to "The Shadow out of Time"]; [Notes to "The Challenge From Beyond"]; MISCELLANEOUS LISTS AND NOTES; [1] Catalogue of Prov. Press Co.; [2] [Catalogue of Works (1902)]; [3] [Postal Expenses]; [4] Old Farmer's Almanacks Wanted by H. P. Lovecraft; [5] [Notes on Clothing Stores]; [6] [Works Desired by H. Warner Munn]; [7] [Works of Weird Fiction]; [8] Tales by H. P. Lovecraft; [9] Basic Books for a Weird Library; [10] [Remembrancer]; [11] [List of Amateur Papers]; [12] [Possible Collections of Tales]; [13] [Magazine Addresses]; [14] [List of Individuals to Be Sent "The Battle That Ended the Century"]; [15] [List of Correspondents to Whom Postcards Have Been Sent]; [16] Suggested Recipients for Dragon Fly Outside Memb. List of NAPA; [17] Fungi from Yuggoth and Other Verses; [18] [Notable Stories in Recent Issues of *Weird Tales*]; [19] "Little Magazines"; [20] [Worthy Stories in Recent Issues of *Weird Tales*]; [21] [Pronunciation Guide]; [22] Tales of H. P. Lovecraft; Weird &c. Items in Library of H. P. Lovecraft; APPENDIX: [Advertisement of Revisory Services]; [Advertisement in the *New York Times*]; The Recognition of Temperance; [Advertisement in *Weird Tales*]; [Biographical Notice]; Preface [to *Old World Footprints*]; [E'ch-Pi-El Speaks]; Robert Ervin Howard: 1906–1936; Chronology of the Works of H. P. Lovecraft; Index of Titles (Volumes 1–5); Index (Volumes 1–5).

Notes. Cover illustration by Virgil Finlay. Interior illustrations by Lovecraft. Hardcover 250 copies, Covington Group. Simultaneously published in hardcover and paperback. The fifth and final volume of the *Collected Essays*, with a cumulative index to all five volumes and chronological listing of all Lovecraft's work. For the CD-ROM of the set, see item 55.

37.   CLARK ASHTON SMITH. *The Complete Poetry and Translations, Volume 3: The Flowers of Evil and Others.* Edited by S. T. Joshi and David E. Schultz. 2007. 442 pp. hc.

Contents. Introduction; *Les Fleurs du mal,* BY CHARLES BAUDELAIRE: Preface/Préface; SPLEEN ET IDÉAL: I. Bénédiction; II. The Albatross/L'Albatros; III. Elevation/Élévation; IV. Correspondences/ Correspondances; V. [Untitled]; VI. The Beacons/Les Phares; VII.

The Sick Muse/La Muse malade; VIII. The Venal Muse/La Muse vénale; IX. The Evil Monk/Le Mauvais Moine; X. L'Ennemi; XI. Le Guignon/Le Guignon; XII. Anterior Life/La Vie antérieure; XIII. Travelling Gypsies/Bohémiens en voyage; XIV. L'Homme et la mer; XV. Don Juan aux enfers; XVI. To Theodore de Banville/A Théodore de Banville; XVII. Chastisement of Pride/Châtiment de l'orgueil; XVIII. Beauty/La Beauté; XIX. The Ideal/L'Idéal; XX. The Giantess/La Géante; XXI. Le Masque; XXII. Hymn to Beauty/Hymne à la beauté; XXIII. Exotic Perfume/Parfum exotique; XXIV. The Chevelure/La Chevelure; XXV. [Untitled]; XXVI. [Untitled]; XXVII. *Sed non satiata*; XXVIII. [Untitled]; XXIX. Le Serpent qui danse; XXX. Une Charogne; XXXI. *De profundis clamavi*; XXXII. The Vampire/Le Vampire; XXXIII. [Untitled]; XXXIV. The Remorse of the Dead/Remords posthume; XXXV. The Cat/Le Chat; XXXVI. The Duel/ *Duellum*]; XXXVII. The Balcony/Le Balcon; XXXVIII. The Possessed/Le Possédé; XXXIX. Un Fantôme; XL. [Untitled]; XLI. *Semper eadem*; XLII. Tout entière; XLIII. [Untitled]; XLIV. Le Flambeau vivant; XLV. Réversibilité; XLVI. Confession; XLVII. The Spiritual Dawn/L'Aube spirituelle; XLVIII. Evening Harmony/ L'Harmonie du soir; XLIX. Le Flacon/Le Flacon; L. The Poison/Le Poison; LI. Doubtful Skies/Ciel brouillé; LII. Le Chat; LIII. Le Beau Navire; LIV. L'Invitation au voyage; LV. The Irreparable/ L'Irréparable; LVI. Causerie; LVII. Song of Autumn/Chant d'automne; LVIII. A une Madone; LIX. Chanson d'après-midi; LX. Sisina; LXI. Vers pour le portrait d'Honoré Daumier; LXII. *Franciscæ meæ laudes*; LXIII. To a Creole Lady/A une Dame créole; LXIV. *Mœsta et errabunda*; LXV. The Phantom/Le Revenant; LXVI. Sonnet d'automne; LXVII. Tristesses de la lune; LXVIII. The Cats/Les Chats; LXIX. The Owls/Les Hiboux; LXX. La Pipe; LXXI. Music/La Musique; LXXII. Sépulture; LXXIII. Une Gravure fantastique; LXXIV. Le Mort joyeux; LXXV. The Barrel of Hate/Le Tonneau de la haine; LXXVI. La Cloche fêlée; LXXVII. Spleen; LXXVIII. Spleen; LXXIX. Spleen; LXXX. Spleen; LXXXI. Obsession; LXXXII. Le Goût du néant; LXXXIII. Alchemy of Sorrow/Alchimie de la douleur; LXXXIV. Sympathetic Horror/Horreur sympathique; LXXXV. Le Calumet de paix; LXXXVI. A Pagan's Prayer/La Prière d'un païen; LXXXVII. The Cover/Le Couvercle; LXXXVIII. L'Imprévu; LXXXIX. Examination at Midnight/L'Examen de minuit; XC. Madrigal of Sorrow/Madrigal triste; XCI. The Adviser/L'Avertisseur; XCII. To a Malabaress/A une Malabaraise; XCIII. The Voice/La Voix; XCIV. Hymn/Hymne; XCV. The Rebel/Le Rebelle; XCVI. The Eyes of Bertha/Les Yeux de Berthe; XCVII. The Fountain/Le Jet d'eau; XCVIII. La Rançon; XCIX. Very Far from Here/Bien loin d'ici; C. Le Coucher du Soleil romantique;

CI. On "Tasso in Prison" by Eugène Delacroix/Sur *Le Tasse en Prison* d'Eugène Delacroix; CII. The Gulf/Le Gouffre; CIII. The Lament of Icarus/Les Plaintes d'un Icare; CIV. Contemplation/Receuillement; CV. *L'Héautontimorouménos*; CVI. The Irremediable/ L'Irrémédiable; CVII. The Clock/L'Horloge; TABLEAUX PARISIENS: CVIII. Paysage; CIX. The Sun/Le Soleil; CX. Lola de Valence; CXI. La Lune offensée; CXII. A une Mendiante rousse; CXIII. Le Cygne; CXIV. Les Sept Vieillards; CXV. Les Petites Vieilles; CXVI. The Blind/Les Aveugles; CXVII. To a Passer-by/A une Passante; CXVIII. The Toiling Skeleton/Le Squelette laboureur; CXIX. Evening Twilight/Le Crépuscule du soir; CXX. The Game/Le Jeu; CXXI. The Dance of Death/Danse macabre; CXXII. The Love of Falsehood/L'Amour du mensonge; CXXIII. [Untitled]; CXXIV. [Untitled]; CXXV. Mists and Rains/Brumes et pluies; CXXVI. Parisian Dream/Rêve parisien; CXXVII. Le Crépuscule du matin; LE VIN: CXXVIII. L'Ame du vin; CXXIX. The Wine of the Rag-Pickers/Le Vin de chiffonniers; CXXX. The Wine of the Assassin/Le Vin de l'assassin; CXXXI. The Wine of the Solitary/Le Vin du solitaire; CXXXII. The Wine of Lovers/Le Vin des amants; LES FLEURS DU MAL: CXXXIII. Epigraph for a Condemned Book/Epigraphe pour un livre condamné; CXXXIV. Destruction/La Destruction; CXXXV. Une Martyre; CXXXVI. Femmes damnées; CXXXVII. The Two Kind Sisters/Les Deux Bonnes Sœurs; CXXXVIII. The Fountain of Blood/La Fontaine de sang; CXXXIX. Allégorie; CXL. Beatrice/La Béatrice; CXLI. Un voyage à Cythère; CXLII. Love and the Cranium/L'Amour et le crâne; RÉVOLTE: CXLIII. The Denial of St. Peter/Le Reniement de Saint Pierre; CXLIV. Abel et Caïn; CXLV. Litany to Satan/Les Litanies de Satan; LA MORT: CXLVI. The Death of Lovers/La Mort des amants; CXLVII. La Mort des pauvres; CXLVIII. La Mort des artistes; CXLIX. La Fin de la journée; CL. La Rêve d'un curieux; CLI. The Voyage/; [JETSAM]: I. Les Bijoux; II. Lethe/Le Léthé; III. To Her Who Is Too Gay/A celle qui est trop gaie; IV. Lesbos; V. Femmes damnées: Delphine et Hippolyte; VI. The Metamorphoses of the Vampire/Les Métamorphoses du vampire; TRANSLATIONS FROM THE FRENCH: MARIE DAUGUET: [Untitled]/ [Epilogue]; THÉOPHILE GAUTIER: The Flower-Pot/Le Pot de fleurs; The Impassible/L'Impassible; Pastel; GÉRARD DE NERVAL: Artemis/Artémis; Golden Verses/Vers dorés; JOSÉ-MARIA DE HEREDIA: Antony and Cleopatra/ Antoine et Cléopâtre; The Coral Reef/Le Récif de corail; La Dogaresse; Nemea/Némée; Oblivion/L'Oubli; On a Broken Statue/Sur un Marbre brisé; The Samurai/Le Samouraï; A Setting Sun/Soleil couchant; The Stained Window/ Vitrail; VICTOR HUGO: Twilight/Crépuscule; What One Hears on the Mountain/ Ce qu'on entend sur la montagne; The Wheel of Omphale/Le Rouet d'Omphale;

TRISTAN KLINGSOR: Plaisir d'Amour; ALPHONSE LOUIS MARIE DE LAMARTINE: The Lake/Le Lac; CHARLES MARIE RENÉ LECONTE DE LISLE: The Black Panther/ La Panthère noire; Ecclesiastes/ L'Ecclésiaste; The Exhibitionists/ Les Montreurs; The Howlers/Les Hurleurs; The Sleep of the Condor/Le Sommeil du condor; Solvet seclum; CHARLES VAN LERBERGHE: Song/Chanson; PIERRE LIÈVRE: Elysian Landscape/Paysage Elyséen [text not found]; The End of Supper/[title unknown; text not found]; STUART MERRILL: A Woman at Prayer/Celle qui prie; ALFRED DE MUSSET: Remember Thee/Rappelle-toi; Song/Chanson; SULLY-PRUDHOMME: Siesta/ Sieste; ALBERT SAMAIN: I Dream/ [Untitled]; [Myrtil and Palemone]/ [Myrtil et Palémone]; FERNAND SEVERIN: Sonnet/Bois sacré; PAUL VERLAINE: IX (Ariettes Oubliées); Il Bacio; La Bonne Chanson; Crimen Amoris; En Sourdine; The Faun/Le Faune; Green; Moonlight/Claire de lune; Song from *Les Uns et les autres*; Spleen [Spleen]; To a Woman/A une femme; TRANSLATIONS FROM THE SPANISH: GUSTAVO ADOLFO BÉCQUER: Invocation/Rimas LII; The Sower/Rimas LX; Where?/Rimas XXXVIII; The World Rolls On/Rimas I (Libro de los gorriones); JOSÉ A. CALCAÑO: The Cypress/El ciprés; JOSÉ SANTOS CHOCANO: The Sleep of the Cayman/El sueño del caimán; RUBÉN DARÍO: The Song of Songs/El Cantar de los Cantares; JUANA DE IBARBOUROU: Rustic Life/Vida aldeana; JORGE ISAACS: Luminary/Luminar; JUAN LOZANO Y LOZANO: Rhythm/Ritmo; AMADO NERVO: Night/Noche; APPENDIX: XXVII. *Sed non Satiata*; LV. L'Irréparable; CXLI. Un Voyage à Cythère; The Peace-Pipe, by Henry Wadsworth Longfellow; Notes; Index of Titles; Index of First Lines.

Notes. Dust jacket illustration by Anastasia Damianakos. Published in a limited hardcover edition of 250 copies (Covington Group). The fruit of many years' work on the part of the editors. This volume, although designated Volume 3, appeared first because it was more convenient for the editors to issue Smith's translations of French and Spanish poetry than to prepare his original poetry (see item 50). Smith's translations (many of them in prose) and the original French and Spanish texts (chiefly from Baudelaire's *Les Fleurs du mal* but also from other poets such as Verlaine, Heredia, and Bécquer) are presented on facing pages. Many of Smith's translations are literal prose renderings that he had not yet versified. Most of the translations were previously unpublished. The recently discovered "The Desire of Loving," a translation of "Le Désir d'Aimer" by Hélène Picard, appeared in Volume 2. For the paperback edition, see item 113.

38.   BARRY PAIN. *An Exchange of Souls.* HENRI BÉRAUD. *Lazarus.* 2007. 105 + 114 pp. tpb.

Notes. Cover illustration by anonymous (from the first edition of Pain's *An Exchange of Souls*) and by Ralph Fabri (Béraud). Part of the Lovecraft's Library series. The first "Hippocampus double," analogous to the "Ace doubles" of the 1950s, in which two short novels were presented in a single volume. Pain's novel was first published in 1911 and manifestly influenced Lovecraft's "The Thing on the Doorstep"; Béraud's novel first appeared in French in 1924 (English translation 1925) and was an influence on Lovecraft's "The Shadow out of Time." Joshi has written separate introductions to both books.

39.   PHILIP HALDEMAN. *Shadow Coast.* 2007. 255 pp. tpb.

Notes. Cover illustration and design by Cassie Barden; photograph by David Haldeman. A haunting novel of horrors in the Pacific Northwest.

40.   *Dead Reckonings* No. 1 (Spring 2007). EDITED BY S. T. JOSHI AND JACK M. HARINGA. 100 pp.

Editorial; Knowing and Observing, by Paula Guran [David J. Schow, *Havoc Swims Jaded*; Glen Hirshberg, *American Morons*]; Cosmic Chess Games and Halloween Horrors, by Hank Wagner [F. Paul Wilson, *Harbingers*; Norm Partridge, *Dark Harvest*]; From Mr. Hands to Mr. Molester, by Tony Fonseca [Gary A. Braunbeck, *Prodigal Blues*]; Mommy Made Me Do It, by S. T. Joshi [Ramsey Campbell, *Secret Stories*]; Retro-pocalypse Now, by Michael Marano [Cormac McCarthy, *The Road*; James Newman, *The Wicked*]; Judgment Day, by Alan Warren [John Shirley, *The Other End*]; Strange Stories, by John Langan [Neil Gaiman, *Fragile Things*]; Ramsey Campbell, Probably; *Dandelion Wine* Redux, by Jim Rockhill [Ray Bradbury, *Farewell Summer*]; Pay No Attention to That Man Behind the Curtain, by June Pulliam [Brian Hodge, *World of Hurt*]; The Critic as Dadaist, by Richard Bleiler [John Clute, *The Darkening Garden*]; The Thing That Haunts the Dormitory, by Darrell Schweitzer [Alexandra Sokoloff, *The Harrowing*]; A Different Stephen King, by Ben Indick [Stephen King, *Lisey's Story*]; Weeding Out Emotion to Cultivate Violence, by Tony Fonseca [Jack Ketchum, *Weed Species*]; The Sheridan Le Fanu of Humor, by Steven J. Mariconda [T. E. D. Klein, *Reassuring Tales*]; A Remarkable Intellectual Figure, by Donald R. Burleson [H. P. Lovecraft, *Collected Essays*]; A New Dark Age?, by Rob Latham [J. G. Ballard, *Kingdom Come*]; Shades of Blackwood and Elgar, by Mike Ashley [Phil Rickman, *The Remains of an Altar*]; Twenty-First-Century Ghosts, by Stefan Dziemianowicz [Joe Hill, *20th-Century Ghosts*; Joe Hill, *Heart-Shaped Box*]; Books into Film and Vice Versa, by Matt Cardin [Tom Piccirilli, *The Dead Letters*; Tim Waggoner, *Darkness Wakes*]; Metaphysical Labyrinths and Fairy-Tale Archetypes, by John Langan [Tim Powers, *Three Days to Never*; John Connolly, *The Book of Lost Things*]; Lights, Camera, Horror, by Jack M. Haringa [Stephen Graham Jones, *Demon Theory*; Mick Garris, *Development Hell*]; A Catalogue of Nightmares, by Robert Morrish [S. T. Joshi, ed., *Icons of Horror and the Supernatural*]; Capsule Reviews.

Notes. Cover illustration by Jason C. Eckhardt (uniform, aside from color, in all subsequent issues). The first issue of Hippocampus's review magazine, designed to carry on in the wake of the defunct *Necrofile* (1991–99), published by Necronomicon Press. It was our feeling that the horror field needed a venue for substantial, thoughtful reviews of contemporary publications. Ramsey Campbell graciously allowed the reprinting of his column, "Ramsey Campbell, Probably," originally published in *Necrofile* and subsequently running in *All Hallows.*

40A.   LESLIE L. LUTHER. *Moravia and Its Past.* Moravia, NY: Cayuga–Owasco Lakes Historical Society, 2007. 414 pp. hc.

Contents. Foreword, by George A. Luther; A Note on This Edition, by S. T. Joshi; Preface (1966); Introduction, by Frederic Luther; Acknowledgments; I. Local Historians; II. Roads, Streets and Buildings; III. Moravia Schools; IV. Moravia Churches; V. Moravians of Note; VI. Various Local Characters Who Have Appeared upon the Scene, Had Their Day, and Been Gathered to to Their Fathers; VII. African Americans; VIII. Tragedies; IX. Patriots; X. Interesting Letters Received; XI. Miscellaneous Items; XII. Montville; XIII. Town of Niles; XIV. Town of Sempronius; XV. Town of Locke; XVI. Town of Genoa; XVII. Town of Venice; XVIII. Town of Scipio; Further Reading about Moravia; Index.

Notes. A reprint of the 1966 edition. Published by arrangement with Hippocampus Press. S. T. Joshi was at the time a resident of Moravia, and lent assistance in reissuing this highly regarded local history, correcting some apparent errors in the first edition, and recompiling the index to include nearly every name, place, and business.

41.   S. T. JOSHI AND ROSEMARY PARDOE, EDITORS. *Warnings to the Curious: A Sheaf of Criticism on M. R. James.* 2007. 338 pp. tpb.

Contents. Introduction, by S. T. Joshi; I. SOME NOTES ON BIOGRAPHY: Montague Rhodes James 1862–1936, by Stephen Gaselee; Montague

Rhodes James, by Shane Leslie; The Strangeness Present: M. R. James's Suffolk, by Norman Scarfe; M. R. James and Livermere, by Michael Cox; II. GENERAL STUDIES: Supernatural Horror in Literature, by H. P. Lovecraft; The Art of Montague James, by Mary Butts; The Ghost Stories of Montague Rhodes James, by L. J. Lloyd; The Toad in the Study: M. R. James, H. P. Lovecraft, and Forbidden Knowledge, by Simon MacCulloch; III. SOME SPECIAL TOPICS: On Not Letting Them Lie: Moral Significance in the Ghost Stories of M. R. James, by Michael A. Mason; Dark Devotions: M. R. James and the Magical Tradition, by Ron Weighell; M. R. James's Women, by David G. Rowlands; "The Rules of Folklore" in the Ghost Stories of M. R. James, by Jacqueline Simpson; "A Warning to the Curious": Victorian Science and the Awful Unconscious in M. R. James's Ghost Stories, by Brian Cowlishaw; "They've Got Him! In the Trees!" M. R. James and Sylvan Dread, by Steve Duffy; Homosexual Panic and the English Ghost Story: M. R. James and Others, by Mike Pincombe; "If I'm Not Careful": Innocents and Not-So-Innocents in the Stories of M. R. James, by John Alfred Taylor; "As Time Goes On I See a Shadow Coming": M. R. James's Grammar of Terror, by Steven J. Mariconda; "What Is This That I Have Done?" The Scapegoat Figure in the Stories of M. R. James, by Scott Connors; IV. STUDIES OF INDIVIDUAL TALES: The Nature of the Beast: The Demonology of "Canon Alberic's Scrap-book," by Helen Grant; A Haunting Presence, by C. E. Ward; "A Wonderful Book": George MacDonald and "The Ash-Tree," by Rosemary Pardoe; Who Was Count Magnus? Notes towards an Identification, by Rosemary Pardoe; A Haunting Vision: M. R. James and the Ashridge Stained Glass, by Nicholas Connell; A Maze of Secrets in a Story by M. R. James, by Martin Hughes; Thin Ghosts: Notes toward a Jamesian Rhetoric, by Jim Rockhill; Nightmares of Punch and Judy in Ruskin and M. R. James, by Roger Craik; An Elucidation (?) of the Plot of M. R. James's "Two Doctors," by Lance Arney; Landmarks and Shrieking Ghosts, by Jacqueline Simpson; Addendum by Rosemary Pardoe; Bibliography; Acknowledgments; Index.

Notes. Cover illustration by Carl Wilton, from *Ghost Stories of an Antiquary* by M. R. James (London: Pan Books, 1953). The first volume ever published that was devoted solely to James's ghost stories. A substantial anthology, including both reprinted pieces (many from *Ghosts & Scholars*, the leading organ of M. R. James studies) and original works.

42. FRANKLYN SEARIGHT. *Lair of the Dreamer: A Cthulhu Mythos Omnibus*. 2007. 307 pp. tpb.

Contents. Tainted Lineage, by Robert M. Price; There Is a Pond; Interlude at the Bridge; The Sorcerer's Pipe; The Innsmouth Head; Armillaria; The Guardian of the Pit; The Closing of the Gate; Mists of Death; Stomach Pains; Lair of the Dreamer.

Notes. Cover and interior illustrations by Robert H. Knox. Substantial collection of the Cthulhu Mythos fiction of Franklyn Searight, son of Richard F. Searight, a correspondent of Lovecraft. Includes the short novel of the title, previously unpublished.

43. SEAN DONNELLY, EDITOR. *W. Paul Cook: The Wandering Life of a Yankee Printer*. 2007. x, 237 pp. tpb.

Contents. Preface; Acknowledgments; ABOUT W. PAUL COOK: W. Paul Cook: "An Ordinary Printer," by Sean Donnelly; Recollections of W. Paul Cook, by Arthur H. Goodenough; The Birth of Drift, by Walter John Coates; The Colossus of the North, by Edward H. Cole; In Memoriam: W. Paul Cook, by Edward H. Cole; A Bibliography of W. Paul Cook, by Sean Donnelly; BY W. PAUL COOK: John DeMorgan; By and about Ourselves; Inconsequentialities; First Impressions; A Thought; Howard P. Lovecraft's Fiction; H. P. Lovecraft; Introducing Vermont Names; More about Names; A Plea for Lovecraft; The Great "What Is It?"; Jim Morton; A Day in the Life of Willis T. Crossman; PROTEST STUFF: Introduction; Rhyme; Futility; Paternalism; The Root; Extermination; Parasites; The Plan; Mission; Confidence; Boomerang; The Butt; Fealty; Vacation; Tabloid; "Not Molested"; Amusement; The Parting; Joy Street; Church; Selections from *Contradictions* (Escape; Rootless; Easter; Awakening; Agnosticism); Waters of Lethe; About the Editor; About the Book; *The Recluse* (cover) (1927); Photograph of Orton, Coates, and Cook; *In Memoriam: Howard Phillips Lovecraft* (cover) (1941); *Monadnock Monthly* (cover) (November 1901); *Vagrant* (cover) (Spring 1927); *A Day in the Life of Willis T. Crossman* (cover) (1934); *Protest Stuff* (title page) (1934).

Notes. Cover illustration by Gale Mueller. A lengthy biographical study of Cook, the amateur printer and close friend of Lovecraft. Also includes memoirs of Cook by his colleagues, a bibliography of his publications, and a rich sampling of Cook's prose and poetic writings. A companion volume to Donnelly's *Willis T. Crossman's Vermont: Stories by W. Paul Cook* (University of Tampa Press, 2005).

44. *Lovecraft Annual* No. 1 (2007). EDITED BY S. T. JOSHI. 160 pp.

Contents. Lovecraft Read This, by Darrell Schweitzer; Lovecraft and Lawrence Face the Hidden Gods: Transformations of Pan in "The Colour out of Space" and *St. Mawr*, by Robert H. Waugh; Memories of Sonia H. Greene Davis, by Martin H. Kopp; Letters to Lee McBride White, by H. P. Lovecraft (ed. S. T. Joshi and David E. Schultz); The Negative Mystics of the Mechanistic Sublime: Walter Benjamin and Lovecraft's Cosmicism, by Jeff Lacy and Steven J. Zani; Unity in Diversity: *Fungi from Yuggoth* as a Unified Setting, by Phillip A. Ellis; "They Have Conquered Dream": A. Merritt's "The Face in the Abyss" and H. P. Lovecraft's "The Mound," by Peter Levi; The Master's Eyes Shining with Secrets: H. P. Lovecraft's Influence on Thomas Ligotti, by Matt Cardin; Thomas Ligotti's Metafictional Mapping: The Allegory of "The Last Feast of Harlequin," by John Langan; REVIEWS: [Review of Michel Houellebecq, *H. P. Lovecraft: Against the World, Against Life*], by Kevin Dole; [Review of Ben J. S. Szumskyj and S. T. Joshi, ed., *Fritz Leiber and H. P. Lovecraft: Writers of the Dark*], by Philip A. Ellis; [Review of Peter Cannon, *The Lovecraft Chronicles*], by S. T. Joshi; [Review of Robert H. Waugh, *The Monster in the Mirror: Looking for H. P. Lovecraft*], by S. T. Joshi; Briefly Noted.

Notes. Cover illustration by Allen Koszowski (uniform, aside from color, in all subsequent issues). The first issue of Hippocampus's scholarly journal devoted to Lovecraft, intended as a replacement of the defunct *Lovecraft Studies* (1979–2005), published by Necronomicon Press.

45. *Dead Reckonings* No. 2 (Fall 2007). EDITED BY S. T. JOSHI AND JACK M. HARINGA. 117 pp.

Contents. The World Down Under, by Sherry Austin [Ekaterina Sedia, *The Secret History of Moscow*]; A Cannibal's Boyhood, by June Pulliam [Thomas Harris, *Hannibal Rising*]; Poe, Poe, and More Poe, by Ben Fisher [Christopher Conlon, *Poe's Lighthouse*; James Robert Smith and Stephen Mark Rainey, ed., *Evermore*]; Green Glows and Trickster Gods, by Tony Fonseca [Thomas Tessier, *Wicked Things*; Philip Haldeman, *Shadow Coast*]; The Ultimate Clark Ashton Smith, by Hubert Van Calenbergh [Clark Ashton Smith, *Collected Fantasies*, Vols. 1 and 2]; Decadence in Verse and Prose, by Steven J. Mariconda [Clark Ashton Smith, *Complete Poems and Translations*, Vol. 3]; Tact and the Ghost Story, by Reggie Oliver [S. T. Joshi and Rosemary Pardoe, ed., *Warnings to the Curious*]; An Anatomist of Technoscience, by Rob Latham [Thomas Pynchon, *Against the Day*]; Ghosts and Scholars, by Brian Showers [Margaret Oliphant, *The Library Window*; Cheiro, *A Study of Destiny*]; Domination of Black, by

John Langan [Laird Barron, *The Imago Sequence*]; Ligotti Redivivus?, by S. T. Joshi [Michael Cisco, *Secret Hours; The Traitor*]; Some Manifestations of Fantasy, by Ben P. Indick [Sean Wallace and Paul Tremblay, ed., *Fantasy;* Scriptus Innominatus, *Zencore!*]; Ramsey Campbell, Probably; Devouring Yet More Flesh, by Darrell Schweitzer [Kim Paffenroth, *Dying to Live*]; Ambrose Bierce's Moral Art, by Donald R. Burleson [*The Short Fiction of Ambrose Bierce: A Comprehensive Edition*]; Hardboiled and Haunted, by Jack M. Haringa; Tom Piccirilli, *The Midnight Road*]; The Yellow House on Benefit Street, by Scott Connors [Caitlin R. Kiernan, *Daughter of Hounds*]; Good, Bad, and Ugly, by Tony Fonseca [Peter Crowther, ed., *PostScripts 10;* Robert Morrish, ed., *Thrillers Two (II, 2)*]; Danger and Loss, by Paula Guran [Elizabeth Hand, *Illyria; Generation Loss*]; Memoirs, Essays, and Frivolities, by Richard Bleiler [Peter Straub, *Sides*]; Confronting the Unknowable, by Jim Rockhill [Lucius Shepard, *Dagger Key and Other Stories; Softspoken*]; Thrillers That Don't Thrill, by Michael Marano [Michael Marshall Smith, *The Servants; The Intruder*]; The Dark Delights of Gnostic Nightmares, by Matt Cardin [Richard Gavin, *Omens*]; Breathing Life into Old Plots, by Hank Wagner [Mary SanGiovanni, *The Hollower;* Sarah Langan, *The Missing*]; Unfinished Business, by Van Viator [John Farris, *You Don't Scare Me;* Lee Thomas, *The Dust of Wonderland*]; Open Mouths, Ready to Feed, by John Langan [Conrad Williams, *The Unblemished*]; Dudsville, by Alan Warren [Jeffrey Thomas, *Deadstock;* with Scott Thomas, *The Sea of Flesh and Ash*]; Enough Ghost Sex, Already, by Sherry Austin [Steve Berman, *Vintage: A Ghost Story*]; In the Garden of Yidden, by Ben P. Indick [Michael Chabon, *The Yiddish Policeman's Union*]; The Sounds of Violence, by Jack M. Haringa [Michael Arnzen, *Audiovile;* Elizabeth Monteleone, ed., *Dark Voices, Vols. 1, 2, 4, & 5;* Gruesome, *Johnny Gruesome*]; A Lasting Object of Contemplation, by Darrell Schweitzer [*Pan's Labyrinth* (film)]; The Darkling Plain, by Stefan Dziemianowicz; Capsule Reviews.

46.   LELAND HALL. *Sinister House.* FRANCIS BRETT YOUNG. *Cold Harbour.* 2008. 108 + 161 pp. tpb.

Notes. Cover and interior illustrations by Haydon Jones (from the original edition of *Sinister House*) and by the anonymous artist of the first American edition of *Cold Harbour.* Part of the Lovecraft's Library series. A reprint of two splendid novels discussed by Lovecraft in "Supernatural Horror in Literature." Neither *Sinister House* (1919) nor *Cold Harbour* (1924) appear to have had any direct influence on Lovecraft's stories, but further investigation may reveal subtle influences here and there. S. T. Joshi has written separate introductions to each novel.

47.　　EDITH MINITER. *Dead Houses and Other Works.* Edited by Kenneth W. Faig, Jr., and Sean Donnelly. 2008. xiii, 369 pp. tpb.

Contents. Introducing Edith Miniter, by Kenneth W. Faig & Sean Donnelly; ABOUT EDITH MINITER: Edith Miniter: A Life, by Kenneth W. Faig, Jr.; Mrs. Miniter—Estimates and Recollections, by H. P. Lovecraft; Edith Miniter, by Edward H. Cole; My Recollections, by William R. Murphy; Memories and Impressions, by Ernest A. Edkins; As I Knew Her, by Arthur H. Goodenough; Some Thoughts of Edith Miniter, by James P. Morton; My Friend Edith Miniter, by Nelson Glazier Morton; My Association with Edith May Miniter, by Truman J. Spencer; Edith Miniter, by H. P. Lovecraft; AMATEUR JOURNALISM: Salutatory; Editorial; Definitions Definitely Defined; Some Benefits of Amateur Journalism: A Hallowe'en Invitation; Hallowe'en Happenings; The Aftermath; Epgephi Musings; Falco Ossifracus; My Mother as She Seemed to Me; The Aftermath; The February Meeting; The Big Event; FICTION: To Thine Own Heart Be True; A Tragedy of the Hills; A Shadow on the Water; The Homecoming of Cleora; He That Will Not When He May: A Tale of Christmas Time; Wonted Fires; The Root of Age; The Emancipation of Elivra; Utilizing a By-Product; A Bunch of Crocuses; Aunt Ann's Bed; Cinderella Soapman; Nobody Home; Tartar Sauce; Thumbs; Dead Houses; About the Editors; About the Book.

Notes. Cover design by Sean Donnelly. A generous selection of Miniter's writings, including both fiction and amateur journalism. Miniter was a leading figure in the amateur journalism movement of the late 19th and early 20th centuries, and her fiction also appeared professionally. The book contains a lengthy biographical introduction by Faig and memoirs of Miniter by friends and colleagues, including Lovecraft.

48.　　DONALD WANDREI. *Sanctity and Sin: The Collected Poems and Prose Poems of Donald Wandrei.* Edited by S. T. Joshi. 2008. 195 pp. tpb.

Contents. Introduction, by S. T. Joshi; ECSTASY AND OTHER POEMS: The Voice of Beauty; Song of Autumn; Ecstasy; Let Us Love Tonight; Vain Warning; On Some Drawings; Sanctity and Sin; To Myrrhiline; Song of Oblivion; In Mandrikor; The Woodland Pool; Death and the Poet: A Fragment; Satiation; In Memoriam: George Sterling; Bacchanalia; Awakening; Red; Hermaphroditus; Aphrodite; Amphitrite; Philomela; A Drinking Song; At the Bacchic Revel; The Challenger; The Greatest Regret; Futility; From the Shadowlands of Memory; The Poet's Language; Nightmare; Valerian; DARK ODYSSEY:

Notes. Cover and interior illustrations by Howard Wandrei. Originally designed for a 6 × 9 inch format, although copies were printed at a smaller trim size, resulting in very tight margins. This was corrected in 2011. An exhaustive revision of Joshi's edition of Wandrei's *Collected Poems* (Necronomicon Press, 1988), augmented by several new poems and a sheaf of Wandrei's prose poems.

49.   CLARK ASHTON SMITH. *The Hashish-Eater.* Edited by Donald Sidney-Fryer. 2008. 85 pp. tpb.

Contents. A Wind from the Unknown, by Ron Hilger; About Clark Ashton Smith and *The Hashish-Eater*; The Crystals, by Clark Ashton Smith; Argument of *The Hashish-Eater*, by Clark Ashton Smith; The Face from Infinity, by Clark Ashton Smith; Excerpt from a letter by Smith, summer 1950; The Hashish-Eater; or, The Apocalypse of Evil, by Clark Ashton Smith; Commentary; The Final Image; Suggested Interpretation; Conclusion.

Notes. Cover illustration by Clark Ashton Smith. Expanded from the editor's privately printed booklet (1990). Offered free with purchase of Smith's *Complete Poetry and Translations*; eventually made available for separate purchase. Audio CD contains hidden tracks of Sidney-Fryer reading a selection of other poems by Smith.
    A thoroughly annotated edition of Smith's longest poem (581 lines) by the leading authority on Smith. The text of the poem comprises the original appearance in *Ebony and Crystal* (1922) and Smith's revised version (dating to the 1940s) from his *Selected Poems* (1971) on facing pages.

50.   CLARK ASHTON SMITH. *The Complete Poetry and Translations.* Edited by S. T. Joshi and David E. Schultz. 2008. 2 vols. hc (xxxix, 846 pp., numbered consecutively).

Contents. VOLUME 1 (*The Abyss Triumphant*): Introduction; THE VOICE OF SILENCE (1910–1911): Cloudland; The Fountain of Youth; The Road of Pain; Reincarnation; Lethe; A White Rose; Death; Companionship; Illusion; The Call of the Wind; The Expanding Ideal; Imagination; The Sunrise; Night; To a Yellow Pine; A Sierran Sunrise; The Sierras; The Wind and the Moon; Moonlight; The Altars of Sunset; To George Sterling; The Voice of Silence; Weavings; The West Wind; Before Sunrise; At Nadir; The Besieging Billows; The Butterfly; The Meaning; To the Nightshade; The Garden of Dreams; Ode to Matter; Ode to Poetry; The Pageant of Music; Autumn Dew; The Eclipse; The Falling Leaves; The Freedom of the Hills; The Hosts of Heaven; Ode on the Future of Song; The Suns and the Void; To George Sterling; Moods of the Sea; Sonnets of the

Autumn; On Re-reading Baudelaire; Lemurienne; You Are Not Beautiful; December; The Pagan; A Meeting; Adventure; Transmutation; The Last Oblivion; To the Chimera; Immortelle; In Autumn; Estrangement; A Catch; Consolation; The Temptation; Apologia; Incognita; Enigma; Query; Loss; Concupiscence; Maya; Dead Love; A Prayer; Enchanted Mirrors; Minatory; Interrogation; Madrigal; Sandalwood; October; The Envoys; Ode; Un Couchant; A Sunset; Un Madrigal; A Madrigal; The Saturnienne; Apostrophe; Chansonette; Idylle païenne; Idylle païenne; Retrospect and Forecast; Sonnet lunaire; Sonnet lunaire; À Mi-Chemin; À Mi-Chemin; L'Abîme; Le Cauchemar; Chanson de rêve; Le Cheveu; Éloignement; Exotique; La Méduse des cieux; To George Sterling: A Valediction; After Armageddon; JUVENILIA: [Untitled]; [Fragment 1]; [Fragment 2]; [Fragment 3]; [Fragment 4]; [Fragment 5]; [Fragment 6]; Benares; The Prayer Rug; The Rubaiyat of Seyyid; Sunrise; The Skull; The Orient; Time; To an Eastern City; Fortune; The Ocean; Allah; Arab Song; Arabian Love-Song; Bedouin Song; The City of the Djinn; The Desert; A Dream of Vathek; A Dream of Zanoni; Eblis Repentant; From the Persian; From the Persian; From the Persian; Haroun Al-Raschid; The Inscription; Jewel of the Orient; Jewel of the Orient; Kismet; Mohammed; The Muezzin; Ode from the Persian; Odes of Alnaschar; Omar's Philosophy; The Palace of the Jinn; The Prayer Rug; The Prince and the Peri; Quatrain; Quatrains; Quatrains; The Snare; Song; Quatrains on Jewels; The Diamond; The Pearl; The Turquoise; The Ruby; The Opal; Rubaiyat; Rubaiyat; Rubaiyat of Saiyed; The Seekers; Some Maxims from the Persian; Stamboul; Suleyman Jan ben Jan; The Temple; The World; Youth and Age; Zuleika; Asia; Aurungzeb's Mosque; The Burning Ghauts; The Burning-Ghauts at Benares; Dawn; Delhi; A Dream of India; The Ganges; Alchemy; The Book of Years; Courage; The Days of Time; The Departed City; A Dream; Fear; The Fear of Death; The Feast; Hate and Love; Hope; The Land o' Dreams; The Leveler; Love; The Lure of Gold; Mercy; The Moon; Perseverance; Poem [?]; Resignation; The River; The River of Life; Sea-Lure; The Sea-Shell; Silence; Solitude; Summer Idleness; To the Best Beloved; The World; [Fragment 7].

VOLUME 2 (*The Wine of Summer*): SPECTRAL LIFE (1927–1929): Les Violons; Au Bord du Léthé; The Nevermore-to-Be; Fantaisie d'antan; Canticle; A Fable; De Consolation; De Consolation; Simile; Trope; Venus; One Evening; Tristan to Iseult; Souvenance; To Antares; Song; Amor Autumnalis; Warning; Temporality; Chansonette; Chansonette; Credo; The Autumn Lake; Le Lac d'automne; On a Chinese Vase; November; Chanson de Novembre; Chanson de Novembre; Exorcism; Winter Moonlight; Connaissance; Harmony; Moon-Sight;

Monacle; Feast of St. Anthony; Paphnutius; Philtre; Borderland; Lethe; Empusa Waylays a Traveller; Perseus and Medusa; Odysseus in Eternity; The Ghost of Theseus; Distillations; Fence and Wall; Growth of Lichen; Cats in Winter Sunlight; Abandoned Plum-Orchard; Harvest Evening; Willow-Cutting in Autumn; Declining Moon; Late Pear-Pruner; Nocturnal Pines; Phallus Impudica; Stormy Afterglow; Geese in the Spring Night; Foggy Night; Reigning Empress; The Sparrow's Nest; The Last Apricot; Mushroom-Gatherers; Spring Nunnery; Nuns Walking in the Orchard; Improbable Dream; Crows in Spring; High Mountain Juniper; Storm's End; Pool at Lobos; Poet in a Barroom; Fallen Grape-Leaf; Gopher-Hole in Orchard; Basin in Boulder; Indian Acorn-Mortar; Old Limestone Kiln; Love in Dreams; Night of Miletus; Tryst at Lobos; Mountain Trail; Future Meeting; Classic Reminiscence; Goats and Manzanita-Boughs; Bed of Mint; Chainless Captive; California Winter; January Willow; Snowfall on Acacia; Flight of the Yellow-Hammer; Sunset over Farm-Land; Flora; Windows at Lamplighting Time; Old Hydraulic Diggings; Hearth on Old Cabin-Site; Builder of Deserted Hearth; Aftermath of Mining Days; River-Canyon; Childhood; School-Room Pastime; Boys Telling Bawdy Tales; Fight on the Play-Ground; Water-Fight; Boys Rob a Yellow-Hammer's Nest; Nest of the Screech-Owl; Grammar-School Vixen; Girl of Six; Mortal Essences; Snake, Owl, Cat or Hawk; Slaughter-House in Spring; Cattle Salute the Psychopomp; Slaughter-House Pasture; Field Behind the Abatoir; Plague from the Abatoir; La Mort des amants; Vultures Come to the Ambarvalia; For the Dance of Death; Berries of the Deadly Nightshade; Water-Hemlock; Felo-de-se of the Parasite; Pagans Old and New; Initiate of Dionysus; Bacchic Orgy; Abstainer; Picture by Piero di Cosimo; Bacchants and Bacchante; Garden of Priapus; Morning Star of the Mountains; Bygone Interlude; Prisoner in Vain; Epitaphs; Braggart; Slaughtered Cattle; The Earth; Miscellaneous Haiku; Illuminatus; Limestone Cavern; Maternal Prostitute; Ocean Twilight; Radio; Tule-Mists; IF WINTER REMAIN (1948–1950): Hellenic Sequel; No Stranger Dream; On the Mount of Stone; Only to One Returned; Sonnet for the Psychoanalysts; Avowal; Tolometh; If Winter Remain; Almost Anything; "That Motley Drama"; Pour Chercher du nouveau; Dans l'univers lointain; In a Distant Universe; High Surf: Monterey Bay; Isaac Newton; La Muse moderne; The Mystical Number; Pantheistic Dream; Rêve panthéistique; Poèmes d'amour; Sandalwood and Onions; The Dark Chateau; Don Quixote on Market Street; The Isle of Saturn; "O Golden-Tongued Romance"; Averoigne; Zothique; Le poéte parle avec ses biographes; The Poet Talks with the Biographers; Beauty; La Hermosura; Las Poetas del optimismo; The Poets of Optimism; El

Cantar de los seres libres; Song of the Free Beings; ¿Donde duermes, Eldorado?; Where Sleepest Thou, O Eldorado?; Los Dueños; Dominium in Excelsis; Parnaso; Parnassus; Las Alquerías perdidas; Lost Farmsteads; Cantar; Song; Eros in the Desert; Dice el soñador; Says the Dreamer; Memoria roja; Red Memory; Dos Mitos y una fábula; Two Myths and a Fable; La Nereida; La Isla de Circe; The Isle of Circe; Lo Ignoto; The Unknown; Leteo; [Lethe]; Añoranza; Melancholia; El Vendaval; El Vendaval; Farmyard Fugue; Didus Ineptus; Amithaine; Malediction; Shapes in the Sunset; Sinbad, It Was Not Well to Brag; El Eros de ébano; Eros of Ebony; THE DEAD WILL CUCKOLD YOU (1950); THE SORCERER DEPARTS (1951–1961): The Stylite; Two on a Pillar; Not Theirs the Cypress-Arch; Alpine Climber; Hesperian Fall; "Not Altogether Sleep"; Seeker; Soliloquy in a Ebon Tower; The Twilight of the Gods; Qu'Importe?; ¿Qué sueñas, Musa?; What Dreamest Thou, Muse?; Que songes-tu, Muse?; Ye Shall Return; Lives of the Saints; Secret Worship; The Song of Songs; STYES WITH SPIRES; In Time of Absence; Nada; Seer of the Cycles; I Shall Not Greatly Grieve; Geometries; Alchemy; Sacraments; Delay; Verity; La Isla del náufrago; Isle of the Shipwrecked; Thebaid; Saturnian Cinema; Dedication: To Carol; The Centaur; Lawn-Mower; Tired Gardener; High Surf; H. P. L.; Cycles; FRAGMENTS AND UNTITLED POEMS: Al borde del Leteo; Ballad of a Lost Soul; The Brook; Demogorgon; Despondency; The Flight of the Seraphim; For Iris; Haunting; The Milky Way; Night; The Night Wind; No-Man's-Land; Ode on Matter; The Regained Past; The Saturnienne; Sonnets of the Desert; The Temptation; To a Comet; To Iris; To Iris; To the Sun; The Vampire Night; [miscellaneous fragments]; Broceliande; [miscellaneous fragments]; Twilight Pilgrimage; [miscellaneous fragments]; Limericks; Ripe Mulberries; From "Ode to Antares"; From "The Song of Xeethra"; From "Song of the Galley Slaves"; From "Song of King Hoaraph's Bowmen"; From "Ludar's Litany to Thasaidon"; From "Ludar's Litany to Thasaidon"; APPENDIX: *Prospective Tables of Contents*. The Jasmine Girdle; The Jasmine Girdle and Other Poems; Incantations; The Abalone Song; *Translations:* The Desire of Loving [a translation of "Le Désir d'Aimer" by Hélène Picard; [Sandalwood]; Voices; Notes; Index of Titles; Index of First Lines.

Notes. Cover photo by Jack Newton (vol. 1) and Anastasia Damianakos (vol. 2). 250 hardcover copies per volume, printed by Covington Group. The first complete edition of Smith's original poetry, completing the set that began with the publication of vol. 3 (Smith's translations) in 2007 (see item 37). The edition was the product of decades of work by Schultz; Joshi contributed editorial guidance only at a late stage of compilation. The edition was based upon the manuscripts of Smith's poetry that form part of the Clark Ashton Smith Papers at the John Hay Library of Brown University; nearly 300 unpublished poems appear here for the first time. The texts have been extensively annotated and arranged in chronological order by date of composition, so far as that can be established. For the paperback edition, see item 113.

51.   PHILLIP A. ELLIS. *A Concordance to the Poetry of Donald Wandrei.* 2008. 462 pp. hc.

Notes. Published in hardcover without dust jacket. A concordance to Wandrei's poetry, based on the texts established in *Sanctity and Sin* (item 48). Surely one of the scarcest Hippocampus Press titles, based on number of copies printed; an electronic version of this title was made available as a free download.

52.   *Dead Reckonings* No. 3 (Spring 2008). EDITED BY S. T. JOSHI AND JACK M. HARINGA. 94 pp.

Contents. A Swift River of Allusion, by Jim Rockhill [Emma Frances Dawson, *An Itinerant House and Other Ghost Stories*]; The Novel as Tumor, by Michael Marano [Stephen King, *Duma Key*]; Exploring the Breadth of Weird Fiction, by June Pulliam [Ann and Jeff VanderMeer, ed., *The New Weird*; Ellen Datlow, ed., *Inferno*]; Die Laughing, by Stefan Dziemianowicz [Ramsey Campbell, *The Grin of the Dark*]; The Self, the Landscape, by John Langan [Conrad Williams, *The Scalding Rooms*; Conrad Williams, *Rain*]; An Opportunity Lost, by Mike Ashley [Ian Alexander Martin, ed., *The First Humdrumming Book of Horror Stories*]; Kitchen-Sink Naturalism, by Rob Latham [Christopher Barzak, *One for Sorrow*]; In, Between, and Around the Genres, by Bernadette Bosky [Peter Straub, *5 Stories*]; More (of the Same) Can Sometimes Be Less, by Tony Fonseca [John Everson, ed., *Sins of the Sirens*; Hank Schwaeble and Gary Braunbeck, ed., *Five Strokes to Midnight*]; Cthulhuism and Yog-Sothothery, by Steven J. Mariconda [H. P. Lovecraft, *Essential Solitude: Letters to August Derleth*; *O Fortunate Floridian: H. P. Lovecraft's Letters to R. H. Barlow*]; Lives and Deaths at the Edge of Noir, by Jack M. Haringa [Brian Hodge, *Mad Dogs*; John Connolly, *The Unquiet*]; Stormy Weather, by Ben Indick [Nicholas Royle, *The Appetite*]; Ramsey Campbell, Probably; Creeping Nihilism, by Alan Warren [Adam-Try Castro, *The Shallow End of the Pool*; Tim Lebbon and Lindy Moore, *Children of the New Disorder*]; The Sublime and the Ridiculous, by S. T. Joshi [Dennis Etchison, *Got to Kill Them All*; Ray Garton, *Slivers of Bone*]; Liebestod in Lower Manhattan, by John Langan [John

Marks, *Fangland*]; Dystopia Now, by Matt Cardin [Thomas Ligotti, *Teatro Grottesco*; Paulo Bacigalupi, *Pump Six and Other Stories*]; Burn This Book, by Hank Wagner [Clive Barker, *The Painter, the Creature, and the Father of Lies*; Clive Barker, *Mister B. Gone*]; It's All in the Telling, by Gary William Crawford [Brian Showers, *The Bleeding Horse and Other Stories*; Reggie Oliver, *Masques of Satan*]; They Know Their South, by Sherry Austin [Beth Massie, *Homeplace*; Will Clarke, *The Worthy: A Ghost's Story*]; Dross in Translation, by Jack M. Haringa [Asa Nonami, *Now You're One of Us*]; Nice Mice, by Ben Indick [Susan Palwick, *The Fate of Mice*]; Heirs to the King?, by Kevin Dole [Brian Keene, *Dark Hollow*; Richard Dansky, *Firefly Rain*]; Two Centuries of American Ghosts, by Richard Bleiler [S. T. Joshi, ed., *American Supernatural Tales*]; Winning the Resurrection Lottery, by Scott Connors [Stephen Mark Rainey, *Blue Devil Island*; Greg Lamberson, *Johnny Gruesome*]; Capsule Reviews.

53.   DONALD SIDNEY-FRYER. *The Atlantis Fragments: The Trilogy of Songs and Sonnets Atlantean*. 2008 hc (tpb edition 2009). 549 pp.

Contents. The Atlantis Fragments: An Introduction, by Brian Stableford; SONGS AND SONNETS ATLANTEAN: THE FIRST SERIES: Introduction, by Dr. Ibid M. Andor; Avalonessys; The Crown and Trident Imperial; Atlantis; The Rose and the Thorn; Rose Escarlate; "O Ebon-Colored Rose"; Your Mouth of Pomegranate; As Buds and Blossoms in the Month of May the Rose; To Clark Ashton Smith; Pavane; When We Were Prince and Princess; The Crown and Trident; Song; "Thy Spirit Walks the Sea"; Recompense; To a Youth; Spenserian Stanza-Sonnet Empourpré; A Symbol for All Splendor Lost; The Ashes in the Rose Garden; To Edmund Spenser (1552?–1599); Rose Verdastre; Ave Atque Vale; Thaïs and Alexander in Persepolis; A Fragment; O Fair Dark Eyes, O Glances Turned Aside; The Cydnus; Golden Mycenae; Lullaby; *Minor Chronicles of Atlantis* (Proem, by Michel de Labretagne; The Hippokamp; The Alpha Huge; The River Called Amphus; The Amphus Delta; The Imperial Crown Jewels of Atlantis; The Atlantean Obelisk; The Garden of Jealous Roses; The Tale of an Olden Love; The Shepherd and the Shepherdess; Reciprocity; The Iffinnix; A Vision of Strange Splendor); Kilcolman Castle: 20 August 1965; Aubade; The Lilac Hedge at Cassell Prairie: 27 May 1967; Black Poppy and Black Lotus; The House of Roses; "The Musical Note of Swans . . . Before Their Death"; Green Sleeves; O Beautiful Dark-Amber Eyes of Old; The Forsaken Palace; For the *Shapes of Clay* of Ambrose Bierce; Connaissance Fatale; For the *Black Beetles in Amber* of Ambrose Bierce; Offrande Exotique; *Sonnets on an Empire of Many Waters*: Legend; I. Here, where the fountains of the

60

Rinaldo for Clark Ashton Smith; Forevermore the Rose; Tableau Sous-Marin; Predicament; Remonstration; Enlightenment; A Rendezvous with Pierrefonds; Rondeau of Winter; Rondeau of Summer; Pierrefonds, Poème en Pierre; A Ballade of Duality; Conundrum; Rondel of Time; Rondel of Space; The Ghost of a Dream; A Fanfare from Atlantis; Appendix; Index of Titles; Register of Subscribers.

Notes. Dust jacket illustration by Gordon R. Barnett. Interior illustrations by William Boddy and Lance Alexander. Paperback edition omits frontispiece of Elizabeth I and endpaper map illustrations by William Boddy. A combined edition of the three volumes of the author's *Songs and Sonnets Atlantean* (1971, 2003, 2005), a scintillating series of poems and prose poems influenced in part by Clark Ashton Smith (whom Sidney-Fryer knew during the latter stages of Smith's life), Edmund Spenser, and others, but also reflecting Sidney-Fryer's vigorously original poetic work. Originally published in a limited hardcover edition by subscription (300 copies, printed by Covington Group) and subsequently issued in paperback.

54.   H. P. LOVECRAFT AND AUGUST DERLETH. *Essential Solitude: The Letters of H. P. Lovecraft and August Derleth: 1926–1931* (vol. 1) and *1932–1937* (vol. 2). Edited by David E. Schultz and S. T. Joshi. 2008 hc (rpt. 2013 [tpb]). 880 pp. (numbered consecutively).

Contents. Volume 1: Introduction; A Note on This Edition; Abbreviations; Letters: Volume 2: Letters; APPENDIX : One for the Black Bag, by H. P. Lovecraft; The Weird Tale in English Since 1890 [excerpt], by August Derleth; A Master of the Macabre, by August Derleth; H. P. Lovecraft, Outsider, by August Derleth; H. P. L.—Two Decades After, by August Derleth. Glossary of Frequently Mentioned Names; Bibliography; Index.

Notes. Cover illustrations (different ones for the two volumes) by David C. Verba. 250 hardcover copies, printed by Covington Group. The first complete publication of Lovecraft's letters to Derleth, including 50 or so extant letters by Derleth to Lovecraft. Exhaustively annotated, with an immense bibliography of the hundreds of literary works (including their own) discussed by the authors. The edition constituted, informally, the commencement of Hippocampus Press's ambitious plan to issue the complete Lovecraft letters in book form. For the paperback edition, see item 121.

55.   H. P. LOVECRAFT. *Collected Essays* (CD-ROM). 2008.

Notes. An electronic edition of the five volumes of *Collected Essays* (see items 18, 19, 29, 30, 36). It includes both text and digital images of all 13 issues Lovecraft's *Conservative*.

56.   *Lovecraft Annual* No. 2 (2008). EDITED BY S. T. JOSHI. 215 pp.

Contents. Dispatches from the Providence Observatory: Astronomical Motifs and Sources in the Writings of H. P. Lovecraft, by T. R. Livesey; The Sickness unto Death in H. P. Lovecraft's "The Hound," by James Goho; Queer Tales? Sexuality, Race, and Architecture in "The Thing on the Doorstep," by Joel Pace; "Clever Lines": Some Thoughts on Lovecraft's "Ad Criticos," by Phillip A. Ellis; "The Rats in the Walls," the Rats in the Trenches, by Robert H. Waugh; Knowledge in the Void: Anomaly, Observation, and the Incomplete Paradigm Shift in H. P. Lovecraft's Fiction, by Kálmán Matolcsy; H. P. Lovecraft and the Archaeology of "Roman" Arizona, by Marc A. Beherec; Reviews: [Review of H. P. Lovecraft, *O Fortunate Floridian: H. P. Lovecraft's Letters to R. H. Barlow*], by Martin Andersson; [Review of H. P. Lovecraft and August Derleth, *Essential Solitude: The Letters of H. P. Lovecraft and August Derleth*], by John D. Haefele; Briefly Noted.

Notes. Of particular note is Livesey's immense and penetrating study of Lovecraft's knowledge of astronomy.

57.   JONATHAN THOMAS. *Midnight Call and Other Stories.* 2008. 258 pp. tpb.

Contents. Foreword, by S. T. Joshi; Eben's Portrait; The Weird Old Hole; The Returns of Johnny Mapleseed; Fingers of Stone; Conjurings and Celtic Holidays (A Thematic Set) (The May Day Melée, Explained; Doctor Farrell's Goddesses; Some Days Before Shadow Damsel; In the Wake of Bridget; Midnight Call); Damn the Wheelwright; The Road to Schwärmerei; McEveety among the Leisure Elect; The Judgment Birds; An Office Nymph; Another Psychic on Comp; Towbear to Hell; The Christmas Clones; Awakening of No Return; A Vampire Heart; Subway of the Dead; Graveside Friday Night; Dappled Ass; An Alternate History of Annette; Tendrils in Formaldehyde; Ariadne's Hair.

Notes. Cover illustration by David C. Verba. A substantial and well-received collection of stories by a writer who met S. T. Joshi when the latter was giving a lecture at Brown University. Joshi at once recognized Thomas's talent and encouraged him to assemble a collection. A few stories had appeared in Thomas's rare collection, *Stories from the Big Black House* (1992), but these were extensively revised; the other stories are previously unpublished.

58. RAMSEY CAMPBELL. *Inconsequential Tales*. [Edited by S. T. Joshi.] 2008. 249 pp. tpb.

Contents. Truth or Consequences; The Childish Fear; The Offering to the Dead; The Reshaping of Rossiter; The Void; The Other House; Broadcast; The Urge; The Sunshine Club; Writer's Curse; Property of the Ring; The Shadows in the Barn; Night Beat; The Precognitive Trip; Murders; Point of View; The Grip of Peace; Only the Wind; Morning Call; Pet; Hain's Island; Bait; Snakes and Ladders; The Burning; A Play for the Jaded.

Notes. Cover and interior illustrations by Jason C. Eckhardt. A volume Joshi had been encouraging Campbell for years to compile. When Joshi assisted Campbell in publishing a bibliography of his writings, *The Core of Ramsey Campbell* (1995), he noticed that many of Campbell's stories remained uncollected, and Joshi at last prevailed upon Campbell to gather them for this volume. Two stories were previously unpublished. The self-deprecating title—modeled, perhaps, on T. E. D. Klein's *Reassuring Tales* (2007)—is Campbell's.

59. *Dead Reckonings* No. 4 (Fall 2008). EDITED BY S. T. JOSHI AND JACK M. HARINGA. 97 pp.

Contents. A Grab-Bag of Perverse Delight, by Donald R. Burleson [Thomas M. Disch, *The Word of God*]; Edge-of-Your-Seat Suspense, by Hank Wagner [Joe R. Lansdale, *Leather Maiden*]; An Epic and Long-Awaited Publication, by Donald Sidney-Fryer [Clark Ashton Smith. *The Complete Poetry and Translations, Volumes 1 and 2.*]; Dissecting Thomas Harris, by Bev Vincent [Benjamin Szumskyj, ed. *Dissecting Hannibal Lecter: Essays on the Novels of Thomas Harris.*]; A Slow-Moving Tsunami, by S. T. Joshi [Caitlín R. Kiernan, *Tales of Pain and Wonder*]; Horror on the Ice, by Rob Latham [Dan Simmons, *The Terror*]; "The Weird Old Hole" and Much More, by Sherry Austin [Jonathan Thomas, *Midnight Call and Other Stories*]; The Nightmares That Cling to Us, by John Langan [Ramsey Campbell, *Thieving Fear* and *Inconsequential Tales*]; Sometimes You Just Have to Gush, by Matt Cardin [Stephen Mark Rainey. *Other Gods*; Michael Shea. *The Autopsy and Other Tales*]; Ramsey Campbell, Probably; A Shadow Across the Heart, by Jack M. Haringa [Jack Ketchum, *Old Flames* and *Book of Souls*]; Faster Than You Can Read Them, by Ben P. Indick [Brian Keene. *Kill Whitey* and *Ghost Walk*]; Torture, Cannibalism, and

Necrophilia, by Tony Fonseca [Bill Breedlove, ed. *Like a Chinese Tattoo*; Nick Mamatas and Sean Wallace, ed. *Realms: The First Year of Clarkesworld Magazine*]; Everyday Horrors, by Javier A. Martínez [Bentley Little, *The Vanishing* and *The Academy*]; Nightmares and Dreamscapes, by Robert Butterfield [Patrick McGrath, *Trauma*; Greg F. Gifune. *Dominion*]; Confessionals, by John Langan [Christopher Conlon, *Midnight on Mourn Street*; Graham Joyce, *How to Make Friends with Demons*]; Vampires Doing Good, by June Pulliam [Tananarive Due, *Blood Colony*; Jewell Parker Rhodes, *Yellow Moon*]; Only an Abundance of Horror, by Tony Fonseca [Weston Ochse, *Scarecrow Gods*]; Erotic Fantasies and Necromantic Mysteries, by Hank Wagner [Polly Frost, *Deep Inside*; Sarah Monette, *The Bone Key*]; The Departure of "Enigma," by Kevin Dole [Nicholas Royle, *The Enigma of Departure*]; Ambitious Reading and Ambitious Feeling, by Michael Marano [Steve Rasnic Tem and Melanie Tem, *The Man on the Ceiling*]; Put-Downable, But Pick-Upable Again, by Darrell Schweitzer [Alexandra Sokoloff, *The Price*]; A Gothic Landscape, by Jim Rockhill [James Doig, ed. *Australian Gothic: An Anthology of Australian Supernatural Fiction, 1867–1939*]; Retrospective Reviews: The Line of Terror, by Arthur Machen [Walter de la Mare, *On the Edge*]; The Weird Scholar, by S. T. Joshi; Capsule Reviews; Correspondence.

60.   KENNETH W. FAIG, JR. *The Unknown Lovecraft.* 2009. 253 pp. tpb.

Contents. Lovecraft: Artist or Poseur?; Quae Amamus Tuemur: Ancestors in Lovecraft's Life and Fiction; Whipple V. Phillips and the Owyhee Land and Irrigation Company; Lovecraft's Parental Heritage; The Friendship of Louise Imogen Guiney and Sarah Susan Phillips; The Unknown Lovecraft I: Political Operative; The Unknown Lovecraft II: Reluctant Laureate; Lovecraft's "He"; "The Silver Key" and Lovecraft's Childhood; The Dream-Quest of Unknown Kadath; Lovecraft's Unknown Friend: Dudley Charles Newton; R. H. Barlow; Robert H. Barlow as H. P. Lovecraft's Literary Executor: An Appreciation; Some Final Thoughts for Readers of This Collection; Sources.

Notes. Cover design (incorporating a photograph of Lovecraft) by Barbara Briggs Silbert. The date of the Lovecraft photo was given as 1936, based on a notation on the back of the photo, though it seems to be the one Lovecraft describes in a letter to R. H. Barlow [January 15, 1935]: "Has Talman sent you any of the surprise snaps he took at the gang meeting? I've just got a partial set—& I fared worst of all! The young rascal caught me as I was looking upward & saying something which put my mouth in an utterly comic position . . . as if I were going to whistle or expectorate!" A small number of copies were printed lacking the "Sources" section, and a few made it into circulation before the error was corrected. A rich collection of Faig's biographical essays on Lovecraft, including his landmark monograph on Barlow, which had never been published in its entirety aside from a limited edition.

61.   S. T. JOSHI. *Classics and Contemporaries: Some Notes on Horror Fiction.* 2009. 291 pp. tpb.

Contents. Preface; I. SOME OVERVIEWS: Arkham House and Its Legacy; The Haunted House; Professionals and Amateurs; Some Thoughts on Weird Poetry; Bram and Bela and Mary and Boris; What the Hell Is Dark Suspense?; The Small Press; II. CLASSICS: Algernon Blackwood: The Starlight Man; Arthur Machen: A Minor Classic; William Hope Hodgson: Writer on the Borderland; E. F. Benson: Spooks and More Spooks; A. M. Burrage: The Ghost Man; Herbert S. Gorman: Where Is the Place Called Dagon?; Andrew Caldecott: The Well-Crafted Ghost; Rescuing Shirley Jackson; III. CONTEMPORARIES: Les Daniels: The Sardonic Vampire; Dennis Etchison and His Masters; Thomas Tryon: The Return of the Posthumous Collaboration; Stephen King and God; Peter Straub and the Blue Pencil; Ramsey Campbell: Alone with a Master; Clive Barker: Weird Fiction as Subversion; David J. Schow: Zombies, Tapeworms, and Kamikaze Butterflies; Donald R. Burleson: Enmeshed in the Bizarre; Norman Partridge: Here to Stay; Thomas Harris: Lecter as Albatross; Thomas Ligotti: The Long and the Short of It; Michael Cisco: Ligotti Redivivus?; Sherry Austin: The Southern Ghost Story; Shades of Edgar and Ambrose; IV. SCHOLARSHIP: The Charting of Horror Literature; Classics and Contemporaries; V. H. P. LOVECRAFT: Some Lovecraft Editions; The Cthulhu Mythos; Lovecraft as a Character in Fiction; Some Lovecraft Scholarship (Barton L. St Armand; Donald R. Burleson; Peter Cannon; Robert M. Price; Kenneth W. Faig, Jr; Edward W. O'Brien, Jr; Robert H. Waugh); Index; Acknowledgements.

Notes. Cover illustration by Allen Koszowski, a playful homage to Virgil Finlay's famous drawing of Lovecraft in periwig and smallclothes (see item 18), with Joshi as the Old Gent. An extensive selection of Joshi's book reviews, chiefly from *Necrofile* but also from *Lovecraft Studies, Studies in Weird Fiction, Weird Tales,* and other periodicals. Although written over a span of more than two decades, the volume forms a kind of foretaste of Joshi's forthcoming comprehensive history of supernatural fiction.

62.   ADAM NISWANDER. *The Hound Hunters*. 2009. 302 pp. tpb.

Notes. Cover illustration by Armand Cabrerra. (There are no interior illustrations, despite what the copyright page says.) An original Cthulhu Mythos novel by Niswander, and a loose sequel to *The Charm* (1993) and *The Serpent Slayers* (1994), published by Integra. *The Hound Hunters* had been scheduled for publication by Integra in 1995, and bound galleys had been issued, but the publisher collapsed before the book could be published. Niswander had outlined a thirteen-volume series of novels adapting the Cthulhu Mythos to a southwestern locale; for the next volume in the series, see item 69.

63.   R. E. SPENCER. *The Lady Who Came to Stay*. ARTHUR RANSOME. *The Elixir of Life*. 2009. 153 + 180 pp. tpb.

Notes. Cover illustration of *The Lady Who Came to Stay* reprinted from the Knopf edition of 1933; cover illustration of *The Elixir of Life* is a detail from *The Alchemist* by Sir William Fettes Douglas. Part of the Lovecraft's Library series. A reprint of two novels that Lovecraft read and may have been influenced by: Ransome's fabulously rare *The Elixir of Life* (1915) and Spencer's *The Lady Who Came to Stay* (1931). Joshi has written separate introductions to each work.

64.   *Dead Reckonings* No. 5 (Spring 2009). EDITED BY S. T. JOSHI AND JACK M. HARINGA. 93 pp.

Contents. The Vampire as Action-Adventure Anti-Hero, by June Pulliam [Rio Youers, *Everdead*]; A Mask Made of Exposition, by Michael Marano [Gene Wolfe, *An Evil Guest*]; The Pathetic and the Mundane, by Kevin Dole [Quentin Crisp, *Shrike*]; Mythos and More Mythos, by Martin Andersson [Richard L. Tierney, *The Drums of Chaos*; Asamatsu Ken, *Queen of K'n-Yan*]; Forget-Me-Nots?, by Tony Fonseca [Ronald Damien Malfi, *Passenger*; Peter Atkins, *Moontown*]; A New Jungle Book, by Hank Wagner [Neil Gaiman, *The Graveyard Book*]; Abandon All Preconceptions, Ye Who Enter Here, by Sherry Austin [Ellen Datlow, ed., *Poe*]; Williams *One*, Clark *Zero*, by Robert Morrish [Simon Clark, *Vengeance Child*; Conrad Williams, *One*]; Mini-collections from Major Talent, by Matt Cardin [Douglas Smith, *Impossibilia*; Mark Samuels, *Glyphotech and Other Macabre Processes*]; Ramsey Campbell, Probably; Listing Towards Horror Paralyzed by Discomfort, by Jack M. Haringa [*British Invasion*, ed. Christopher Golden, Tim Lebbon, and James A. Moore]; Passing the Baton, by Ben P. Indick [*New Dark Voices II*, ed. Brian Keene; Jeremy C. Shipp, *Sheep and Wolves*]; Genius Loci, by John Langan [Cherie Priest, *Fathom*]; Enter Ghost, by Bev Vincent [Stieg Larsson, *The Girl with the*

Dragon Tattoo; David Wroblewski, *The Story of Edgar Sawtelle*]; The Lovecraft Cult, by S. T. Joshi [Kenneth Hite, *Tour de Lovecraft: The Tales*; Robert M. Price, *Blasphemies & Revelations*]; Two Unique Visions of Horror, by Robert Butterfield [Scott Nicholson, *Scattered Ashes*; Tony Richards, *Shadows and Other Tales*]; Living on a Powder Keg, by Bev Vincent [Joe Hill, *Gunpowder*]; Can You Murder a Dream?, by John Edgar Browning [Jeffrey Ford, *The Drowned Life*]; Doing Your Homework, by Hank Wagner [F. Paul Wilson, *By the Sword*]; Waking to Nightmares, by Jack M. Haringa [Paul Tremblay, *The Little Sleep*]; The Supernatural in Prose and Verse, by Donald R. Burleson [S. T. Joshi, *Emperors of Dreams: Some Notes on Weird Poetry*; S. T. Joshi, *The Rise and Fall of the Cthulhu Mythos*; S. T. Joshi, *Classics and Contemporaries: Some Notes on Horror Fiction*]; The Perfect Museum Edition, by Darrell Schweitzer [Henry S. Whitehead, *Passing of a God and Other Stories*]; The Weird Scholar, by S. T. Joshi; Capsule Reviews.

65.   *Lovecraft Annual* No. 3 (2009). EDITED BY S. T. JOSHI. 206 pp.

Contents. Lovecraft and the Ray-Gun, by T. R. Livesey; What Is "the Unnamable"? H. P. Lovecraft and the Problem of Evil, by James Goho; Some Notes on the Topographical Poetry of H. P. Lovecraft, by Phillip A. Ellis; The Theme of Distance in the Tales of H. P. Lovecraft, by Lorenzo Mastropierro; Lovecraft's Avatars: Azathoth, Nyarlathotep, Dagon, and Lovecraftian Utopias, by Brandon Reynolds; Self, Other, and the Evolution of Lovecraft's Treatment of Outsideness, by Massimo Berruti; Some Notes on Lovecraft's "The Transition of Juan Romero," by Leigh Blackmore; "The Shadow out of Time" and Time-Defiance, by Will Murray; Poems Not in *The Ancient Track*, by H. P. Lovecraft (ed. S. T. Joshi); Lovecraft and the Polar Myth, by John M. Navroth; REVIEWS: [Review of Kenneth Hite, *Tour de Lovecraft*], by Donald R. Burleson; [Review of S. T. Joshi, *The Rise and Fall of the Cthulhu Mythos*], by Leigh Blackmore; Briefly Noted.

66.   H. L. MENCKEN. *Collected Poems.* Edited by S. T. Joshi. 2009. 145 pp. tpb.

Contents. Introduction, by S. T. Joshi; To R. K.; The Four-Foot Filipino: A Ballad of the Trenches; The Tin-Clads; Joe and Bobs; Auroral; One Man Band; A Frivolous Rondeau; A Few Lines; The Roorback and the Canard; Chrysanthemum; Canzonette; [Untitled]; An Ante-Christmas Rondeau; The Dawn of Love; [Untitled]; Fidelis ad Urnum; [Untitled]; A Ballad of Impecuniosity; A War Song; A Madrigal; A Song for Autumn; Nocturne; An Ode to a "Stein"; The Filipino Maiden; A Rondeau of Two Hours; When the Pipe Goes Out;

Thanksgiving Day; Adlai; A Dirge; A Bacteriologal Romance; To O. P. K.; And Now Comes Congress; The Man That Guards the Grub; A Ballad of Looking; Well Buried; The Orf'cer Boy; A Paradox; Madrigal; The Song of the Slapstick; An Old, Old Story; Love and the Rose; The Coming of Winter; Outside, Old Year!; To Isaackhanmofakhammeddovlet; The Boy and the Man; The Donation Party; To Kruger; A Rondeau of Statesmanship; In Eating Soup; Serenade; Im Hinterland; The Snow; A Ballad of Fierce Fighters; The Pantoum of Congress; To Mrs. Nation; In Vaudeville; A Slug of Pessimism; An Ode to Nelson A.; To G. W.; A Sonnet to a Wienerwurst; The Ballade of the Rank and File; To Wu Ting Fang, Envoy Extraordinary and Minister Plenipotentiary; On Phyllis at the Play; Theatrical Alphabet; April; Dawn; A Villanelle; The Transport Gen'ral Ferguson; Faith; The Spanish Main; The Rondeau of Riches; A Ballade of Protest; Preliminary Rebuke; The Song of the Olden Time; The Ballad of Ships in Harbor; The Violet; September; Arabesque; The Rhymes of Mistress Dorothy; Roundel; Within the City Gates; Il Penseroso; Finis; War; On Passing the Island of San Salvador; Starting for the Play; Good-By, Divine Sarah!; The Old Trails; The Ballade of Cockaigne; Song; Invocation; The Voices; APPENDIX: A Kruger, by Edmond Rostand; Notes; Index of Titles; Index of First Lines.

Notes. Cover design (incorporating a photograph of Mencken) by Barbara Briggs Silbert. Perhaps an odd publication for Hippocampus Press, as both the author and the work are well outside the realms of horror or fantasy fiction; but the press has always sought to issue collected editions of poetry, and Mencken's poetry contains substantial merits. Mencken himself issued only 33 of his poems in his first published book, *Ventures into Verse* (1903). The others (most of them published in various columns in the *Baltimore Herald*) are uncollected.

67.   JOSEPH S. PULVER, SR. *Blood Will Have Its Season.* 2009. 284 pp. tpb.

Contents. Foreword, by S. T. Joshi; Choosing; Carl Lee & Cassilda; A Line of Questions; PITCH nothing . . .; I, Like the Coyote; Blood Will Have Its Season; mr wind sits; The Prisoner; An American Tango Ending in Madness; Orchard Fruit; The Songs Cassilda Shall Sing, Where Flap the Tatters of the King; The Night Music of Oakdeene; Dogs Begin to Bark All Over My Neighborhood; Chasing Shadows; But the Day Is a Tomb of Claws; In This Desert Even the Air Burns; And She Walks into the Room . . .; a certain Mr. Hopfrog, Esq., Nightwalker; The Black Litany of Nug and Yeb; Erendira; An Engagement of Hearts; An Event Without Knives or Rope; One

Side's Ice, One's Fire; A Spider in the Distance; PAIN; A Night of Moon and Blood, Then Holstenwall; Under the Mask Another Mask; W a t e r l i l i e s; Yvrain's Black Dancers; No Exit Sign; Lovecraft's Sentence; Midnight on a Dead End Street in Noir City; The Master and Margeritha; Hello Is a Yellow Kiss; The Faces of She; Good Night and Good Luck; Patti Smith, Lovecraft, & I; The Collector and the Hand Puppet; The Only Thing We Have to Fear . . .; The Corridor; Stone Cold Fever.

Notes. Cover illustration by Thomas S. Brown. A scintillating collection of weird and fantasy tales by Pulver, previously known to the public as the author of the Lovecraftian novel *Nightmare's Disciple* (Chaosium, 1999).

68.   H. P. LOVECRAFT AND ROBERT E. HOWARD. *A Means to Freedom: The Letters of H. P. Lovecraft and Robert E. Howard: 1930–1932* (vol. 1) and *1933–1937* (vol. 2). Edited by S. T. Joshi, David E. Schultz, and Rusty Burke. 2009. 1004 pp. hc (numbered consecutively).

Contents. Volume 1: Introduction; A Note on This Edition; Abbreviations; Letters; Volume 2: Letters; APPENDIX: With a Set of Rattlesnake Rattles; The Beast from the Abyss; Dr. I. M. Howard: Letters to H. P. Lovecraft; Glossary of Frequently Mentioned Names; Bibliography; Index.

Notes. Cover illustrations (different for the two volumes) by David C. Verba. Limited edition of 345 hardcover copies, printed by Covington Group. A project long in the works—the collected correspondence of Lovecraft and Howard over an intense six-year period. The wordage of Howard's letters exceeds that of Lovecraft's, in part because some of Lovecraft's letters do not survive. Many logistical and legal issues had to be resolved before the edition could be published. For the paperback edition, see item 91.

69.   ADAM NISWANDER. *The War of the Whisperers.* 2009. 341 pp. tpb.

Notes. Cover illustration by Ron Leming. The fourth novel in Niswander's series of thirteen southwestern Cthulhu Mythos novels, and the second to be published by Hippocampus Press (see item 62).

70. DAN CLORE. *Weird Words: A Lovecraftian Lexicon.* 2009. 568 pp. tpb.

Notes. Cover illustration by Howard Wandrei. An immense dictionary of words used by Lovecraft and other writers of horror and fantasy fiction, with examples and citations extending back to the Tudor era. A monument of scholarship—a kind of *Oxford English Dictionary* for weird fiction.

71. MICHAEL ARONOVITZ. *Seven Deadly Pleasures.* 2009. 247 pp. tpb.

Contents. Foreword, by S. T. Joshi; How Bria Died; The Clever Mask; Quest for Sadness; The Legend of the Slither-Shifter; The Exterminator; Passive Passenger; Toll Booth.

Notes. Cover and interior art by Thomas S. Brown. The debut collection of short stories by a dynamic new writer, who had submitted his work to Joshi a year or so before.

72. NORA MAY FRENCH. *The Outer Gate: The Collected Poems of Nora May French.* Edited by Donald Sidney-Fryer and Alan Gullette. 2009. 254 pp. tpb.

Contents. Acknowledgments; Nora May French: One Still, Small Voice out of Time and Space; Sources; THE OUTER GATE: THE COLLECTED POEMS OF NORA MAY FRENCH: The Outer Gate; Rain; Best-Loved; The Rose; Between Two Rains; The Message; By the Hospital; "Oh, Dryad Thoughts"; My Maid of Dreams; Music in the Pavilion; Rebuke; In Camp; The Nymph; Vivisection; The Stranger; The Constant Ones; Instinct; The Lost Chimneys; San Francisco, New Year's, 1907; The Panther Woman; The Poppy Field; Poppies; You; Just a Dog; Mirage; Dusk; *The Spanish Girl;* PART I: I. The Vine; II. The Chapel; III. The Garden; IV; V; VI; VII; PART II; I; II; III; IV; V; VI; VII; PART III: I; II; III; IV; V; VI; VII; VIII; The Garden of Dolores; Answered; Indifference; After-Knowledge; Be Silent, Love; Two Spendthrift Kings; Growth; Change; Wistaria; How Ends the Day?; My Nook; When Plaintively and Near the Cricket Sings; The Little Memories; Pass By; In Empty Courts; Down the Trail; "Bells from Over the Hills Sound Sweet"; In Town; Moods; A Misty Morning; Two Songs; Noon; Your Beautiful Passing; By Moonlight; A Dream-Love; One Day; The Mission Graves; Along the Track; A Place of Dreams; Think Not, O Lilias; The Suicide; "To Rosy Buds . . . ."; Yesterday; The Mourner; Ave atque Vale; At the End; Notes; NOTICES: General Note; San Francisco *Bulletin,* Friday evening, 15 November 1907; San Francisco *Call,* Friday, 15 November 1907;

San Francisco *Chronicle*, Friday, 15 November 1907; San Francisco *Chronicle*, Friday, 15 November 1907, notes; San Francisco *Examiner*, Friday, November 15, 1907; Los Angeles *Times*, Friday, November 15, 1907; Los Angeles *Times*, Sunday, November 17, 1907; Los Angeles *Times*, Monday, 18 November 1907; *Town Talk*, Saturday, 23 November 1907; *Current Literature*, June 1908; San Francisco *Call*, Sunday, June 12, 1910; *The New Age, A Weekly Review of Politics, Literature and Art*, Thursday, 14 July 1910; *Current Literature*, September 1910; *Die Nieuwe Gids* [*The New Guidebook*], November 1910; Poems by Nora May French, *The California Literary Pamphlets*, Number 2; Helen (Augusta) French Hunt (1883–1973): A Little Memoir (A Friendship, 1968–1973); TRIBUTES: General Note; Sources; Untitled, by Henry Anderson Lafler; Sonnet, by Henry Anderson Lafler; Sonnet, by Henry Anderson Lafler; The Pearl, by Henry Anderson Lafler; Nora May French, by George Sterling; The Ashes in the Sea, by George Sterling; Nora May French, In Memoriam, by Louise Gebhard Cann; To Nora May French, by Clark Ashton Smith; "Thy Spirit Walks the Sea," by Donald Sidney-Fryer; [Nora May French], by Dorothy Jesse Beagle; For Nora May in Paradise, by Mary Rudge; Nora May, by Alan Gullette; For Nora May French, by Val Beatts; Quicksilver, by Do Gentry; November, by Do Gentry; The Poet Replies, by Do Gentry; Dear Critic, Dear Abstraction, by Do Gentry; The Poet with Us: Nora May French, by Marvin R. Hiemstra. Index of Titles; Index of First Lines.

Notes. Cover photograph of Nora May French by Arnold Genthe, cover design by Barbara Briggs Silbert. A landmark of scholarship: the editors not only unearthed numerous poems by French (1881–1907) not included in her lone posthumous volume, *Poems* (1910), but also included a generous sampling of reviews of that book along with other interesting matter. French was a beautiful and talented poet in George Sterling's literary circle who committed suicide at the age of 26. Her delicate and sensitive poetry retains a following to this day.

73.   *Dead Reckonings* No. 6 (Fall 2009). EDITED BY S. T. JOSHI AND JACK M. HARINGA. 94 pp.

Contents. Crooked House, by Bev Vincent [Sarah Langan, *Audrey's Door*]; From the Sensuous to the Sophomoric, by Zachary Z. E. Bennett [David Niall Wilson, *Ennui and Other Stories of Madness*]; Ending the World: Do's and Don'ts, by Kevin Dole [Lavie Tidhar and Nir Yaniv, *The Tel Aviv Dossier*; Tim Lebbon, *Bar None*]; For Aficionados Only, by Robert Butterfield [Simon Stranzas, *Cold to the Touch*; Alan M. Clark and Elizabeth Massie, *D. D. Murphry, Secret Po-*

liceman]; Destined for the Remainder Shelves, by Scott David Briggs [Brian Knight, *Reservoir Gods*; Seamus Cooper, *The Mall of Cthulhu*]; The Way of Escape, by Sherry Austin [Barbara Roden, Northwest Passages; Kealan Patrick Burke, The 121 to Pennsylvania and Others]; More Than Just Tentacles, by Martin Andersson [Henrik Harksen, ed., *Eldritch Horrors*; Ellen Datlow, ed., *Lovecraft Unbound*]; Apocalypse Nowadays, by John Edgar Browning [Greg F. Gifune, *Children of Chaos*; Greg F. Gifune, *Blood in Electric Blue*]; Gold, Silver, and Bronze, by Hank Wagner [Stephen Jones, ed. *The Mammoth Book of Best New Horror 20*; Charles Black, ed. *The Fourth Black Book of Horror*; Richard Chizmar, ed. *Shivers V.*]; Ramsey Campbell, Probably: The Edited Version; Impalements at Piccadilly Circus, by John Edgar Browning [Dacre Stoker and Ian Holt, *Dracula the Un-Dead*]; Horror as an Afterthought, by Tony Fonseca [John Harwood, *The Séance*; Gemma Mawdsley, *The Paupers' Graveyard*]; Of Fishmen and Lovecraftian Place-Names, by John M. Navroth [James A. Moore, *Deeper*]; A Modern "Heart of Darkness," by S. T. Joshi [Caitlín R. Kiernan, *The Red Tree*]; The Banality of Evil, by June Pulliam [Bentley Little, *His Father's Son*]; Two (or More) Tales of Dark Religion, by Matt Cardin [Leopoldo Gout, *Ghost Radio*; Brian Evenson, *Last Days*]; Robert Bloch: *Psycho* and Beyond, by Henrik Sandbeck Harksen [Benjamin Szumskyj, ed., *The Man Who Collected Psychos: Critical Essays on Robert Bloch*]; Tradition Viewed through Different Lenses, by Jim Rockhill [Scott Thomas, *The Garden of Ghosts*; John Langan, *Mr. Gaunt and Other Uneasy Encounters*]; Formula and Geography, by Richard Bleiler [Graham Masterton, *Basilisk*; Danel Olson, ed., *Exotic Gothic 2: New Tales of Taboo*]; A Window onto the Real Poe, by Benjamin F. Fisher [John Ward Ostrom, ed., *The Collected Letters of Edgar Allan Poe*]; Vampires, the Holocaust, and 9/11, by Michael Marano [Guillermo del Toro and Chuck Hogan, *The Strain*]; The Weird Tradition in Poetry, by Darrell Schweitzer [Donald Wandrei, *Sanctity and Sin*; Rain Graves, *Barfodder*]; The Perfect Length for Horror, by Hank Wagner [Sarah Pinborough. *The Language of Dying*; Terry Lamsley. *R.I.P.*; Joel Lane. *The Witnesses Are Gone*]; The Weird Scholar, by S. T. Joshi.

Notes. The last issue with Haringa as coeditor.

74.   DONALD R. BURLESON. *Wait for the Thunder: Stories for a Stormy Night*. 2010. 300 pp. tpb.

Contents. Tumbleweeds; One-Night Strand; Hopscotch; Jigsaw; Country Living; Sheep-Eye; Tummerwunky; A Student of Geometry; Fwoo; Down in the Mouth; Crayons; The Weeping Woman of White

Crow; Spider Willie; Jack O'Lantern Jack; The Watcher at the Window; Desert Dreams; Grampa Pus; Gramma Grunt; Sheets; Up and About; Blessed Event; The Cryptogram; Leaves; Pump Jack; Lujan's Trunk; Wait for the Thunder; Papa Loaty.

Notes. Cover illustration by Thomas S. Brown. A substantial collection of stories by Burleson, who has established himself both as a leading literary scholar (especially of H. P. Lovecraft) and a short story writer and novelist. The volume includes stories published since the issuance of his previous collection, *Beyond the Lamplight* (Jack o' Lantern Press, 1996).

75.　　H. B. DRAKE. *The Shadowy Thing.* 2010. 245 pp. tpb.

Notes. Cover illustration taken from the 1928 A. L. Burt reprint of *The Shadowy Thing.* Part of the Lovecraft's Library series. A reprint of the novel first published in the UK as *The Remedy* (1925) and in the US as *The Shadowy Thing* (1928). Lovecraft read it not long after publication, and it manifestly influenced "The Thing on the Doorstep" (1933). Contains an introduction by S. T. Joshi.

76.　　ROBERT M. PRICE, EDITOR. *The Tindalos Cycle.* 2010. 365 pp. tpb.

Contents. Chock Full o' Mutts (introduction), by Robert M. Price; The Maker of Moons, by Robert W. Chambers; The Death of Halpin Frayser, by Ambrose Bierce; The Space-Eaters, by Frank Belknap Long; The Hounds of Tindalos, by Frank Belknap Long; The Letters of Halpin Chalmers, by Peter Cannon; The Death of Halpin Chalmers, by Perry M. Grayson; The Madness out of Time, by Lin Carter; The Hound of the Partridgevilles, by Peter Cannon; Through Outrageous Angles, by David C. Kopaska-Merkel and Ronald McDowell; Firebrands of Torment, by Michael Cisco; The Shore of Madness, by Ann K. Schwader; Gateway to Forever, by Frank Belknap Long; The Gift of Lycanthropy, by Frank Belknap Long; The War Among the Gods, by Adrian Cole; The Ways of Chaos, by Ramsey Campbell; Juggernaut, by C. J. Henderson; Scarlet Obeisance, by Joseph S. Pulver, Sr.; The Horror from the Hills, by Frank Belknap Long; Pompelo's Doom, by Ann K. Schwader; Confession of the White Acolyte, by Ann K. Schwader; When Chaugnar Wakes, by Frank Belknap Long; The Elephant God of Leng, by Robert M. Price; Death Is an Elephant, by Robert Bloch; The Dweller in the Pot by Frank Chimesleep Short, by Robert M. Price; But It's A Long Dark Road, by Joseph S. Pulver, Sr.; Nyarlatophis: A Fable of Ancient Egypt, by Stanley C. Sargent; Mind-Pilot, by William Laughlin.

Notes. Cover illustration by Thomas S. Brown. A rich collection of stories (some of them parodies) playing off of the Hounds of Tindalos, as created in the story of that title by Frank Belknap Long.

77.   THOMAS LIGOTTI. *The Conspiracy against the Human Race.* 2010 hc (rpt. 2011 [tpb]). 219 pp.

Notes. Cover design and photograph of the author by Jennifer Gariepy; cover production by Barbara Briggs Silbert. Limited hardcover edition of 1150 copies, printed by Covington Group. For the first time, we also issued roughly 100 uncorrected proof copies in paperback, in advance of publication of the hardcover. A remarkable philosophical treatise by Ligotti, best known as one of the most dynamic and innovative writers of supernatural literature to emerge in recent years. The volume (which includes its share of literary criticism, including discussions of Lovecraft and other weird writers) is a searching examination of the fundamental wretchedness of the human race.

78.   JONATHAN THOMAS. *Tempting Providence and Other Stories.* 2010. 261 pp. tpb.

Contents. Foreword, by Sherry Austin; Dead Men's Shoes; Into Your Tenement I'll Creep; Tempting Providence; A Different Kind of Heartworm; Gumball Man; The Silence in the Copse; The Lord of the Animals; The Salvage Saints; Passenger Bastion; Power of Midnight; The Men at the Mound; Three Ounces over Advent.

Notes. Cover illustration by Thomas S. Brown. The second collection of Thomas's short fiction featuring a number of richly evocative novelettes, following the well-received *Midnight Call* (see item 57). Most of the stories were previously unpublished.

79.   *Dead Reckonings* No. 7 (Spring 2010). EDITED BY S. T. JOSHI AND TONY FONSECA. 120 pp.

Contents. Realms of Perilous Delight, by Jim Rockhill [Richard Gavin, *The Darkly Splendid Realm*; Matt Cardin, *Dark Awakenings*]; The Red and the Blue, by Scott Connors [H. P. Lovecraft and Robert E. Howard, *A Means to Freedom*; Robert E. Howard, *The Horror Stories of Robert E. Howard* and *Heroes in the Wind: From Kull to Kane*]; A Macabre Display, by Javier A. Martínez [Jeffrey Thomas, *Thirteen Specimens: A Collection of the Bizarre*]; The Evil That Lurks Inside Us, by Jonathan Johnson [Michael Aronovitz, *Seven Deadly Pleasures*]; The Eldritch and the Cosmic, by Martin Andersson [S. T. Joshi, ed., *Black Wings: New Tales of Lovecraftian Horror*]; Rain, Rain, Everywhere, by S. T. Joshi [Ramsey Campbell, *Creatures of the Pool* and *Just Behind You*]; My Dear Watson, It's a Zombie Raccoon!, by Tony Fonseca [Martin H. Greenberg and Kerrie Hughes, ed., *Zombie Raccoons and Killer Bunnies*; John Joseph Adams, ed., *The Improbable Adventures of Sherlock Holmes*]; Where's the Plot?, by Andy K. Trevathan [L. A. Banks, *Undead on Arrival* and "Ev'ry Shut Eye Ain't Asleep"]; Living in a Topolganger, by Rob Latham [China Miéville, *The City & ytiC ehT*]; B-Grade and Z-Grade, by Matt Cardin [Richard Laymon, *Flesh and Dark Mountain*]; Lesser Straub, But Still Worth Reading, by Richard Bleiler [Peter Straub, *A Dark Matter*]; Ramsey Campbell, Probably: Restyling for Our Time; Bloodbath and Mayhem, by Lisa Nunn [Graham Masterton, *Death Mask* and *Blind Panic*]; Road Dogs and Iron Dead, by S. T. Joshi [Norman Partridge, *Lesser Demons*]; Horrors Down Under, by Leigh Blackmore [Felicity Dowker, *Phantasy Made Grotesk*; Robert Hood, *Creeping in Reptile Flesh*]; The Dead Return and They Have Bite, by Van Viator [Edward Lee, *The Golem*; Ray Garton, *Bestial*]; Less Artful Than Enthusiastic, by Robert Butterfield [Gord Rollo, *Crimson* and *Strange Magic*]; All That Glitters . . ., by Kevin Dole [Ellen Datlow, ed., *The Best Horror of the Year, Volume One*; William F. Nolan and Jason V Brock, ed., *The Bleeding Edge*]; Post-Columbine and the Gothic, by John Edgar Browning [Gary A. Braunbeck, *Far Dark Fields*]; Cautionary Tales, by Antoinette Winstead [Dean R. Koontz, *Dean Koontz's Frankenstein: Dead and Alive*; Conrad Williams, *Decay Inevitable*]; A Matheson Sampler, by Darrell Schweitzer [Richard Matheson, *The Box*]; The Permeability of Flesh, by Vicky Gilpin [Brian Keene, *Castaways* and *Urban Gothic*]; Lycanthropes and Rotters, by Kendra Kuss Ditto [Laurell K. Hamilton, *Skin Trade*; Cherie Priest, *Boneshaker*]; Scarifyingly Assured, by Matt Cardin [John Langan, *House of Windows*]; Weaponized Affluence, by Michael Marano [Suzanne Collins, *The Hunger Games* and *Catching Fire*]; Skipping the Light Fandango, by Melissa Ursula Dawn Goldsmith [Michael Long, *Beautiful Monsters: Imagining the Classic in Musical Media*]; Cthulhu in San Francisco, by Scott David Briggs [Michael Shea, *Copping Squid and Other Mythos Tales*]; Capsule Reviews.

Notes. The first issue with Fonseca as coeditor.

80. S. T. JOSHI. *I Am Providence: The Life and Times of H. P. Lovecraft.* 2010. 2 vols. hc (x, 1151 pp., numbered consecutively).

Notes. Cover illustrations consist of photographs of H. P. Lovecraft (different for each volume). Unabridged and updated version of Joshi's *H. P. Lovecraft: A Life* (Necronomicon Press, 1996), with more than

150,000 words restored to the text and much of it brought up to date to take account of recent discoveries in Lovecraft's life and work. Published in a limited hardcover edition (1000 copies) by subscription. For the paperback edition, see item 114.

81.   *Lovecraft Annual* No. 4 (2010). EDITED BY S. T. JOSHI. 206 pp.

Contents. Lovecraft's "The Bride of the Sea" and the Uses of Bathos, by Manuel Pérez-Campos; Following "The Ancient Track," by Jonathan Adams (includes musical composition, "The Ancient Track," by Adams); Letters to Carl Ferdinand Strauch, by H. P. Lovecraft (ed. S. T. Joshi and David E. Schultz); Appendix: A Library Goes Regionalist, by Carl F. Strauch; The Construction of Race in the Early Poetry of H. P. Lovecraft, by Phillip A. Ellis; The Ecstasies of "The Thing on the Doorstep," "Medusa's Coil," and Other Erotic Studies by Robert H. Waugh; Notes on a Nonentity, by H. P. Lovecraft; In Memoriam: Dr. Harry K. Brobst (1909–2010), by Christopher M. O'Brien; Time, Space, and Natural Law: Science and Pseudo-Science in Lovecraft, by S. T. Joshi; REVIEWS: [Review of H. P. Lovecraft and Robert E. Howard, *A Means to Freedom: The Letters of H. P. Lovecraft and Robert E. Howard*], by Martin Andersson; [Review of S. T. Joshi *H. P. Lovecraft: A Comprehensive Bibliography*], by Donald R. Burleson; [Review of S. T. Joshi, *I Am Providence: The Life and Times of H. P. Lovecraft*], by Steven J. Mariconda; Briefly Noted.

Notes. Of note are the lengthy and penetrating discussion of Lovecraft's poetry by Pérez-Campos and the musical setting of "The Ancient Track" by Adams, a professional composer.

82.   *Dead Reckonings* No. 8 (Fall 2010). EDITED BY S. T. JOSHI AND TONY FONSECA. 114 pp.

Contents. His Best in Years: King in Fine Form, by Hank Wagner [Stephen King, *Just After Sunset;* Stephen King, *Under the Dome*]; A Sheaf of Horrific Delights, by Leigh Blackmore [Richard L. Tierney, *Savage Menace and Other Poems*]; Motels, Arachnids, and High Heels, by Scott David Briggs [Donald R. Burleson, *Wait for the Thunder*]; Custer's Last Stand, by Bev Vincent [Dan Simmons, *Black Hills*]; Is the Soul Changeless?, by Kendra Ditto [Michael Schiefelbein, *Vampire Maker;* Gail Carriger, *Changeless*]; Doubly Disappointing, by Tony Fonseca [Robert R. McCammon, *Mystery Walk;* Jeffrey Thomas, *Thought Forms*]; Horrors Cosmic and Personal, by Javier A. Martínez [Brian Keene, *Darkness on the Edge of Town;* Ray Garton, *Scissors*]; On the Rack, by Michael Marano [Michael Marshall Smith, *What Happens When You Wake Up in the Night;* Tom Fletcher, *The Safe*

Children; Joel Lane, *Black Country*; Alison Moore, *When the Door Closed, It Was Dark*]; A Portrait of the Artist, by Steven J. Mariconda [S. T. Joshi, *I Am Providence: The Life and Times of H. P. Lovecraft*]; The Men Behind the Curtain, by Matt Cardin [Thomas Ligotti, *The Conspiracy against the Human Race*; H. P. Lovecraft, *Against Religion*]; Ramsey Campbell, Probably: The Missing Bits; What If Cthulhu Won?, by Martin Andersson [Darrell Schweitzer, ed., *Cthulhu's Reign*]; Shock or Schlock?, by Hank Wagner [Joe R. Lansdale, *Sanctified and Chicken-Fried*; John Skipp and Cody Goodfellow, *Jake's Wake*]; Horror and Fantasy for the Impecunious, by S. T. Joshi [Michael Kelahan, ed., *The Screaming Skull*; Michael Kelahan, ed., *The End of the World*; Sir Arthur Conan Doyle, *The Horror of the Heights*; Washington Irving, *The Legend of Sleepy Hollow*; Bram Stoker, *Dracula's Guest*; Oscar Wilde, *The Picture of Dorian Gray*]; A Werewolf Story with (Sharp) Teeth, by Robert Butterfield [Tom Fletcher, *The Leaping*]; Writing Above the Zombie Line, by Vicky Gilpin [Darrell Schweitzer and Martin H. Greenberg, ed., *Full Moon City*; Scott Edelman, *What Will Come After*]; Nutrition for the Dead, by Leigh Blackmore [Chris Lane, *Zombies: A Record of the Year of Infection*]; The United States of the Undead, by John Edgar Browning [Robin Becker, *Brains: A Zombie Memoir*]; Two Anthologies, 45 Stories, by Richard Bleiler [Ellen Datlow, ed., *Darkness: Two Decades of Modern Horror*; Stephen Jones, ed., *The Mammoth Book of the Best of Best New Horror*]; A Broad Range of Strange, by Jonathan Johnson [Jonathan Thomas, *Tempting Providence*]; Darkness with Depth, by Robert Butterfield [Maurice Broaddus and Jerry Gordon, ed., *Dark Faith*]; What Lurks in the Dark, by Van P. Viator [Alyson Hagy, *Ghosts of Wyoming*; Daniel McGachey, *They That Dwell in Dark Places*]; New Writers, New Horror, by John Edgar Browning [Jeani Rector, ed., *And Now the Nightmare Begins: The Horror Zine*]; Dante of the Dead, by Matt Cardin [Kim Paffenroth. *Valley of the Dead: The Truth Behind Dante's Inferno*]; Sympathy for Ig, by John Langan [Joe Hill, *Horns*]; Living in London Is Overrated, by Andy Trevathan [Tim Lebbon, *30 Days of Night: Fear of the Dark*]; A Ghost Melodrama, by June Pulliam [Simon Clark, *Ghost Monster*]; What If?, by Antoinette Winstead [Tananarive Due, *Blood Colony*]; Murder Most Macabre, by Tony Fonseca [Joe R. Lansdale, *The Bottoms*]; The Weird Scholar, by S. T. Joshi; Capsule Reviews.

83.   JOSEPH S. PULVER, SR. *Sin & Ashes.* 2010. 325 pp. tpb.

Contents. Death's Head Blues, by Laird Barron; Love Her Madly; She's Waiting . . .; *First There Is a Mountain . . . Then*; In This Desert Even the Air Burns; Even Night; Crow in Trick Town; When the Deal

Goes Down; Devil's Got the Walkin' Blues; Dead 'Round Here To-night; The Delirium of a Worm-Wizard; As the Sun Still Burns Away; Caligari, Again; Long-Stemmed Ghost Words; When the Moon Comes to Call; After Reading Michaux's "In the Land of Magic"; The Walking Man Walks; Silent No Longer; The Maiden of the Pines; Last Year in Carcosa; Scarlet Obeisance; Rendezvous Under Shadow Bridge; in front of an empty house in dead city; Ain't No Love on the Street; Perfect Grace; Kynothrabian Dirge; The Exorcism of Iagsat; Lonesome Separate Ways; Just Another Desert Night with Blood; After Death; I Often Dream of Words; Forever Changes; In the White Walls of Silence; Mother Stands for Comfort; Blow Wind Blow; 8's & Aces; A One-Way Fare; Don't Look Back; Long is the way and hard . . .; huddled in rags in a Kingsport alley . . .; Dead Ends and Empties; Sharp Fangs + Blood = Murder; Saint Nicholas Hall; Funeral in a Hate Field; An Orange Tick-Tick-Tick- Tick-Tick; Engravings; The Last Few Nights in a Life of Frost; Epilogue for Two Voices; To Live and Die in Arkham; The Last Twenty Miles of Wandering Again; Acknowledgments.

Notes. Cover illustration by J. Karl Bogartte. A second collection of horrific, fantastic, and surrealistic fiction by Pulver, following on his well-received first collection (item 67).

84.   FRED PHILLIPS. *From the Cauldron.* 2010. 132 pp. tpb.

Contents. THE FAIR FOLK: The Fair Folk; Metamorphosis; Giliniel; Sleep; De la Marche; One More; The Little Stone; Fleeting Hours; Frederick of Holland; On the Heath; Madrigal to Dian Alene; A Winter Night's Sleep; The Old Tavern; Ode to Asbjorn Gustavsson Haarfagr; Final Quest; Bane of Aeacus; The Gathering of Clan Creachain; The Formula; The Tale of the Scribe; Burleycon 1973; Chanson de Guerre; The Printed Grail; The Inn at the Side of the Road; The Mask; Yesudai; The Honour of Princes; Moira; They Also Rule, Who Only Stand and Baste; The Ballad of the Four Sons; Aisling for Mary Radich; Sonnet LIII. R.E.H. Style #3; Quest; Stand or Fall; The Price of Blood; Tiresias; WEIGHED IN THE SCALES: Origin; Ephemera; Chagrin; Sortilege; A Fragrance; Apathy; Futility; Damozel Alayne; Epitaph on an Unknown Howe in the Foothills of Wales; The Poet to His Bed; Angelique Perdue; Rendezvous; Toilette d'Angelique; Meistersang; At the Inn; Samhain; A Peek at Dürer; Discovery; Wrapped in Fabrics Red; Weighed in the Scales; To Clark Ashton Smith; Conundrum; Anomaly; Raw, New Things; PHANTASMS: The Pathways of the Dead; The Lost Legend of Ingoldsby; A Lovecraftian's Eye-View of Kipling; The Elder Ones;

The Lost City; The Book; Janandra; Predecessors; Buried Truths; Caveat; The Presence; The Codex; Outpost; Somnambulist; Witness; A Lovecraftian Reads Caesar Midnight on Hallowe'en; Silent Watchers; The Shop; The Steeple; Recompense; Chiaroscuro; Impasse; Volte-Face; The Sword; Pale Visitor; The House; The Street; Wyckham; Phantasm; Erato; The Wanderer; The Donjon; Rubaiyat of Rub al-Khali; The Journey; Off the Beaten Track; The Pit; The Keep; The Travelers.

Notes. Cover illustration by Howard Wandrei. A distinctive collection of weird and fantastic poetry by Phillips, an elder statesman in the world of Lovecraftian and fantasy fandom.

85. S. T. JOSHI, EDITOR. *A Weird Writer in Our Midst: Early Criticism of H. P. Lovecraft.* 2010. 264 pp. tpb.

Contents. Introduction, by S. T. Joshi; I. RECOLLECTIONS OF LOVECRAFT: Howard P. Lovecraft [1890–1937], by Walter J. Coates; Amateur Affairs, by Hyman Bradofsky; [Letter to the Editor], by Robert Bloch; Interlude with Lovecraft, by Stuart M. Boland; Howard Phillips Lovecraft, by Muriel E. Eddy; I Met Lovecraft, by Paul Livingston Keil; The Man Who Came at Midnight, by Ruth M. Eddy; II. CRITICISM IN LOVECRAFT'S LIFETIME: A Note on Howard P. Lovecraft's Verse, by Rheinhart Kleiner; Howard P. Lovecraft's Fiction, by W. Paul Cook; The Vivisector, by Zoilus [Alfred Galpin]; Preface to *The Shunned House*, by Frank Belknap Long, Jr.; A Weird Writer Is in Our Midst, by Vrest Orton; The Sideshow, by B. K. Hart; What Makes a Story Click?, by J. Randle Luten; III. COMMENTS FROM READERS; IV. CRITICISM FROM THE FAN WORLD: H. P. Lovecraft, Outsider, by August Derleth; A Master of the Macabre, by August Derleth; Disbelievers Ever, by R. W. Sherman; The Last of H. P. Lovecraft, by J. B. Michel; What of H. P. Lovecraft? or, A Commentary upon J. B. Michel, by Autolycus; H. P. Lovecraft: Strange Weaver, by J. Chapman Miske; Lovecraft and Benefit Street, by Dorothy Walter; [Letters to the Editor], by Thomas Ollive Mabbott; A Plea for Lovecraft, by W. Paul Cook; Let's All Jump on H.P.L., by P. Schuyler Miller; Howard Phillips Lovecraft, by Michael Harrison; The Lovecraft Cult, by Arthur F. Hillman; Lovecraft Is 86, by Francis T. Laney; Rusty Chains, by John Brunner; Some Notes on HPL, by Sam Moskowitz, Fritz Leiber, Edward Wood, and John Brunner; V. NOTICES FROM THE LITERARY COMMUNITY: Mystery and Adventure, by Will Cuppy; Horror Story Author Published by Fellow Writers, by Anonymous; [Review of *The Outsider and Others*], by T. O. Mabbott; Such Pulp as Dreams Are Made On, by Robert Allerton Parker; Macabre,

Lyrical and Weird, by Peter De Vries; Mystery and Adventure, by Will Cuppy; Nightmare in Cthulu, by William Poster; Books Alive, by Vincent Starrett; Bookman's Holiday, by Charles Collins; Mystery and Adventure, by Will Cuppy; Poesque Doodles, by Marjorie Farber; Books Alive, by Vincent Starrett; The Phoenix Nest, by William Rose Benét; [Review of *Supernatural Horror in Literature*], by Fred Lewis Pattee; Pilgrims through Space and Time, by J. O. Bailey; Imagination Runs Wild, by Richard B. Gehman; Books Alive, by Vincent Starrett; A Bookman's Notebook, by Joseph Henry Jackson; Sabbat-Night Reading, by E. O. D. Keown; Of Good and Evil, by [Anthony Powell]; The Genius Who Lived Backwards, by Vincent H. Gaddis; APPENDIX: Some Vignettes; Notes; Index.

Notes. Cover illustration by Jason C. Eckhardt. An extensive collection of criticism of Lovecraft—early articles in the amateur and fan press, readers' comments from *Weird Tales* and *Astounding Stories,* and reviews in magazines and newspapers—charting Lovecraft's emergence from a pulp writer to an established literary figure.

86.   DERRICK HUSSEY, S. T. JOSHI, AND DAVID E. SCHULTZ. *Ten Years of Hippocampus Press: 2000–2010.* 2010. 80 pp. tpb.

Contents. Foreword, by Derrick Hussey; My Years with Hippocampus Press, by S. T. Joshi; Publications of Hippocampus Press: 2000–2010; Index of Authors, Editors, and Artists.

Notes. Cover design by Barbara Briggs Silbert, featuring the distinctive spiderweb logo designed by Anastasia Damianakos. In the grand tradition of August Derleth and Arkham House, the leading figures behind Hippocampus Press provide a history and bibliography of the firm's publications during its first ten years of existence.

87.   *Dead Reckonings* No. 9 (Spring 2011). EDITED BY S. T. JOSHI AND TONY FONSECA. 85 pp.

Contents. Sculptures in Prose, by S. T. Joshi [Caitlín R. Kiernan, *The Ammonite Violin*]; They Grow Up So Fast, The Little Monsters, by June Pulliam [M. T. Anderson, *Thirsty*; Patrick McCabe, *Emerald Germs of Ireland*]; Imagination as Arbiter, by Jim Rockhill [Laird Barron, *Occultation*]; Attack of the Subgenre Anthologies: Female Vampires and Southern Shamblers, by Vicky Gilpin [Ty Schwamberger and Jessy Marie Roberts, ed., *Fem-Fangs*; Jessy Marie Roberts, ed., *Gone with the Dirt: Undead Dixie*]; Not Your Average Minas, by Tony Fonseca [Charity Becker, *Presence: Wolf Moon*; Karen Essex, *Dracula in Love*]; E'ch-Pi-El and Two-Gun Bob, by Leigh

Blackmore [S. T. Joshi, ed., *A Weird Writer in Our Midst: Early Criticism of H. P. Lovecraft*; Darrell Schweitzer, ed., The Robert E. Howard Reader]; Weird Japan, by Darrell Schweitzer [Higashi Masao, ed., *Kaiki: Uncanny Tales from Japan*]; Killed by a Big Ol' Book, by Andy Trevathan [Paula Guran, ed., *The Year's Best Dark Fantasy and Horror 2010*]; Savoring the Tragic, by Richard Bleiler [Steve Duffy, *Tragic Life Stories*; Frances Oliver, *The Ghosts of Summer*]; Bring Out Your Undead, by June Pulliam [Paula Guran, ed., *Zombies: The Recent Dead*]; Down Dark and Lonesome Highways, by Richard Gavin [Joseph S. Pulver, Sr., *Sin & Ashes*]; Ramsey Campbell, Probably: The Poetry of Shadows; The Shadow Theatre of One's Memory, by John Edgar Browning [Otto Penzler, ed., *Coffins: The Vampire Archives, Volume 3*; Peter Crowther and Nick Gevers, ed., *The Company He Keeps*]; Two Authors with Their Own Voice, by Robert Butterfield [Brian James Freeman, *The Painted Darkness*; Mark Howard Jones, *Songs from Spider Street*]; The Dawning of the Age of Bradbury, by Matt Cardin [Ray Bradbury, *The Collected Stories of Ray Bradbury: A Critical Edition*]; Unhappily Ever After, by Hank Wagner [Stephen King, *Full Dark, No Stars*]; Jack the Ripper Goes Graphic, by Van Viator [Robert Bloch, Joe R. Lansdale, John L. Lansdale, and Kevin Colden, *Robert Bloch's Yours Truly, Jack the Ripper*]; Bricks and Marble, by Jim Rockhill [Andrew Smith, *The Ghost Story, 1840–1920: A Cultural History*; Helen Conrad O'Briain and Julie Anne Stevens, ed., *The Ghost Story from the Middle Ages to the Twentieth Century*]; A Cornucopia of the Weird, by Leigh Blackmore [S. T. Joshi, ed., *Weird Fiction Review No. 1*]; Cheesy Demons and Whiny Vampires, by Tony Fonseca [Michael Laimo. *The Demonologist*; Jemiah Jefferson. *Fiend*. Vampire Quartet Series.]; Retrospective Reviews: Tales of a Mystic, by Joseph Wood Krutch [Arthur Machen, *The House of Souls*; Arthur Machen, *The Secret Glory*; Arthur Machen, *The Terror*]; The Weird Scholar, by S. T. Joshi; Capsule Reviews.

88.   MASSIMO BERRUTI. *Dim-Remembered Stories: A Critical Study of R. H. Barlow.* 2011. 400 pp. tpb.

Contents. Foreword, by S. T. Joshi; Abbreviations; 1. Some Notes on an Entity; 2. Dunsanianism; 3. Vagueness; 4. Cosmicism; 5. Time; 6. Nature; 7. Irony; 8. Forbidden/Furtive Search; 9. Poetry; Conclusion. Bibliography.

Notes. Cover illustration by Pete Von Sholly. A penetrating semiotic analysis of Barlow's fiction and poetry by Berruti, an Italian literary critic who has written several substantial articles on Lovecraft.

89.   DAVID E. SCHULTZ AND S. T. JOSHI, EDITORS. *An Epicure in the Terrible: A Centennial Anthology of Essays in Honor of H. P. Lovecraft.* 2010. 380 pp. tpb.

Contents. Preface; Introduction, by S. T. Joshi; I. BIOGRAPHICAL: The Parents of Howard Phillips Lovecraft, by Kenneth W. Faig, Jr.; The Cosmic Yankee, by Jason C. Eckhardt; H. P. Lovecraft and the Pulp Magazine Tradition, by Will Murray; II. THEMATIC STUDIES: On Lovecraft's Themes: Touching the Glass, by Donald R. Burleson; Letters, Diaries, and Manuscripts: The Handwritten Word in Lovecraft, by Peter Cannon; Outsiders and Aliens: The Uses of Isolation in Lovecraft's Fiction, by Stefan Dziemianowicz; Lovecraft's Cosmic Imagery, by Steven J. Mariconda; From Microcosm to Macrocosm: The Growth of Lovecraft's Cosmic Vision, by David E. Schultz; Landscapes, Selves, and Others in Lovecraft, by Robert H. Waugh; III. COMPARATIVE AND GENRE STUDIES: Lovecraft's "Artificial Mythology," by Robert M. Price; Lovecraft and the Tradition of the Gentleman Narrator, by R. Boerem; The Artist as Antaeus: Lovecraft and Modernism, by Norman R. Gayford; Synchronistic Worlds: Lovecraft and Borges, by Barton Levi St. Armand; Bibliography.

Notes. Cover illustration by Virgil Finlay. A reprint of the volume first published by Fairleigh Dickinson University Press (1991). A substantial collection of original essays by leading Lovecraft scholars, written to commemorate the centennial of Lovecraft's birth. The original edition, published only in hardcover, was widely purchased by libraries but not easily affordable to individuals.

90.   BARRY PAIN. *The Undying Thing and Others.* Edited by S. T. Joshi. 2011. 373 pp. tpb.

Contents. Introduction by S. T. Joshi; "Bill"; The Glass of Supreme Moments; Exchange; The Diary of a God; This Is All; The Moon-Slave; The Green Light; The Magnet; The Case of Vincent Pyrwhit; The Bottom of the Gulf; The End of a Show; The Undying Thing; The Gray Cat; The Four-Fingered Hand; The Tower; The Unfinished Game; The Unseen Power; The Widower; Smeath; Linda; Celia and the Ghost; The Tree of Death; Not on the Passenger-List; The Reaction; The Missing Years; The Shadow of the Unseen (with James Blyth).

Notes. Cover illustration by Allen Koszowski. Extensive selection of Pain's short fiction, including the complete contents of the early collection *Stories in the Dark* (1901); also the first reprint of the scarce novel *The Shadow of the Unseen* (1907), cowritten with James Blyth.

91. H. P. LOVECRAFT AND ROBERT E. HOWARD. *A Means to Freedom: The Letters of H. P. Lovecraft and Robert E. Howard: 1930–1932* (vol. 1) and *1933–1937* (vol. 2). Edited by S. T. Joshi, David E. Schultz, and Rusty Burke. 2011. 1004 pp. tpb (numbered consecutively).

Notes. Limited paperback edition (1000 copies) of item 68, with sewn signatures and French flaps.

92. *Lovecraft Annual* No. 5 (2011). EDITED BY S. T. JOSHI. 246 pp.

Contents. Locked Dimensions out of Reach: The Lost Stories of H. P. Lovecraft, by J.-M. Rajala; Cosmic Maenads and the Music of Madness: Lovecraft's Borrowings from the Greeks, by John Salonia; Blacks, Boxers, and Lovecraft, by Gavin Callaghan; On H. P. Lovecraft's "The House," by J. D. Worthington; From Bodily Fear to Cosmic Horror (and Back Again): The Tentacle Monster from Primordial Chaos to Hello Cthulhu, by T. S. Miller; Lovecraft and I, by Caitlín R. Kiernan; Lovecraft and the Sublime: A Reinterpretation, by Alex Houstoun; Lovecraft: A Gentleman without Five Senses, by Roland Hölzing; Endless Bacchanal: Rome, Livy, and Lovecraft's Cthulhu Cult, by Dennis Quinn; "Cool Air," the Apartment Above Us, and Other Stories, by Robert H. Waugh; Lovecraft's "The City," by R. Boerem; Briefly Noted.

93. ROBERT H. WAUGH. *A Monster of Voices: Speaking for H. P. Lovecraft.* 2011. 384 pp. tpb.

Contents. Introduction; PART I: FIRST PRINCIPLES: Lovecraft's Hands; Documents, Creatures, and History; PART II: SORTIES: "The Picture in the House": Images of Complicity; *At the Mountains of Madness*: The Subway and the Shoggoth; PART III: MEDITATIONS ON "THE OUTSIDER": "The Outsider," the Terminal Climax, and Other Conclusions; Lovecraft and Keats Confront the "Awful Rainbow"; The Outsider, the Autodidact, and Other Professions; PART IV: MATERIALISM, THEOLOGY, AND IMAGINATION: Lovecraft and Leopardi: Sunsets and Moonsets; Lovecraft Born Again: An Essay in Apologetic Criticism; Works Cited; Index.

Notes. Cover illustration by Philip Fuller. A second collection of Waugh's always stimulating papers on Lovecraft, following on *The Monster in the Mirror* (item 31 above).

94.   ANN K. SCHWADER. *Twisted in Dream: The Collected Weird Poetry of Ann K. Schwader*. 2011. 206 pp. tpb.

Contents. Foreword, by Robert M. Price; Introduction; I. MEMORIES OF THE WORM: The Worms Remember; Out of Corruption; Power Failure; The Ghoul-Queen; Out of Egypt; Abul Al-Hol; Ech-Pi-El's Ægypt; Lord of the Land; Dream-Gates; The Coming of Chaos; The Elder Lords; Out of the Nameless City; Asylum Sestina; Night Hungers; Hydra's Daughters; Asenath: A Cautionary Tale (On the Doorstep); Inheritrix; Mad Star Rising; Fear-Stars; The Burrowers Beyond; The Gate Between the Stars; The Wind Beyond; Night Terrors; Night Terrors II; Moot Question; Night Glyphs; Of Stonehenge & Star-Myths; Barrow-Walkers; The Last Betrayal; Auld Leng Signs; The Companion; Tonight on the Late, Late Show . . .; Night Lives; Life Studies; Moon-Fears; The Gatekeeper; Sarnath Remembered; In Memoriam Arthur Jermyn; A Man of Many Parts; Yule-Thoughts in Kingsport; The Whippoorwills; Lavinia in Springtime; Stargazing Along the Miskatonic; Untimely Observation; Sestina: To the Audient Void; Neighborly Whispers; If We Return; The Darkness Whispers; Wide Enough; Elder Signs; Ancient Echoes; The Ones Who Come; Faint Echoes; Blood Calls; Shunned Things; Jaded; Less Famous Last Words; Doorway to Madness; Not Alone; Star-Turn; The Quiet One; Darkest Mother; Handmaidens of the Worm; The Coming of Ammutseba; II. ANCESTORS & ACOLYTES: The Weighing of the Soul; The Tomb of Nephren-Ka; Namesake; The Old Ones Whisper; Yig Country; Survivals; Drums of the Father; Guardians of the Mound; Pompelo's Doom; Confession of the White Acolyte; The Shore of Madness; Art Imitates, All Too Well; The Fane of Mordiggian; At the Yielding of Twilight; Rede of the Gray Weavers; Voormi Hymn of Deliverance; Postscript: *The King in Yellow*; A Phantom Walks; Autumn, Lake Hali; Stargazing, Lake Hali; A Lost Song of Cassilda; Evening Reflections, Carcosa; A Queen in Yellow; III. AFTER INNSMOUTH: I. Flight; II. Discovery; III. Decision; IV. CHARLES DEXTER UNWARDED; I. "Who Shal Looke Backe"; II. "Of Whither He Voyag'd"; III. "Do Not Calle Up . . ."; IV. "From Dead Saltes"; V. "Of Humane Dust"; V. PICKMAN'S PROGRESS: I. Admiration; II. Revelation; III. Encounter. VI. LAVINIA: I. Forgotten; II. The Female Line; III. Child of Shadows; IV. Predestined; V. May-Eve; VI. The Other One; VII. His Father's Voice; VIII. Locked Out; IX. Whippoorwill Night; X. Final Signs; XI. Hallowmas Rite; XII. Resemblance; VII. IN THE YADDITH TIME: I. [The Long Waiting]; II. The Finding; III. The Recognition; IV. [The First Visions]; V. The First Sacrifice; VI. A Fatal Flaw; VII. The Departure; VIII. [The Call of Yuggoth]; IX. On Na'morha's Plain; X. Sacrifice Eyes; XI. Inside the Ghooric Zone;

XII. [In Na'morha's Halls]; XIII. Between Strange Stars; XIV. A Dream of Ægypt; XV. The Messenger; XVI. Into the Red Land; XVII. The Walls of Prophecy; XVIII. The Price of Vision; XIX. A Dream of Home; XX. Lost Celaeno; XXI. The Fate of Wisdom; XXII. [The Will of Yaddith]; XXIII. The Crystal Wind; XXIV. Where Black Stars Rise; XXV. A Dream of Sisters; XXVI. The Restoration; XXVII. Sight Past Sight; XXVIII. Sounds of Change; XXIX. A Dream of Prophecy; XXX. The Mutineers; XXXI. Minions of Chaos; XXXII. A Dream of Entropy; XXXIII. [Yaddith's Witness]; XXXIV. Confrontation; XXXV. Revelation; XXXVI. Voices of Yaddith; VIII. PRIVATE SHADOWS: She Hears Them Howling; Pomegranate Winter; Child of the Dark Mother; Lamia of the Mind; Waiting for the Angels; Ophelia's Moon; Coming Forth by Twilight; The Moon Is a Mask; Premonitions I; Premonitions VIII; Dream Tongues; Midnight on the Dark Angel Watch; In the Night Garden; Worm Moon; Rolled in That Dark Dirt; Sunset, Dia de los Muertos; At Lamanai; Viaduct Shrines; Gargoyle of Grief; Come the Mourning; Mutant Autumn; After Too Long Gray; Falling Away; Approaching the Celestial Necropolis; There Is a Darkness; Gargoyle of Longing; Crying from Twilight; The Dark in Dreams; Falling from Grace; The Dead Come Back; Child-Charm; A Thawing of Ghosts; In This Season; Sophie, Dying; Death Envy; Brief Darkness; Nachthexen; Eminence Grise; The Night Priests; Mount Pacho; Spirits of Caral; In a Lost City; After the Show at Karnak; Shadows of Kom Ombo; Where Autumn Brings Us; In the Valley of the Kings; Unkindness of Ravens; The Laughter of Small Bones; On This Last Night of Voices; Maiden & Raven; Six Tailors; Chilled Red; Blood Maidens; Breathless Reunion; Nosferatu Surrenders; Sanguine Taggers; For a Deathless Diva; Of Vanity & the Vein; Her Muse Is a Raven; Diving Xibalba; What Remains; Bones of the God; The Dying Year; Summer of Ravens; Whitechapel Autumn, 1888; Specter Moon; In Webs of Autumn.

Notes. Cover illustration by Loretta Young-Gautier; interior illustrations by Steve Lines. A substantial volume of the collected weird poetry of Schwader, perhaps the leading fantasy poet of our time. Includes the complete contents or extensive selections from such earlier volumes as *The Worms Remember* (2001), *In the Yaddith Time* (2007), and others.

95.   *Dead Reckonings* No. 10 (Fall 2011). EDITED BY S. T. JOSHI AND TONY FONSECA. 98 pp.

Contents. Two Masterful Collections, by Hank Wagner [R. B. Russell, *Literary Remains;* Catherine M. Valente, *Ventriloquism*]; The

Discovery of Sarban, by Darrell Schweitzer [Mark Valentine, *Time, a Falconer: A Study of Sarban*; Sarban, *Discovery of Heretics: Unseen Writings*]; Pitch-Perfect Grotesquerie, by Robert Butterfield [Brendan Connell, *Metrophilias*; Brendan Connell, *Unpleasant Tales*]; The Australian Horror Tradition, by Leigh Blackmore [James Doig, ed., *Australian Ghost Stories*; James Doig, ed., *Australian Hauntings: Colonial Supernatural Fiction*; Angela Challis and Dr. Marty Young, ed., *Macabre: A Journey through Australia's Darkest Fears*]; A Biography of the Mind, by S. T. Joshi [Jonathan R. Eller, *Becoming Ray Bradbury*]; From Short Story to Novel, by Tony Fonseca [Gary A. Braunbeck, *Mr. Hands*]; A Kinship with Monsters, by Scott Connors [W. H. Pugmire, *The Tangled Muse*]; Fear and Loathing in Suburbia, by Jim Rockhill [Bernice M. Murphy, *The Suburban Gothic in American Popular Culture*]; Ramsey Campbell, Probably: Ramsey's Rant; Horrific Hallucinations, by Van Viator [Stephen M. Irwin, *The Dead Path*; Simon Clark, *King Blood*]; The Vampires of Our Age, by Vicky Gilpin [Paula Guran, ed., *Vampires: The Recent Undead*; Laurell K. Hamilton, *Hit List*]; Dead on Arrival, by June M. Pulliam [Steven E. Metze, *The Zombie Monologues*]; The Return of Cosmic Horror, by S. T. Joshi [Kevin Ross, ed., *Dead But Dreaming 2*]; Look Out, Ole Jack Is Back!, by Robert Butterfield [Jack Ketchum, *Off Season*; Jack Ketchum, *Offspring*]; Frankie Goes Down Under, by Andy Trevathan [*Midnight Echo* (The Australian Horror Writers Association), February 2011]; Wondrous Wolves and Quirky Quarks, by Richard Bleiler [Kit Reed, *What Wolves Know*; Elton Elliott and Bruce Taylor, ed., *Like Water for Quarks: Science Fiction Meets Magic Realism*]; Horror Film Collection Hits Discordant Note, by Melissa Goldsmith [Neil Lerner, ed., *Music in the Horror Film: Listening to Fear*]; Weird Verse Over the Ages, by Benjamin F. Fisher [Janie Hofmann, *The Engagement of the Spur*; Ann K. Schwader, *Wild Hunt of the Stars*; Brett Rutherford, ed. *Tales of Wonder*]; Retrospective Reviews: A Novel by Mr. Oscar Wilde, by Walter Pater [Oscar Wilde, *The Picture of Dorian Gray*]; The Weird Scholar, by S. T. Joshi; Capsule Reviews; Index to *Dead Reckonings* 1–10.

Notes. The last issue of *Dead Reckonings* with S. T. Joshi as editor; the cover (in flat black) was intended to reflect mourning at his departure.

96.   H. P. LOVECRAFT. *Letters to James Ferdinand Morton.* Edited by David E. Schultz and S. T. Joshi. 2011. 493 pp. tpb.

Contents. Introduction; Letters to James Ferdinand Morton; APPENDIX: LOVECRAFT AND MORTON: "Conservatism" Gone Mad;

The Isaacsonio-Mortoniad; Save the Old Brick Row; [Christmas Greetings to James F. Morton]; CORRESPONDENCE WITH WILLIAM L. BRYANT; WRITINGS BY JAMES F. MORTON: Fragments of a Mental Autobiography; My Intellectual Evolution; A Few Memories; WRITINGS ABOUT JAMES F. MORTON; [James F. Morton in *Who's Who*]; Memorial of James F. Morton, by O. Ivan Lee; James Ferdinand Morton, Jr., by Edward H. Cole; Mortonius, by E. Hoffmann Price; Comments on Mr. Price's Article, by Pearl K. Morton; Jim Morton, by W. Paul Cook; James Morton, by Rheinhart Kleiner. Glossary of Frequently Mentioned Names; Bibliography; Index.

Notes. Cover design by Anastasia Damianakos (uniform with item 13). The first unabridged publication of Lovecraft's surviving letters to Morton, who was in many ways the most intellectually distinguished of Lovecraft's correspondents. The letters are thoroughly annotated by the editors. The volume is part of the *Collected Letters* series.

97. GARY WILLIAM CRAWFORD, JIM ROCKHILL, AND BRIAN J. SHOWERS, EDITORS. *Reflections in a Glass Darkly: Essays on J. Sheridan Le Fanu.* 2011.473 pp. tpb.

Contents. Foreword, by W. J. Mc Cormack; Introduction, by Gary William Crawford, Jim Rockhill, and Brian J. Showers; I. SOME NOTES ON BIOGRAPHY: A Memoir of Joseph Sheridan Le Fanu, by Alfred Perceval Graves; Anecdotes from Seventy Years of Irish Life, by W. R. Le Fanu; Extracts from *Wilkie Collins, Le Fanu and Others*, by S. M. Ellis; Portraits of Joseph Sheridan Le Fanu, by Jim Rockhill, Brian J. Showers, and Douglas A. Anderson; A Void Which Cannot Be Filled Up: Obituaries of J. S. Le Fanu, by Brian J. Showers; II. GENERAL STUDIES: M. R. James on J. S. Le Fanu, by M. R. James; A Forgotten Creator of Ghosts—Joseph Sheridan Le Fanu, Possible Inspirer of the Brontës, by Edna Kenton; Sheridan Le Fanu, by E. F. Benson; From *The Supernatural in Fiction*, by Peter Penzoldt; An Irish Ghost, by V. S. Pritchett; Excerpts from the "Prologue" and "Epilogue" to *Madam Crowl's Ghost*, by M. R. James; Doubles, Shadows, Sedan-Chairs, and the Past: The "Ghost Stories" of J. S. Le Fanu, by Patricia Coughlan; III. SOME SPECIAL TOPICS: Making Light in the Shadow Box: The Artistry of Le Fanu, by Kel Roop; Le Fanu's House by the Marketplace, by Wayne Hall; Sheridan Le Fanu and the Spirit of 1798, by Albert Power; H. P. Lovecraft's Response to the Work of Joseph Sheridan Le Fanu, by Jim Rockhill; "A Regular Contributor": Le Fanu's Short Stories, *All The Year Round*, and the Influence of Dickens, by Simon Cooke; A Shared Vision: Le Fanu's *In A Glass Darkly* and Carl Theodor Dreyer's *Vampyr*, by Gary William Crawford;

Dreyer, *Vampyr,* and Sheridan Le Fanu, by Mark Le Fanu; IV. CONTEMPORARY REVIEWS; V. STUDIES OF INDIVIDUAL WORKS: "Green Tea": The Archetypal Ghost Story, by Jack Sullivan; Introduction to *The House by the Church-Yard,* by Elizabeth Bowen; Three Ghost Stories: "The Judge's House," "An Account of Some Strange Disturbances in an Old House in Aungier Street," and "Mr. Justice Harbottle," by Carol A. Senf; Introduction to *Uncle Silas,* by M. R. James; Conversations in a Shadowed Room: The Blank Spaces in "Green Tea", by John Langan; Introduction to *Uncle Silas,* by Elizabeth Bowen; "Addicted to the Supernatural": Spiritualism and Self-Satire in Le Fanu's *All in the Dark,* by Stephen Carver; In the Name of the Mother: Perverse Maternity in "Carmilla," by Jarlath Killeen; Crossing Boundaries, Mixing Genres in *The Wyvern Mystery,* by Sally C. Harris; "I Resolved To Play the Part of a Good Samaritan": Metafiction in "The Room in the Dragon Volant," by William Hughes; "The Child That Went with the Fairies": The Folk Tale and the Ghost Story, by Peter Bell; The "Smashed Looking-Glass": Fragmentation and Narrative Perversity in *Willing to Die*, by Victor Sage; Bibliography; Sources; Biographical Notes; Index.

Notes. Cover illustration by Jason Van Hollander from a photograph by Laura Anzuoni. Large volume of both original and reprinted criticism of the great Irish fantaisiste, including an extensive selection of early reviews, memoirs by those who knew him, and much other interesting work. A finalist for the 2011 Bram Stoker Award for nonfiction.

98.   ADAM NISWANDER. *The Nemesis of Night.* 2011. 344 pp. tpb.

Notes. Cover illustration by Ron Leming. Another installment in the author's Shaman Cycle, where Lovecraftian entities manifest themselves in the American Southwest. The last novel completed by the author before his death on August 12, 2012.

99.   PETER CANNON. *Forever Azathoth: Parodies and Pastiches.* 2012. 260 pp. tpb.

Contents. Introduction; FOREVER AZATHOTH: I. Azathoth in Arkham; II. The Revenge of Azathoth; III. The House of Azathoth; IV. Azathoth in Analysis; V. Bride of Azathoth; VI. Son of Azathoth; SCREAM FOR JEEVES: I. Cats, Rats, and Bertie Wooster; II. Something Foetid; III. The Rummy Affair of Young Charlie; PARODIES AND PASTICHES: Tender Is the Night-Gaunt; The Sound and the Fungi; All Moon-Beasts Amorphous and Mephitic; The Undercliffe Sentences; The Arkham Collector; Old Man; Nautical-Looking Negroes; The Madness out of Space. A Reading Group Guide to *Forever Azathoth.*

Notes. Cover illustration by Jason C. Eckhardt. A generous selection of the Lovecraftian tales of one of the leading scholars on Lovecraft as well as one of the most engaging writers of Lovecraftian humor. This volume is an expansion of a book of the same title published in 1999 by Tartarus Press.

100.   W. H. PUGMIRE. *Uncommon Places: A Collection of Exquisites.* 2012. 270 pp. tpb.

Contents. An Identity in Dream; Artifice; Cesare; The Host of Haunted Air; Hempen Rope; Cathedral of Death; House of Legend; Inhabitants of Wraithwood; In Memoriam: Oscar Wilde; The Zanies of Sorrow; In Remembrance: Edgar A. Poe; Keepsake; Postcard from Prague; Necronomicon; Sickness of Heart; The Tangled Muse; Chamber of Dreams; Some Distant Baying Sound; Some Buried Memory; Your Ghost on Glass; Letters from an Old Gent; Uncommon Places; Acknowledgments.

Notes. Cover and interior illustrations by Gwabryel. A collection of stories and prose-poems by one of the leading contemporary writers of Lovecraftian fiction.

101.   H. P. LOVECRAFT. *The Annotated Supernatural Horror in Literature.* Edited by S. T. Joshi. 2nd ed. 2012. 228 pp. tpb.

Contents. Preface; Introduction; Supernatural Horror in Literature, by H. P. Lovecraft; Appendix: The Favourite Weird Stories of H. P. Lovecraft; Notes; Bibliography of Authors and Works; Index.

Notes. Cover illustration by Vrest Orton. Extensive revision of the first Hippocampus Press title, with exhaustive updating of the bibliography and notes and an overhauling of the overall design.

102.   JOSHI, S. T. *Lovecraft's Library: A Catalogue.* 3rd rev. ed. 2012. 180 pp. tpb.

Contents. Introduction; Explanatory Notes; Lovecraft's Library; Weird &c. Items in Library of H. P. Lovecraft; Indices.

Notes. Cover illustration by Jason C. Eckhardt. Revised version of the listing of titles in Lovecraft's library (for the 2nd ed. of 2002, see item 4), with the addition of 24 new titles.

103. *Dead Reckonings* No. 11 (Spring 2012). EDITED BY JUNE M. PULLIAM AND TONY FONSECA. 102 pp.

Contents. Horror's International Voices, by Hank Wagner [Lavie Tidhar, *Osama*; John Aivide Lindqvist, *Harbor*]; Successes, Excesses, and Failures, by Javier A. Martínez [Reza Negarestani, Cyclonopedia: Complicity with Anonymous Materials; Michael Cisco, *The Great Lover*]; An Ordinary Darkness, by John Edgar Browning [Ellen Datlow, ed., The Best Horror of the Year, Volume 3; Peter Crowther and Nick Gevers, ed. The New and Perfect Man]; The Horror of Revelation, by Robert Butterfield [Steven Savile, *London Macabre*; Michael McBride, *Blindspot*]; Old and New Cthulhu, by S. T. Joshi [Ross E. Lockhart, ed., *The Book of Cthulhu*; Paula Guran, ed. *New Cthulhu*]; Lovecraft Fans Rejoice, by Robert Butterfield [Simon Strantzas, *Nightingale Songs*; James Chambers, *The Engines of Sacrifice*]; Mainstreaming the Zombie Narrative, by June M. Pulliam [Colson Whitehead, *Zone One*; Jonathan Maberry, *Dead of Night*]; Fascination with Tragic Horror, by Tony Fonseca [Charlee Jacob, *This Symbiotic Fascination*]; Literary Nostalgia, with Some Great Fun, by Hank Wagner [Kenneth Robeson, *Doc Savage: The Desert Demons*; Tim Champlin, *Tom Sawyer and the Ghosts of Summer*]; Seductive Vampire with a Heart, by Van Viator [Andrea Dean Van Scoyoc, *Dante's Diary*]; Sacre Bleu! C'est Le Diable (Encore), by Tony Fonseca [J. K. Huysmans, *La-Bas (Down There)*]; Fifty Years of Ramsey Campbell, by S. T. Joshi [Ramsey Campbell, *The Inhabitant of the Lake & Other Unwelcome Tenants,* and *Ghosts Know*]; The Dark Waters of Capitalism, by Vicky Gilpin [Todd Grimson, *Brand New Cherry Flavor*]; "True" Crime, Stranger Than Fiction, by June M. Pulliam [Susan Mustafa and Sue Israel. *Dismembered*; Susan Mustafa, Tony Clayton, and Sue Israel, *Blood Bath*]; Whip Me, Beat Me, Bite Me, PLEASE!, by Andy Trevathan [Jemiah Jefferson, *Wounds*]; Bridging the YA-Mainstream Gap, by June M. Pulliam [Ransom Riggs, *Miss Peregrine's Home for Peculiar Children*]; A Barlow Primer for Attentive Readers, by Scott Connors [Massimo Berruti, *Dim-Remembered Stories: A Critical Study of R. H. Barlow*]; Got Gothic?, by June M. Pulliam [John Sears, *Stephen King's Gothic*]; Something Beyond Comprehension, by Bev Vincent [Joseph Aisenberg, *Carrie*; Danel Olson, ed. *The Exorcist*]; Re-Possessed, by Andy Trevathan [William Peter Blatty, *The Exorcist*; William Friedkin, *The Exorcist.*]; Silent House Tricks and Treats, by June M. Pulliam [Chris Kentis and Laura Lau, dir., *Silent House*]; Hooked on Maniacs and Bloody Hooks, by Tony Fonseca [Bob Harper, Twisted Rhymes]; Female Trouble, by June M. Pulliam [James Watkins, dir., *The Woman in Black*]; Horrors on the Small Screen, by June M. Pulliam [Ryan Murphy and Brad Falchuk,

American Horror Story; Frank Darabont, *The Walking Dead*]; A Pair of Kings: Two Views of Time Travel, by Robert Butterfield and Hank Wagner [Stephen King, *11/22/63*]; From Bad Dreams May Come Beauty, by Margi Curtis and Kenneth W. Faig, Jr. [Kyla Lee Ward, *The Land of Bad Dreams*]; Tales of Unease, by Matthew McEver and Hank Wagner [Christopher Fowler, *Red Gloves*]; Ramsey Campbell, Probably: Granted by *Granta*; The Weird Scholar, by S. T. Joshi; Notes on Contributors.

104.   DONALD SIDNEY-FRYER. *The Atlantis Fragments: The Novel.* 2012. 322 pp. hc.

Notes. Cover illustration by Gordon R. Barnett. Fantasy novel set in the world of DSF's poetry omnibus *The Atlantis Fragments* (item 53). While technically a reprint of an edition issued by the author by Phosphor Lantern Press, very few copies of that state were ever distributed.

105.   DONALD SIDNEY-FRYER. *The Golden State Phantasticks—The California Romantics and Related Subjects: Collected Essays and Reviews.* Associate Editors Leo Grin and Alan Gullette. 2012. 428 pp. tpb.

Contents. Foreword/Forward in a Phantastick Mode!; The Sorcerer Departs; Clark Ashton Smith, Poet in Prose (1893–1961); George Sterling (1869–1926): Hesperian Laureate; A Garland of Poems by George Sterling; A Memoir of Timeus Gaylord; A Visionary of Doom: Ambrose Bierce, Poet (1842–1914); Clark Ashton Smith: The Last of the Great Romantic Poets; A Statement for Imagination; The Last Lutenist: Christian Gottlieb Scheidler; Francis Marion Crawford: A Neglected But Not a Forgotten Master; F. Marion Crawford: Romantist Nonpareil; Robert E. Howard: Frontiersman of Letters; Robert E. Howard: Epic Poet in Prose; The Alleged Influence of Lord Dunsany on Clark Ashton Smith; Klarkash-Ton and E'ch-Pi-El: On the Alleged Influence of H. P. Lovecraft on Clark Ashton Smith; Nora May French: Somewhere Between Eulalie and Edna St. Vincent Millay; APPENDIX OF LESSER REVIEWS AND MISCELLANEA: Addendum: Another "Smith"; Don Herron: Echoes and Yet Again Echoes; L. Sprague de Camp: The Art of Modern Enchantment; Frank Belknap Long, *In Mayan Splendor;* Celeste Turner Wright, *Seasoned Timber;* William Hope Hodgson, *The Dream of* X: A Creative Alternative to *The Night Land;* Jesse F. Knight, *The Romantic Revival;* Clark Ashton Smith, *The City of the Singing Flame* (Introduction); Clark Ashton Smith, *The Last Incantation* (Introduction); Clark Ashton Smith, *The*

Monster of the Prophecy (Introduction); G. Sutton Breiding, *Autumn Roses* (Introduction); H. P. Lovecraft, *Fungi From Yuggoth*; "Klarkash-Ton" versus "Clark Ashton": A Minor Issue for Controversy; G. Sutton Breiding, *Journal of an Astronaut* (Introduction); *O Amor atque Realitas!* Clark Ashton Smith's First Adult Fiction; Frank Belknap Long, *The Darkling Tide* (Introduction); Keith Allen Daniels, *What Rough Beast, What Rough Book*; In Memoriam: Keith Allen Daniels (1956–2001); Acknowledgments.

Notes. Cover illustration by Alan Gullette. Compendium of Sidney-Fryer's articles on the California poets of the past century and weird poets of various sorts, written over decades. While technically a reprint of an edition issued by the author via Phosphor Lantern Press, very few copies of that state were ever distributed.

106.   RICHARD A. LUPOFF. *Dreams*. 2012. 260 pp. tpb.

Contents. Introduction: Into the Weird Blue Yonder, by Cody Goodfellow; The Adventure of the Voorish Sign; At the Esquire; Nothing Personal; Tee Shirts; Dingbats; The River of Fog; Cairo, Good-Bye; Report of the Admissions Committee; Fourth Avenue Interlude; Sergeant Ghost; The Law; The Green Fairy; THE WEBSTER SLOAT STORIES: dreemz.biz; wyshes.com; heaven.god. Afterword.

Notes. Cover illustration by Steven Gilberts. Reprint of a collection (first published by Mythos Books in 2011) of Lupoff's variegated Lovecraftian tales, with the addition of the tale "The Green Fairy," which appeared in print for the first time here.

107.   RICHARD A. LUPOFF. *Visions*. 2012. 268 pp. tpb.

Contents. Introduction by Peter S. Beagle; THE BEN ZACCHEUS CASE FILES: Hebrews Have No Horns; There Are Kings; Steps Leading Downward; April Dawn; Ankareh Minu; MYSTERIES, HORRORS, AND ADVENTURES: Petroglyphs; Brackish Waters; A Freeway for Draculas; The Peltonville Horror; Simeon Dimsby's Workshop; Villaggio Sogno; Tangaroa's Eye; Snow Ghosts. Afterword.

Notes. Cover illustration by Steven Gilberts. Reprint of another volume of Lupoff's Lovecraftian tales, first published by Mythos Books in 2009, with the addition of the tale "April Dawn," which appeared in print for the first time here.

108.   ALLAN GULLETTE. *Intimations of Unreality: Weird Fiction and Poetry.* 2012. 386 pp. tpb.

Contents. Gullette's Ritual, by Robert M. Price; INTIMATIONS OF UN-REALITY; The Old Man up the Road; The Admiral's Tale; Derrick's Ritual; Knocker-Over; Within the Machinery of Light; The Door in Lheil; The Desolation of Falithra; The Twilight Necropolis; The Shadow from Yith; In the Realm of Ying; House of Morning, House of Dream; The Legend of the Seeker; The Summons of Hastur; The Tomb of Nyarlathotep; Charles Nathan's Pipe; A Visit from Ray Bradbury; The Axe of the Executioner; Phases; THE GREEN TRANS-FER; THE MORE, THE MARIGOLD; INTO THE BEYOND: Dusk; Thoughts I; On a Rainy Eve; Poem to Polymnia; Arcanesia; Lunar Liturgy; For Fear; Song of the Old Ones; Hidden Realization; Flight; Lost Refuge; Song to Helios; Carven Faces; The Witness's Account; Cataclysm; The Portal; Oblivion; Awakening; Vision; Revelation of Night; Home in Autumn; Game; Painting: Dreamscape I; The Sorcerer's Lament; Down to the Harbor; Praise to the Sunrise; Sojourn; Solitude; Selene; I Ask the Fortune Teller; On the Mass Destruction of Starlings Near Fort Campbell, Kentucky; Thoughts II; Vidya; She; Requiem; The Mere Weather Sends Transport; The Absolute Sameness of Change; Lizard Life; Alchemy; Vest; Portal II; Burial Instructions; Epitaph; In-vocation: On the 100th Mailing of the Esoteric Order of Dagon; The Face of Death; Seer; The Last Sonnet; The Menace from the Wood-work; Song for the End of Time; To Keith Allen Daniels (1956–2001); Absinthe; The Dead Priest; Into the Beyond; Stripped to the Bone; The Truth of the Ages; Nora May; I Hitched My Wagon to a Shooting Star; A Trip to the Hypnotist; Acknowledgments.

Notes. Cover and interior illustrations by Denis Tiani. Generous selection of the prose and poetry of Gullette, who has emerged as a leading critic and follower of the San Francisco weird fictionists and poets, notably George Sterling and Clark Ashton Smith.

109.   JOSEPH A. PULVER, SR. *Portraits of Ruin.* 2012. 384 pp. tpb.

Contents. Introduction, by Matt Cardin; No Healing Prayers; Lena . . . cries; So Into You; (a piece) about angels left out in the rain; Time . . . and Forever, by Joseph S. Pulver, Sr., and Tara Vanflower; Before and After Science; A Hand at the Door; Le Festin de l'araignée; Herding Fire: A Murder Mystery; THE RUSS MEYER TRIPTYCH: The Director's Cut; Skin Flick sans Money Shot; When There's a Riot Goin' On . . .; But Not for Me, by Joseph S. Pulver, Sr., and Laurence Amiotte; kris-tamas as an exhibition; Small Ocean After Solar; Lonely . . . and a long way from home; Listen to a Country Song; Memories Can Wait; Jolene;

6 ... 6—; ... LIES ...... Thunder ...... ashes ....;
Rune Grammofon poem [U.N/umbered))))); Marks and Scars and
Flags; Mrs. Spriggs' Easter Attire, by Joseph S. Pulver, Sr., and Tara
Vanflower; Each Night Begins a New Journey That Leads Only to an
End with No Between; BACK to—; Catch Tomorrow; When a Sigh
Visits Skin; By the Light ... of; Her Lips Were Wet with Venom;
Now (a parade); After Plath's "Goatsucker"; Tark Left Santiago; How
I Survived the Cowboy Movie [or When the Barron Opened His Eye];
In Her Forest Garden Dreaming; Icarus Above ...; My Mirage; And
this is where I go down into the darkness; Acknowledgments.

Notes. Cover illustration by J. Karl Bogartte. A third collection of Pulver's weird work, highlighted by a deft use of prose-poetry and a focus
on the paradoxical beauties of terror and death. The final, novella-
length tale presciently anticipated the eventual mass appeal of Thomas Ligotti's *The Conspiracy against the Human Race* (item 77).

110.   *Lovecraft Annual* No. 6 (2012). EDITED BY S. T. JOSHI. 238 pp.

Contents. Race and War in the Lovecraft Mythos: A Philosophical Reflection, by César Guarde Paz; Of Regner Lodbrog, Hugh Blair, and
Mistranslations, by Martin Andersson; The Shadow over "The Lurking Fear," by Michael Cisco; The Aboriginal in the Works of H. P.
Lovecraft, by James Goho; Envisaging the Cosmos: A Note on "The
Dreams in the Witch House," by Scott Connors; Lovecraft, Absurdi-
ty, and the Modernist Grotesque, by Sean Elliot Martin; Sources of
Anxiety in Lovecraft's "Polaris," by J. D. Worthington; *Tekeli-li!* Dis-
turbing Language in Edgar Allan Poe and H. P. Lovecraft, by Lynne
Jamneck; Lovecraft's 1937 Diary, by Kenneth W. Faig, Jr.; The Case
for "How the Enemy Came to Thlunrana" and *The Case of Charles
Dexter Ward,* by Peter Levi; Misperceptions of Malignity: Narrative
Form and the Threat to America's Modernity in "The Shadow over
Innsmouth," by Anna Klein; Elementary, My Dear Lovecraft: H. P.
Lovecraft and Sherlock Holmes, by Gavin Callaghan; [Review of H.
P. Lovecraft, *The Annotated Revisions and Collaborations*], by Steven J.
Mariconda; Briefly Noted.

111.   RICHARD GAVIN. *At Fear's Altar.* 2012. 256 pp. tpb.

Contents. Prologue: A Gate of Nerves; Chapel in the Reeds; The Ab-
ject; Faint Baying from Afar; The Unbound; A Pallid Devil, Bearing
Cypress; King Him; The Plain; Only Enuma Elish; The Word-Made
Flesh; Annexation; Darksome Leaves; The Eldritch Faith; Acknowledgments; About the Author.

Notes. Cover illustration and frontispiece by Harry O. Morris. Substantial collection of weird tales by a leading Canadian author of supernatural and Lovecraftian fiction.

112.   *Dead Reckonings* No. 12 (Fall 2012). EDITED BY JUNE M. PULLIAM AND TONY FONSECA. 96 pp.

Contents. Children of Bram and Poesy *du Macabre*, by John Edgar Browning [Stephen Jones, ed., *The Mammoth Book of Dracula*; Michael A. Arnzen, *The Gorelets Omnibus: Collected Poems, 2001–2011*]; Horror Authors Get Religion, by Kendra Kuss Ditto [Stacia Kane, *Sacrificial Magic*; Michele Lang, *Dark Victory*]; Uttering the Unutterable, by Tony Fonseca [S. T. Joshi, *Unutterable Horror: A History of Supernatural Fiction*]; Time and Time Again, by Antoinette Winstead [Dean Koontz, *The Dead Town: A Novel* and *Odd Apocalypse: An Odd Thomas Novel*]; Weird Poetry, Then and Now, by S. T. Joshi [Matthew Gregory Lewis (ed.), *Tales of Wonder*; Brett Rutherford (ed.), *Last Flowers: The Romance and Poetry of Edgar Allan Poe & Sarah Helen Whitman*; Brett Rutherford, *Whippoorwill Road: The Supernatural Poems of Brett Rutherford*]; The Return of the Old-Fashioned Tale of Terror, by Robert Butterfield [Scott Thomas, *Urn and Willow*; William Meikle, *Dark Melodies*]; Sweet Zombie Jesus!, by June Pulliam [Daryl Gregory, *Raising Stony Mayhall*]; Martin's Classic Vampire Still Lives, by Braden Dauzat [George R. R. Martin, *Fevre Dream*]; Vampire Sluts, Doppelgangers, and Impossible Abodes, by Javier A. Martínez [Blake Butler, *There Is No Year*; Grace Krilanovich, *The Orange Eats Creeps*]; A Shadow of His Best Work, by Tim Lucas [Tim Burton, dir., *Dark Shadows*]; Shelley's Monster Lives, by Matthew McEver [Mary Shelley, *Frankenstein*]; The Heart of Darkness, by Bev Vincent [Peter Straub, *The Ballad of Ballard and Sandrine*; Graham Joyce, *Some Kind of Fairy Tale*]; Ramsey Campbell, Probably: A Can of Heinz; Love(crafty)an Eccentrics, by Darrell Schweitzer [Peter Cannon, *Forever Azathoth: Parodies and Pastiches*; W. H. Pugmire, *Uncommon Places: A Collection of Exquisites*]; Callers from Hell, by Van Viator [Tom Fletcher, *The Leaping* and *The Thing on the Shore*]; A Brilliant Idea Poorly Executed, by Jim Rockhill [John C. Tibbetts, *The Gothic Imagination*]; The Wonderful World of Nihilism, by Antoinette Winstead [Dean Koontz, *77 Shadow Street*; Adam Nevill, *The Ritual*]; Rekindling Interest in Two Novels, by Tony Fonseca [Ramsey Campbell, *The Seven Days of Cain*; Graham Masterton, *Petrified*]; Two Views of Two Classics, by Hank Wagner, with Bev Vincent [Ray Bradbury, *Dandelion Wine and Something Wicked This Way Comes*]; Vampires on Ice, by Hank Wagner [Matt Forbeck, *Carpathia*; Barbara Hambly, *The Magistrates of Hell*]; Lesser Powers?, by

Darrell Schweitzer [Tim Powers, *The Bible Repairman and Other Stories*]; Of Mirrors and Lakes, by Tony Fonseca [Eric A. Jackson, *A Blind Eye to the Rearview*; Ronald [Damien] Malfi, *Floating Staircase*]; Werewolf Novel a Real Dog, by June Pulliam [Anne Rice, *The Wolf Gift*]; Giron "Classic" Promises, But Doesn't Deliver, by Andy Trevathan [Sephera Giron, *The Birds and the Bees*]; The Weird Scholar, by S. T. Joshi; Notes on Contributors.

Notes. The first issue of *Dead Reckonings* with editor June M. Pulliam at the helm. Under her editorship, the journal expanded its scope to cover horror in all media.

113. CLARK ASHTON SMITH. *The Complete Poetry and Translations*. Edited by S. T. Joshi and David E. Schultz. Vols. 1 and 2: xxxix, 846 pp., numbered consecutively; Vol. 3. 2013. 442 pp. tpb.

Notes. See items 37 and 50. This paperback edition includes "The Canyon" and "Dawn," discovered after publication of the hardcover addition, as well as the original French poems "Paysage Elyséen" and "Fin de souper" by Pierre Lièvre. "The Desire of Loving" by Hélène Picard was moved from volume 2 to volume 3 for the paperback edition.

114. S. T. JOSHI. *I Am Providence: The Life and Times of H. P. Lovecraft*. 2013. 2 vols. tpb (x, 1151 pp., numbered consecutively).

Notes. Paperback edition of item 80.

115. WILLIAM F. NOLAN. *Nolan on Bradbury: Sixty Years of Writing about the Master of Science Fiction*. Edited by S. T. Joshi. 2013. 270 pp. tpb.

Contents. Preface; Introduction, by Jason V Brock; Editor's Introduction, by S. T. Joshi; About Bill Nolan, by Ray Bradbury; ARTICLES: R. B.: A Biographical Sketch; Portrait of a Writer; The Bradbury Years; Bradbury: Prose Poet in the Age of Space; The Great White Whale; The Best of Ray Bradbury; Ray Bradbury; Leigh Brackett and Ray Bradbury; Ray Bradbury: Space Age Moralist; Bradbury in the Pulps; Introduction to *The Last Circus and The Electrocution*; Afterword to "The Fireman"; Introduction to *Ray Bradbury Review* (1988 edition); A Half-Century of Creativity; Behind the Illustrations: The Real Ray Bradbury; Fifty Years with Bradbury: A Birthday Tribute; Ray Bradbury: Space-Age Legend; Ray, Ray, and Ray; William F. Nolan Interviews Ray Bradbury; A Bradbury Top Ten, Plus Fifty: My Personal Evaluation of; Ray's Finest Stories; STORIES: The Immortal

Ones; Mr. B. Goes to Hollywood; The Joy of Living; And Miles to Go Before I Sleep; To Serve the Ship; Dead Call; Fair Trade; The Dandelion Chronicles; TRIBUTES TO RAY BRADBURY: Goodbye, Old Pal; Kneeling at the Dandelion Shrine, by Jason V Brock; Ray Bradbury's Good Companions, by John C. Tibbetts; A Master of Symbol and Metaphor, by S. T. Joshi; Afterword: The Return of Ray B., by Greg Bear; Select Bibliography.

Notes. Cover illustration ("The Pedestrian") by Joesph Mugnaini, an artist long associated with editions of Bradbury's work. Cover design by Jessica Forsythe. Compendium of articles on Bradbury by Nolan, who knew the great fantaisiste for more than sixty years; also a selection of stories by Nolan influenced by Bradbury and genial parodies of Bradbury's work. Winner of the Bram Stoker Award for best nonfiction book of 2013.

116. S. T. JOSHI AND STEVEN J. MARICONDA, EDITORS. *Dreams of Fear: Poetry of Terror and the Supernatural.* 2013. 358 pp. tpb.

Contents. Introduction; I. THE ANCIENT WORLD: Homer, *From the* Odyssey; Euripides, *From* Medea; Catullus, Attis; Horace, Epode 5; II. FROM THE MIDDLE AGES TO THE EIGHTEENTH CENTURY: Dante Alighieri, *From* Inferno; Christopher Marlowe, *From* Dr. Faustus; William Shakespeare, *From* Hamlet; *From* Macbeth; John Donne, The Apparition; John Milton, *From* Paradise Lost; John Gay, A True Story of an Apparition; David Mallet, William and Margaret; William Collins, Ode to Fear; III. THE GOTHICS AND ROMANTICS: Johann Wolfgang von Goethe, The Erl-King, The Bride of Corinth, The Dance of Death; Mary Robinson, The Haunted Beach; William Blake, Fair Elenor; Robert Burns, Tam o' Shanter; Friedrich von Schiller, A Funeral Fantasie; Nathan Drake, Ode to Superstition; James Hogg, The Witch of the Gray Thorn; Sir Walter Scott, William and Helen, The Wild Huntsman; Samuel Taylor Coleridge, The Rime of the Ancient Mariner, Kubla Khan; Robert Southey, To Horror; Matthew Gregory Lewis, Alonzo the Brave and Fair Imogene; Thomas Moore, The Lake of the Dismal Swamp; George Gordon, Lord Byron, Darkness; Percy Bysshe Shelley, Sister Rosa: A Ballad; John Clare, The Nightmare; John Keats, La Belle Dame sans Merci: A Ballad; Heinrich Heine, The Lorelei; Thomas Hood, The Demon-Ship; IV. THE LATER NINETEENTH CENTURY: Victor Hugo, The Vanished City; Thomas Lovell Beddoes, The Ghosts' Moonshine, The Boding Dreams, Doomsday; Henry Wadsworth Longfellow, Haunted Houses, The Haunted Chamber; Edgar Allan Poe, The City in the Sea, The Haunted Palace, The Conqueror Worm, Dream-Land,

Ulalume; Alfred, Lord Tennyson, The Kraken; Oliver Wendell Holmes, The Broomstick Train; or, The Return of the Witches; Robert Browning, Chillde Roland to the Dark Tower Came; James Russell Lowell, The Ghost-Seer; Charles Baudelaire, The Phantom, The Irremediable; William Allingham, A Dream; George MacDonald, The Homeless Ghost; George Meredith, Phantasy; Thomas Bailey Aldrich, Eidolons, The Lorelei, Apparitions; Algernon Charles Swinburne, The Witch-Mother; Thomas Hardy, The Dead Man Walking; Ambrose Bierce, A Vision of Doom; Julian Hawthorne, Were-Wolf; W. E. Henley, [Untitled]; Guy de Maupassant, Horror; Edwin Markham, Wail of the Wandering Dead, The Wharf of Dreams; Emile Verhaeren, The Miller; A. E. Housman, Hell Gate; Katharine Tynan, The Witch; Madison Cawein, The Forest of Shadows, The Wood Water, The Night-Wind, Hallowmas; W. B. Yeats, The Phantom Ship; Dora Sigerson Shorter, The Skeleton in the Cupboard, The Fetch; Æ (George William Russell), A Vision of Beauty; V. THE TWENTIETH CENTURY: George Sterling, A Dream of Fear, A Wine of Wizardry, The Thirst of Satan; Edwin Arlington Robinson, The Dead Village, The Dark House; Christopher Brennan, [Untitled]; Paul Laurence Dunbar, The Haunted Oak; Walter de la Mare, Fear, The Listeners, Drugged; Robert W. Service, The Cremation of Sam McGee; Robert Frost, Ghost House, The Demiurge's Laugh; William Hope Hodgson, Storm; Park Barnitz, Mad Sonnet, Mankind; Edward Thomas, Out in the Dark; Herman George Scheffauer, Phantasmagoria, Lilith of Eld, The Shadow o'er the City; Lord Dunsany, Songs from an Evil Wood, The Watchers; Wilfrid Wilson Gibson, The Whisperers, The Lodging House; John Masefield, The Haunted; John G. Neihardt, The Voice of Nemesis; Siegfried Sassoon, Haunted, Goblin Revel; Vincent Starrett, Villon Strolls at Midnight; Georg Heym, The Demons of the Cities; Rupert Brooke, Dead Men's Love; Samuel Loveman, Ship of Dreams; Conrad Aiken, La Belle Morte; H. P. Lovecraft, Despair, To a Dreamer, The Wood, *From* Fungi from Yuggoth; Harold Vinal, Apparition, Ghostly Reaper; Clark Ashton Smith, Ode to the Abyss, The Eldritch Dark, The Medusa of Despair, The Tears of Lilith, A Vision of Lucifer; Robert Graves, The Haunted House; Frank Belknap Long, The Goblin Tower, The Abominable Snow Men; Robert E. Howard, Dead Man's Hate, Recompense; Donald Wandrei, Nightmare, *From* Sonnets of the Midnight Hours; Joseph Payne Brennan, The Scythe of Dreams; Stanley McNail, The House on Maple Hill; Donald Sidney-Fryer, Midnight Visitant; Richard L. Tierney, The Evil House, To the Hydrogen Bomb; Bruce Boston, The Nightmare Collector, Ghost Blood; Brett Rutherford, Fête; G. Sutton Breiding, The Worm of Midnight, Black Leather Vampyre;

W. H. Pugmire, The Outsider's Song; Gary William Crawford, The Formicary; Keith Allen Daniels, Stonehenge; Leigh Blackmore, Terror Australis; Ann K. Schwader, The Coming of Chaos; Index of Poets; Acknowledgments.

Notes. Cover illustration by Charles E. Burchfield ("Tree," 1946). Comprehensive new historical anthology of weird poetry from classical antiquity to the present, meant to be an updating of August Derleth's noteworthy anthology *Dark of the Moon* (1947).

117.   GEORGE STERLING. *Complete Poetry, Volume 1: Chords of Fire.* Edited by S. T. Joshi and David E. Schultz. 2013. 438 pp. hc.

Contents. Preface, by Kevin Starr; Introduction: The Poet of the Skies; THE TESTIMONY OF THE SUNS AND OTHER POEMS: Dedication; Memorial Day; Poesy; The City of Music; To One Loved; The Summer of the Gods; The Lords of Pain; The Fog Siren; To Miss Constance Crawley in "Everyman"; To Imagination; To a Lily; "With the Strength of Dreams"; The Testimony of the Suns; Music; A White Rose; The Soul's Exile; In the Beginning; Memory of the Dead; To My Wife; The Haunting; War; Nightmare; The Spirit of Beauty; To Katherine; Mystery; To My Sister; The Poets; The Reincarnation; On Reading the Poems of Father Tabb; The Parting; Words for Lange's "Blumenlied"; The Altar-Flame; To One Asking Lighter Songs; The Sea-Fog; The Nile; Darkness; The Ideal; To Colonel John S. Engs; "Sad Sea-Horizons"; Evening; Ultima Thule; The Swoon; The City and the Silence; The Directory; The Triumph of Bohemia; A WINE OF WIZARDRY AND OTHER POEMS: A Wine of Wizardry; The Islands of the Blest; The Lover Waits; To Edgar Allan Poe; In Extremis; Romance; The Forest Mother; A Violet; The Wild Iris; To an Elder Poet; The Homing of Drake; The Cloud; Three Sonnets on Oblivion; Oblivion; The Dust Dethroned; The Night of Gods; Helen Peterson; Tasso to Leonora; Of America; Beauty; The Soul Prismatic; Pride and Conscience; An April Morning; Madrigal; To Ina Coolbrith; A Mood; A Visitor; A Dream of Fear; Night in Heaven; Personal Sonnets; To My Wife as May Queen; To Ambrose Bierce; Nora May French; To Robert I. Aitken; To Charles Rollo Peters; The Man I Might Have Been; THE HOUSE OF ORCHIDS AND OTHER POEMS: Duandon; Three Sonnets of the Night Skies; I. Aldebaran at Dusk; II. The Chariots of Dawn; III. The Huntress of Stars; The Evanescent; Memory; The Moth of Time; The Black Vulture; The House of Orchids; Sonnets on the Sea's Voice; Autumn; Stars of the Noon; The Apothecary's; The Swimmers; Beneath the Redwoods; Music at Dusk; The Tides of Change; Morning Twilight; An Altar of the West; The Faun; The

Voices; A Character; The Guerdon of the Sun; The Gardens of the Sea; The Sibyl of Dreams; The Music of Sleep; Duty; The Echo and the Quest; Justice; The Fleet; Remorse; Moonlight in the Pines; At the Grave of Serra; White Magic; Three Sonnets by the Night Sea; After the Storm; The Harlot's Wakening; The Midges; Personal Poems; To Ambrose Bierce; To Hall B. Rand; To Vernon L. Kellogg; Charles Warren Stoddard; The Ashes in the Sea; The Forty-Third Chapter of Job; SONNETS TO CRAIG: Repentance; Thy Picture; To Craig; The Unalterable; Foreboding; Question; From the Gloom; Lost Music; Resurrection; The Heart of Music; Verses to Craig; Parting; A Prayer; Lonely; Autumn; Absence; Worship; Homeward; The Kiss; By Lonely Waters; Passion's Hour; Intimation; Shadows of Thee; The Unattainable; The Font of Beauty; Hope's Paradise; The Soul-Giver; The Inexorable Hour; At the Lily's Heart; The Joys Unchanging; Love the Transmuter; Search Rewarded; Bliss Decreed; The Burden of the Past; Past Flesh and Soul; Sunset; Love's Companions; Love's Shadow; At Dusk; The Spirit of Dusk; Eros in Heaven; The Star of Separation; A Midnight; Transmutation; God's Lily; From Dawn to Dream; Fire of Dreams; Thy Child-Picture; Evanescence; Sorrow and Joy; Beauty Afar; From Arcady; Loneliest; Belovéd; Hesperia; The Eternal Visitant; Evening Music; Love and Joy; Doubt and Worship; Love's Sacrament; Divinity; Enchantment; Coronation; Revelation; Adoration; My Love; The Unavailing; Love's Primacy; To Thy Heart; From Two Skies; The Abiding Presence; Love Complete; By the Western Ocean; A Vision; Love Desolate; The Pain of Beauty; A Constancy of Sleep; Dream's Alchemy; Soul of the World; Dreamland; The Shadow of Immortality; Until Thou Comest; Reborn; The Silent Fane; The Lute-Player; The Heritage of the Skies; Love and Sorrow; In Vain; The Hidden Goddess; Love's Mercy; Song's Futility; At Sunset; The Immortal; Blossom or Bird; Longing; The New Goddess; To the Moon; Lost in Light; The Path to Paradise; Appendix; Worship's Acme; Before Dawn; Separation; [Untitled]; POEMS TO VERA: To Vera; Inclusion; The Song-Font; My Songs; To Vera; "I Loved Thee, Atthis, Long Ago!"; To Vera; To Vera; Intimation; At Noon; The Cup-Bearer; Iphigenia; The Face of the Star; Afterward; Confession; To Vera; Absence; Mystery; "Out of the Night"; Star of the Soul; Before Dawn; To Vera at Night; To Vera (Birthday Ode); To Vera (Blank Verse); BEYOND THE BREAKERS AND OTHER POEMS: The Master-Mariner; The Voice of the Dove; Night-Sentries; The Muse of the Incommunicable; The Coming Singer; At the Grand Cañon; Nightfall; Ode on the Centenary of the Birth of Robert Browning; Afterward; "Tidal, King of Nations"; The Last Monster; Christmas Under Arms; War; Ascension; The Thirst of Satan; Scrutiny; Ballad of Two Seas; Ballad of St. John of Nepomuk; The Rack; Willy Pitcher; "Beyond the Sunset"; Respite; Kindred; "That Walk in Darkness"; In the Market-Place; The Palette; The Hunting of Dian; A Winter Dawn; A Winter Sunset; Forenoon by the Pacific; A Legend of the Dove; Said the Wind:; The Mission Swallows; "Omnia Exeunt in Mysterium"; "On a Western Beach"; Then and Now; Menace; The Secret Room; Past the Panes; From the Mountain; Discord; Lineage; To One Self-Slain; Night on the Mountain; The Abandoned Farm; To H. G. Wells; Caeli Enarrant; "You Never Can Tell"; Dawn from a Western Mountain; The Setting; The Sleepers; The Sleep of Birds; Spring in Monterey; The Last Days; Natural History Items; Father Coyote; The Lagoon; Relativity; The Plaint of the Cotton-Tails; A Possibility; YOSEMITE: AN ODE; THE CAGED EAGLE AND OTHER POEMS: The Slaying of the Witch; To Twilight; Henri; Conspiracy; Indian Summer; Ballad of the Fatal Word; On the Sale of the Love-Letters of a Dead Poet; Mediatrix; A Dog Waits His Dead Mistress; Humility in Art; An Autumn Thrush; The Fall of the Year; October; In Autumn; The Caged Eagle; Time and Tears; To an Old Nurse; To the Mummy of the Lady Isis; The Ramparts and the Rose; On a Portrait of Lincoln; The Tryst; A Yellow Rose; Shakespeare; The Shadow of Nirvana; The Return; Moloch; Three Sonnets on Sleep; Man; On a City Street; Illusion; Essential Night; The Gleaner; California; Poems on the Panama-Pacific International Exposition; Ode on the Opening; The Builders; The Evanescent City; Personal Poems; Frank Unger; To Xavier Martinez, Painter; The Light-Giver; To Margaret Anglin; On the Great War; The Song of the Valkyrs; The Dream of Wilhelm II; Earth's Anthem; To Germany; Betrayal; Belgium, August, 1914; England, August, 1914; To the War-Lords; The War-God; The Little Farm; The House of War; "As It Was in the Beginning"; To Belgium; The Two Prayers; Aftermath; The War-Machine; Bombardment; Germany; The Death-Chords; The Feast; War's Music; The Aeroplane; Before Dawn; The Turk; The New Kings; To France; The Night of Man; To the Allied Arms; The Battlefield at Night; Kingship; The Death of Rupert Brooke; The Helots; The Crown-Prince at Verdun; Before Dawn in America; Gun-Practice; To England; Civilization at Bay; The Day of Decision; Broadway, New York, 1916; The "Lusitania"; War: The Past; War: The Present; War: The Future; ADDITIONAL WAR POEMS FROM *The Binding of the Beast and Other Poems:* To Germany [VI]; The Binding of the Beast; To France at Verdun; In a Thousand Years; Germany in Belgium; Germany on the Seas; A Vision of Germania; To the Hun; THE PLAY OF EVERYMAN.

118.   GEORGE STERLING. *Complete Poetry, Volume 2: To a Girl Dancing.*
Edited by S. T. Joshi and David E. Schultz. 2013. 384 pp. hc.

Contents. ROSAMUND; LILITH; SAILS AND MIRAGE AND OTHER PO-
EMS: The Queen Forgets; Saul; Ocean Sunsets; Sanctuary; Spring in
Carmel; The Setting of Antares; The Deserted Nest; Kingship; The
First Food; The Wind; A Lost Garden; The Glass of Time; Reason;
Sonnets by the Night-Sea; Sails; Mirage; The Skull of Shakespeare;
Two Met; The Common Cult; The Lost Nymph; The Wine of Illu-
sion; To Life; The Roman Wall; "His Own Country"; Lost Colors;
The Passing of Bierce; Everest; Afternoon; A Compact?; Autumn in
Carmel; Poe's Gravestone; The Secret Garden; Norman Boyer; Of
One Asleep; To a Girl Dancing; The Far Feet; Hesperian; The Face
of the Skies; The Morning Star; The Evening Star; To Charles Rollo
Peters; To Ruth Chatterton; The Cool, Grey City of Love; The Prin-
cess on the Headland; To the Moon; The Hidden Pool; The Death of
Circe; The Pathway; The Last Island; Infidels; Vox Humana; An Ele-
gy; Sonnets on the Sea's Voice; The Dead Captain; Wind in Pines;
TRUTH; TRUTH: A GROVE PLAY; STRANGE WATERS; APPENDIX:
Light; By Carmel Mission; A Poet Has Risen, by Ambrose Bierce; A
Poet and His Poem, by Ambrose Bierce; An Insurrection of the Peas-
antry, by Ambrose Bierce; Introduction to Lilith, by Theodore Dreiser.
Notes; Index of Titles; Index of First Lines.

119.   GEORGE STERLING. *Complete Poetry, Volume 3: The Stranger at
the Gate.* Edited by S. T. Joshi and David E. Schultz. 2013. 500
pp. hc.

Contents. DATED POEMS: Farewell; The Sea Waif; The Spaniards in
Cuba; To ———; The Furies; In Farewell; To Leopold of Belgium;
Brotherhood; Feb. 21, '08; To Mrs. J. B. C; Love's Shrine; The Cliff
Dwellers; Inauguration Day, 1909; Romance! Romance!; The Pinions;
To Artemis Hunting; Song in Family Club Jinks for 1912; The Golden
Past; The Abalone Song; The Loosing; The Seasons; The Path of Por-
tola; R. L. S; Hope; The Star of Love; To Stella; "Seasonal to Date";
To Albert Bierce; To the Goddess of Liberty; The Vision of Portola;
Heat in the City; August 1st, 1914; The Blind; At Morning; Night
Sounds; The Fish Hawk; At the Last; On Fifth Avenue; The Lifted
Wings; Stress of Beauty; Ships of a Day; Under the Rainbow; Back to
Back against the Mainmast; Ballad of the Bells; The First Snow; The
Beach by Winter Twilight; Easter Dawn on Rubidoux; Lilies of Stone;
Rendezvous; To the Unknown Goddess; "57"; Transmutation; Art;
Joan of Arc; To Jack London; A Brother to Christ; Butterflies; Farmer
Haynes' Niece; California to the Artist; Before Dawn; Holy River of

Sleep; A Star; To Jack; To Robinson Jeffers; Democracy; The Passing of Buffalo Bill; To Sir Ernest Shackleton; The Revenge; The Friends of Wilhelm; "You Coward!"; To General White and Visiting Officers; The Path of Gold; The Immutable; You Are So Beautiful; The Symboled Spirit; Song of the Swineherds; "The White Logic"; The Flag; Moll; *Songs from* The Twilight of the Kings (1918); A Morning Hymn; The Messenger; Ever of You; We're A-Going; The Dust Hopes; Service; Nov. 11, 1918; The World-Rachel; Lucifer; To Joyce Kilmer; Outward; Visual Beauty; Altars of War; The Modern Muse; Memorial Day, 1919; [The Doughboy's Love Song]; From the Train; Morning in the Pines; To Raphael Weill; To Rachmaninoff; To Science; My Brook; Three Voices; Art and Life; Witch-Fire; Autumnal Love; To One Asleep; To Ned Greenway; To Louis Untermeyer; "Indulge the Genial Hour!"; Incarnation; Good and Evil; The Three Gifts; To Frank Mathieu; Distance; Rainbow's End; The "Bohemian Club"; Beyond the Music; Love and Time; Careless; The Wiser Prophet; Lost Sunsets; Three Sonnets on Beauty; The Parting of the Ways; The Day of Decision; Youth and Time; The Gulls; At Midnight; Flame; Happiest; The Kiss of Consummation; To an Irate Father; Problem; The Twilight of the Grape; Pumas; Ode to Shelley; Beauty Renounced; To Edwin Markham on His Seventieth Birt; The Wild Swan; Warning; The Killdee; The Night Migration; The Voice of the Wheat; The Trapping of Rung; To a Water-Fowl; The Midway Peace; Penitence; The Tracker; A Moth; To Serra of Carmel; The Stranger at the Gate; Ephemera; Shelley at Spezia; Sorcery; Venus Letalis; Song; A Critic; The Sailor Turns Street-Sweeper; The City by the Sea; Long Island Pebbles; The Wings of Beauty; Waste; The Kiss; To a Stenographer; Gulls at Night; By Another Sea; Mystery; Suppose Nobody Cared; The Fog-Sea; The Housebreaker; Fog-Horns; The Black Hound Bays; The Dog; Return, Romance!; Chivalry; The Stranger; Eidolon; To Carl Sandburg; The Strange Bird; A Sceptic's Fate; After Sunset; A Lumberjack Yearns; The First-Born; The Flight; A Knee Is Bent; The Last of Sunset; Old Partings; The Pirate's Grave; Amber; The Daughters of Disillusion; The Young Witch; The Pony Express; Paradox; Transition; One Poem; Wet Beaches; Three Mysteries; Vigil; What Porridge Had John Keats?; Nepenthe; The Night-Watch; To a Reformer; A Face in the Crowd; High Noon; To Wordsworth; From the Valley; The Voice of the Deep; "The Ice-Age"; To Charles Warren Stoddard; Two Pictures by Dickman; The Little Hills; The Unconditioned; Dear to Me; Old Anchors; The Street; Three That Knew Helen; Solitude; Farm of Fools; A Deserted Farm; Once; Caucasus; The Sailing of Keats; Which Was, and Never Shall Be; The Aëroplane; To Bernice di Pasquali; "The Grizzly Giant"; Hostage; Life,

Toil, and Love; Wayfarers; Disillusion; Ballad of the Seeker; Compensation; An Old Pine; To a Monk's Skull; Miocene; The Dreamer; Hope; An Old Road; The Fleet Comes; The Hawk's Nest; The Oldest Book; The Faithful; The Transfusion; The Steelyard; Familiar Beauty; Seismos; Sierran Dawn; Yerba Buena: July 9, 1846; To George Edwards; A Day of Truce; Ballad of the Grapes; Ballad of the Swabs; The Way to the West; The Grey Man; Infusion; The Unborn; The Meteor; Beauty and Truth; The Caravan; Echo; An Old Poem; The Pathfinders; To Friend W. Richardson; The Last Man; Late Tidings; Repartee; The Balance; North Wind; The Quarrel; Peace; Love and Custom; Lost Companion; Implication; On Certain Verses; Grasshopper; Safe; Insincerities; To California; Wings; The Restoration; The Seventh Veil; Coup de Grace; Counsel; Silence; An Old Indian Remembers; Adullam; My Swan Song; Abraham Lincoln; "And on Earth Peace, to Men of Good Wil; At Villa Montalvo; The Ballad of the Ghost-Arrow; Contributor; The Dark Nation; The Dweller in Darkness; The Final Faith; Sacrament; Sorrow; The Sowers; To Pain; To Ray Coyle; UNDATED POEMS: Above the Sea; Above the Stream; After Sunset; Amara; Annus Mirabilis; Answering; Arabian Lullaby; Archer and Arrow; The Ashes of Astarte; At the Club; At the Keyboard; At the Sea's Verge; Autumn; Autumn in California; Autumnal Hope; Before an Ocean; Beyond the Tides; Blue Ranges; Breakers; By the Sea of Time; The Carmel Millionaire; The Castaways; Change; The City and the Night; The Cocktail Song; Cold Altars; The Coming of Helen; Communion; Comparison; Completion; Comradeship; Conclusion; Confiteor; Contrition; Conviction; Coronal; A Couch of Love; A Cry of the Heart; The Cynic; "Dad" Tatlow Advises; Darling!; Dawn; A Day; Deep-Sea Limericks; The Desert; Devotion; Division; A Dream of Arcady; The Dusks of Destiny; Earth-Worms; Endearment; Enigma; Entreaty; Exiles; "A Fair Exchange"; Far and Near; Far Day; The Far Goddess; Far Peace; Farewell and Meeting; Fate's Flower; Flags o' Truce; For E. H. Sothern; Foreshadowed; Forest Music; Forever and Ever; From Dawn to Dusk; From Sun to Star; The Fugitives; Fulfillment; The Futile Song; The Glory of the Globe; The Goal; Goddess-Love; Good-Bye; Haunted; Heart-ache; Her Welcome; Here and Now; The Hidden Garden; The Horse in War; Hotaling's Fancy Farm; A Hymn for Americans; The Immortal Moment; In the Shadow; In the Valley; In the Valley; Inarticulate; Inclusion; Interpeace; Journey's End; June; The Last Mirage; The Last of Beauty; The Last of the Year; The Last Veil; Lilies of Lethe; A Listener; Lonely Beauty; The Lost Empire; Love Adoring; Love and Faith; Love and the Sea; Love at Sunset; Love at Twilight; Love Inexhaustible; Love Song; Love's Consummation; Love's Farewell; Love's Hunger; Love's

Silence; The Lutes of Exile; Magdalene; Man and Woman; Martyrdom; Meeting; Melodie in E; Memory and Rain; The Merciful Man; The Messenger; The Mirror; The Moon of Memory; The Music of Memory; Myrrh; Night-Separation; The Night-Wind; Nimrod; November Carol; The Oceans; "The Old Black-a Bull"; "Old Cats o' Carmel"; On His Blindness; On the Late Payment of Rent—Followed b; One Day; Origin; Pain and Joy; The Palace of the Moon; Parted; Parted; Passion's Prayer; Pavement; The Peace of the Hills; A Prayer; Protest; The Quest; The Rain; Recompense; Recompense; The Redwoods; Redwoods by Morning; The Redwoods Wait; Reflections on the Cat; Regret; Relatives; Remembered; Renouncement; "The Return of Faith"; Revealing Music; Revelation; Rosa Mystica; Rosa Mystica; Rose of the Winds; Roses of Sunset; Sarah the Whale; The Sea; Separation; Serenade; Silver Sword; The Sisters; Song; Song; Song; Song; Song; The Song of Henry Maxwell; Song of the Pirates; Song's Lesson; Sonnets of Realization; Sonnets of the True Beauty; The Sphinx; Spontaneity 37; Spontaneity 40; Spontaneity 42; Spontaneity 44; Spontaneity 92; Star and Storm; Starlight; Stars; Surety; The Swimmer; Tears; Testimony; That Which Abides; Thou and I; Through Love's Eyes; Thy Lineage; To a Dusk-Rose; To Anne Bremer; To Antonoë; To Astarte; To Love the God; To Mrs. Phoebe A. Hearst; To One Who Passed; To Stella; To the Bosom of Antonoë, Handmaiden of; To the True Heart; To Wilhelm II; To Ylla; To You; To You; Together; Too Late; Transfiguration; Twilight at Midway Point; Twilight Song; The Two Buzzards; The Unattainable; Until the Dawn; Valerie; A Visitant; A Voice; The Wayfarer; The Wayside Garden; Western Twilight; What It's Like; What Shall Be; Willy Smith at the Ball Game; Wind and Rain; "With Brief Thanksgiving"; Wonderment; The Woof of the Stars; The Word-Shrine; Yearning; Young Love; [Untitled Poems]; [Untitled Fragments]; [Untitled Fragmentary Poetic Drama]; Appendix; Holy River of Sleep; We're A-Going; A Christmas Hymn; [Untitled], by François Coppée; Notes; Index of Titles; Index of First Lines.

Notes. Bound in hardcover (no dust jacket) in an edition of 300 sets by Covington Group, including a slipcased edition of 50 sets that was released by subscription. Facsimile signature of George Sterling stamped in foil on the front cover of each volume. First complete edition of the poetry by the great California poet (1869–1926). Volumes 1 and 2 contain the complete contents of the volumes of poetry published in Sterling's lifetime, from *The Testimony of the Suns* (1903) to *Sails and Mirage* (1921), as well as his verse dramas and individually published poems; Volume 3 contains unpublished or uncollected poems. The edition features commentary on each of the poems and full bibliographical information on their publication during and shortly after Sterling's lifetime.

120.   JOHN LANGAN. *The Wide, Carnivorous Sky and Other Monstrous Geographies*. 2013. 324 pp. tpb.

Contents. Introduction: Reading Langan, by Jeffrey Ford; Kids; How the Day Runs Down; Technicolor; The Wide, Carnivorous Sky; City of the Dog; The Shallows; The Revel; June, 1987. Hitchhiking. Mr. Norris.; Mother of Stone; Story Notes; Afterword: Note Found in a Glenfiddich Bottle, by Laird Barron; Acknowledgments.

Notes. Cover illustration by Santiago Caruso. The second collection of Langan's short fiction, following on *Mr. Gaunt and Other Uncanny Encounters* (Prime, 2008).

121.   H. P. LOVECRAFT AND AUGUST DERLETH. *Essential Solitude: The Letters of H. P. Lovecraft and August Derleth, 1926–1931* (vol. 1) and *1932–1937* (vol. 2). Edited by David E. Schultz and S. T. Joshi. 2013. tpb (880 pp., numbered consecutively).

Notes. Paperback edition of item 54.

122.   JASON V BROCK. *Simulacrum and Other Possible Realities*. 2013. 248 pp. tpb.

Contents. Foreword: Man of Many Talents, by William F. Nolan; Preface; Introduction, by James Robert Smith; What the Dead's Eyes Behold; Pathologist's Roulette; The Central Coast; Passage; One for the Road; Palindrome Syndrome; The Hex Factor; Valve: The Heart as a Metaphor for Postmodern Blight; Valor: A Fable; Dragon; Object Lesson; Dream Poem #00; Where Everything That Is Lost Goes; Godhead: How to Become a God/Goddess in Six Steps; The Underground; Frac/tion; Van Helsing: His True Story; Story of a Blade; P.O.V.; People After Their Murder by the U.S. CIA; "By Any Other Name . . ."; Fever/Wart; Red-Wat-Shod; Poem from the Future; The History of a Letter; Wind; Black Box; Milton's Children; Simulacrum; Acknowledgments; About the Author.

Notes. Cover design, cover illustration, and interior artwork by Jason V Brock. The first short story collection by a dynamic young writer of weird fiction, including stories that range from psychological suspense to Lovecraftian horror to a melding of weirdness and science fiction. Also features examples of Brock's striking free verse.

123.   S. T. JOSHI. *The Assaults of Chaos: A Novel about H. P. Love-craft*. 2013. 246 pp. hc.

Notes. Cover illustration by Pete Von Sholly. Printed in a limited hardcover edition (500 copies, Covington Group). A novel that envisions Lovecraft, in the summer of 1914, encountering Ambrose Bierce and then venturing to England to team up with Arthur Machen, Lord Dunsany, M. R. James, Algernon Blackwood, and William Hope Hodgson to battle a cosmic threat posed by Nyarlathotep. Many of the words uttered by the various characters are taken from their essays, letters, and other writings.

124.   S. T. JOSHI. *Suicide in Brooklyn*. 2013. 36 pp. tpb.

Notes. Cover illustration by Daniele Serra. A short story included as a bonus to the first 200 purchasers of *The Assaults of Chaos*. A detective story without supernatural elements, but featuring covert references to details of Lovecraft's life and work.

125.   DAVID GOUDSWARD. *H. P. Lovecraft in the Merrimack Valley*. 2013. 192 pp. tpb.

Contents. Foreword, by Kenneth W. Faig, Jr.; Preface; Acknowledgments; 1. Transformations; 2. First Visits: 1921; 3. Whittierland and Newburyport; 4. Intermezzo: 1924–26; 5. Innsmouth Ascendant: 1927–31; 6. Dreams and Eclipses: 1932–33; 7. Shadows out of Haverhill: 1934–36; 8. Coda; APPENDIXES: A. The Haverhill Convention, by H. P. Lovecraft; B. First Impressions of Newburyport, by H. P. Lovecraft; C. Tryout's Return to Haverhill; Plaistow, N.H., by C. W. Smith; The Return, by H. P. Lovecraft; D. The Published Works of Myrta Alice Little Davies; E. Howard Prescott Lovecraft, by C. W. Smith; F. The Publications of Charles W. Smith; G. H. P. Lovecraft, "The Dunwich Horror," and Mystery Hill; H. Sites Open to the Public; Notes; Lovecraft: A Sense of Place and High Strangeness, by Chris Perridas; Bibliography; Index.

Notes. Cover photograph by Logan Seale, with copious interior illustrations. Interesting treatise on Lovecraft's travels in Massachusetts and New Hampshire and his encounters with such colleagues as Charles W. Smith and Myrta Alice Little, with a discussion of the influence of these visits on his fiction.

126.   STEVEN J. MARICONDA. *H. P. Lovecraft: Art, Artifact, and Reality*. 2013. 306 pp. tpb.

Contents. Introduction; I. GENERAL STUDIES: H. P. Lovecraft: Consummate Prose Stylist; Lovecraft's Concept of "Background"; Toward a Reader-Response Approach to the Lovecraft Mythos; Lovecraft's Cosmic Imagery; H. P. Lovecraft: Art, Artifact, and Reality; H. P. Lovecraft: Reluctant American Modernist; "Expect Great Revelations": Lovecraft Criticism in His Centennial Year; II. ESSAYS ON SPECIFIC WORKS: On "Amissa Minerva"; "The Hound"—A Dead Dog?; "Hypnos": Art, Philosophy, and Insanity; *Curious Myths of the Middle Ages* and "The Rats in the Walls"; Lovecraft's "Elizabethtown"; On the Emergence of "Cthulhu"; The Subversion of Sense in "The Colour out of Space"; Tightening the Coil: The Revision of "The Whisperer in Darkness"; Lovecraft's Role in "The Tree on the Hill"; Some Antecedents of the Shining Trapezohedron; III. REVIEWS: The Corrected Texts of Lovecraft's Tales; Lovecraft's Essays, Poems, and Letters; Some Lovecraft Scholars; Anodyne. Amusing Appendix; Afterword; Works Cited; Sources; Index.

Notes. Cover illustration by Charles E. Burchfield ("Afterglow", 1916). Rich collection of the collected essays and reviews of one of the leading Lovecraft scholars over the past thirty years. A radical expansion of Mariconda's earlier essay collection, *On the Emergence of "Cthulhu" and Other Observations* (Necronomicon Press, 1995).

127.   KENNETH W. FAIG, JR. *Lovecraft's Pillow and Other Strange Stories*. 2013. 234 pp. tpb.

Contents. Preface; TALES OF THE LOVECRAFT COLLECTORS: Introduction; Collector the First—Major Geoffrey Hopkinton-Smith (1857–1943); Collector the Second—Dean Alan Edgerton Noble (1876–1959); Collector the Third—Charles Wilson Hodap (1842–1944); Collectors the Fourth and Fifth—David Parkes Boynton (1897–1956) and Another Gentleman of the Hope Club; Collectors the Sixth and Seventh—Miss Susan M. Rounds (1780–1878) and James N. Arnold (1844–1927). Life and Death; The Squirrel Pond; Innsmouth 1984; Boy in Summer; The Haunting of Huber's; Lovecraft's Pillow; Leng; Gothic Studies; Sources.

Notes. Cover illustration by Daniele Serra. A substantial—and perhaps surprising—collection of stories by a writer who has distinguished himself as a leading authority on Lovecraft's life. Faig here brings that knowledge to bear in many of these stories, especially in an expanded version of *Tales of the Lovecraft Collectors* (first published by Necronomicon Press in 1995), as well as in other tales.

128.   JONATHAN THOMAS. *Thirteen Conjurations*. 2013. 278 pp. tpb.

Contents. In Situ: Excavating the Art of Jonathan Thomas, by Barton Levi St. Armand; FROM OUT OF THE MYTHOS: Mobymart After Midnight; King of Cat Swamp; Pictures of Lily; The Last Jar; FROM ELSEWHERE: The Copper God's Treat; Sympathy for the Deadbeats; Way Up When; The Comeuppance Hour; A Retouch in Camonica; Election Roundup; SWEDISH-AMERICAN TRIPTYCH: Missing the Boat (The Promised Land); Harm Like Water (The Undiscovered Country); Taking the Plunge (The Old Country).

Notes. Cover illustration by Jason C. Eckhardt. Thomas's third story collection, containing ingenious elaborations of the Lovecraft Mythos as well as other tales of terror and strangeness.

129.   H. P. LOVECRAFT. *The Ancient Track: The Complete Poetical Works of H. P. Lovecraft*. Edited by S. T. Joshi. 2013. 604 pp. tpb.

Contents. Introduction; I. JUVENILIA: 1897–1905: The Poem of Ulysses, or The Odyssey; Ovid's Metamorphoses; H. Lovecraft's Attempted Journey betwixt Providence & Fall River on the N.Y.N.H. & H.R.R.; *Poemata Minora, Volume II:* Ode to Selene or Diana; To the Old Pagan Religion; On the Ruin of Rome; To Pan; On the Vanity of Human Ambition; C. S. A.: 1861–1865; De Triumpho Naturae; II. FANTASY AND HORROR: To the Late John H. Fowler, Esq.; The Unknown; The Poe-et's Nightmare; The Rutted Road; Nemesis; Astrophobos; Psychopompos: A Tale in Rhyme; The Eidolon; A Cycle of Verse (Oceanus, Clouds, Mother Earth); Despair; Revelation; The House; The City; To Edward John Moreton Drax Plunkett, Eighteenth Baron Dunsany; Bells; The Nightmare Lake; On Reading Lord Dunsany's *Book of Wonder;* To a Dreamer; With a Copy of Wilde's Fairy Tales; [On *The Thing in the Woods* by Harper Williams]; The Cats; Primavera; Festival; Hallowe'en in a Suburb; [On Ambrose Bierce]; The Wood; The Outpost; The Ancient Track; The Messenger; *Fungi from Yuggoth:* I. The Book; II. Pursuit; III. The Key; IV. Recognition; V. Homecoming; VI. The Lamp; VII. Zaman's Hill; VIII. The Port; IX. The Courtyard; X. The Pigeon-Flyers; XI. The Well; XII. The Howler; XIII. Hesperia; XIV. Star-Winds; XV. Antarktos; XVI. The Window; XVII. A Memory; XVIII. The Gardens of Yin; XIX. The Bells; XX. Night-Gaunts; XXI. Nyarlathotep; XXII. Azathoth; XXIII. Mirage; XXIV. The Canal; XXV. St. Toad's; XXVI. The Familiars; XXVII. The

coul Verelst of Manhattan; The Return; Hedone; To Miss Beryl Hoyt; Dirge of the Doomed; To a Sophisticated Young Gentleman,; Veteropinguis Redivivus; To a Young Poet in Dunedin; [Metrical Example]; The Odes of Horace: Book III, ix; Gaudeamus; The Greatest Law; [Sonnet Study]; Verses Designed to Be Sent by a Friend of the Author to His Brother-in-Law on New-Year's Day; [To a Cat]; IV. SATIRE: Providence in 2000 A.D.; Fragment on Whitman; [On Robert Browning]; Ad Criticos; Frustra Praemunitus; De Scriptore Mulieroso; On a Modern Lothario; The End of the Jackson War; Gryphus in Asinum Mutatus;; The Power of Wine: A Satire; The Simple Speller's Tale; [On Slang]; Ye Ballade of Patrick von Flynn; The Isaacsonio-Mortoniad; Unda; or, The Bride of the Sea; [On "Unda; or, The Bride of the Sea"]; Gems from In a Minor Key; The State of Poetry; The Magazine Poet; My Lost Love; The Beauties of Peace; Epitaph on yᵉ Letterr Rrr. . . . . .; The Dead Bookworm; Ad Balneum; [On Kelso the Poet]; Futurist Art; The Nymph's Reply to the Modern Business Man; The Poet of Passion; On the Death of a Rhyming Critic; To the Incomparable Clorinda; To Saccharissa, Fairest of Her Sex; To Rhodoclia—Peerless among Maidens; To Belinda, Favourite of the Graces; To Heliodora—Sister of Cytheraea; To Mistress Sophia Simple, Queen of the Cinema; The Introduction; Grace; To Col. Linkaby Didd:; Amissa Minerva; [On Prohibition]; Monody on the Late King Alcohol; The Pensive Swain; To Phillis; The Poet's Rash Excuse; On Religion; The Pathetick History of Sir Wilful Wildrake; Medusa: A Portrait; Simplicity: A Poem; Plaster-All; To Zara; Waste Paper; [On a Politician]; [On a Room for Rent]; [On J. F. Roy Erford]; Lines upon the Magnates of the Pulp; Dead Passion's Flame; Arcadia; Lullaby for the Dionne Quintuplets; The Decline and Fall of a Man of the World; [Epigrams]: On a Poem for Children, Writ by J. M. W.; On —'s Gaining in Weight; Lines on a Dull Writer Having Insomnia; On a Pathetick Poem, by J. M. W.; Idle Lines on a Poetick Dunce; On the Habit of Letter-Writing; Life's Mystery; On Mr. L. Phillips Howard's Profound Poem Entitled "Life's Mystery"; On an Accomplished Young Linguist; "The Poetical Punch" Pushed from His Pedestal; The Road to Ruin; Sors Poetae; V. SEASONAL AND TOPOGRAPHICAL: Quinsnicket Park; New England; March; A Mississippi Autumn; A Rural Summer Eve; Brumalia; On Receiving a Picture of the Marshes at Ipswich; A Garden; April; On Receiving a Picture of yᵉ Towne of Templeton, in the Colonie of Massachusetts-Bay, with Mount Monadnock, in New-Hampshire, Shewn in the Distance; Autumn; Sunset; Old Christmas; A Summer Sunset and Evening; A Winter Wish; Ver Rusticum; A June Afternoon; The Spirit of Summer; August; Spring; April Dawn; January; October; Christmas; [On Marblehead];

bus Communis, by Sonia H. Greene; Alone, by Jonathan E. Hoag; Unity, by Unknown; The Dweller, by William Lumley; Dreams of Yith, by Duane W. Rimel; [On John Donne], by Lee McBride White; The Wanderer's Return, by Wilson Shepherd; Appendix 2: Poems by Others: *Metamorphoses* 1.1–88, by Ovid (P. Ovidius Naso); Our Apology to E. M. W., by John Russell; Florida, by John Russell; Regner Lodbrog's Epicedium, by Olaus Wormius, tr. Hugh Blair; A Prayer for Universal Peace, by Robert L. Selle, D.D.; To Mary of the Movies, by Rheinhart Kleiner; A Prayer for Peace and Justice, by Henry F. Thomas; The Modern Business Man to His Love, by Olive G. Owen; His Frank Self-Expression, by Paul Shivell; To a Movie Star, by Rheinhart Kleiner; [On the Duke of Leeds], by Unknown; Ruth, by Rheinhart Kleiner; Only a Volunteer, by Sergt. Hayes P. Miller; John Oldham: 1653–1683, by Rheinhart Kleiner; To Miriam, by Rheinhart Kleiner; Ethel: Cashier in a Broad Street Buffet, by Rheinhart Kleiner; Pastorale, by Hart Crane; Odes 3.9, by Horace (Q. Horatius Flaccus); [On John Donne], by Lee McBride White; Irony, by Wilson Shepherd; Notes; Bibliography; A Chronology of Lovecraft's Poems; Index of Titles; Index of First Lines.

Notes. Cover illustration by Charles E. Burchfield ("The Sphinx and the Milky Way," 1946). A thorough overhauling of Joshi's edition of Lovecraft's collected poetry (first published by Night Shade Books in 2001), containing several new poems and poem fragments and with an exhaustive revision of notes, bibliography, and other matter. The first and to date only Hippocampus Press book to be released in an oversized (7 × 10 in.) trim size.

130. *Lovecraft Annual* No. 7 (2013). EDITED BY S. T. JOSHI. 218 pp.

Contents. New Deal Politics in the Correspondence of H. P. Lovecraft, by Tyler L. Wolanin; Letters between H. P. Lovecraft and Orville L. Leach, edited by Donovan K. Loucks; Lovecraft's Rats and Doyle's Hound: A Study in Reason and Madness, by Robert H. Waugh; Lovecraft's Travelogues of Foster, Rhode Island, by Kenneth W. Faig, Jr.; Reappraising "The Haunter of the Dark," by John D. Haefele; Department of Public Criticism: July 1918, by H. P. Lovecraft; A Mountain Walked or Stumbled, by Stephen Walker; Excised Passages from "The Thing on the Doorstep," by S. T. Joshi; Additions and Corrections for "Lovecraft's 1937 Diary," by David Haden; Lovecraft, Reality, and the Real: A Žižekian Approach, by Juan Luis Pérez de Luque; REVIEWS: [Review of H. P. Lovecraft, *The Classic Horror Stories*], by S. T. Joshi; [Review of Robert H. Waugh, ed., *Lovecraft and Influence*], by Scott Connors; Briefly Noted.

131.   *Dead Reckonings* No. 13 (Spring 2013). EDITED BY JUNE M.
        PULLIAM AND TONY FONSECA. 106 pp.

Contents. Wagner and Vincent on King, by Hank Wagner and Bev
Vincent [Stephen King, *Doctor Sleep*]; A Dazzling Collection of Weird
Fiction Gems, by Robert Butterfield [Peter Bell, *Strange Epiphanies*];
Ramsey Campbell, Probably: A Ghostly Poll; Rhyme, Rhythm, and
Revenants, by Leigh Blackmore [S. T. Joshi and Steven J. Mariconda,
ed., *Dreams of Fear: Poetry of Terror and the Supernatural*]; Don't Play
It Again, Sam, by Tony Fonseca [Ed Kurtz, *Catch My Killer!*]; From
Forties Noir to Cheesy Sci-Fi, by Robert Butterfield [Brandon Zuern,
The Last Invasion]; Future Zombies and Past Scary-otypes, by June
Pulliam [Marc Forster, dir., *World War Z*; James Wan, dir., *The Con-
juring*]; A Distinctive Talent, by S. T. Joshi [W. H. Pugmire, *The
Strange Dark One: Tales of Nyarlathotep; Bohemians of Sesqua Valley;*
W. H. Pugmire and Jeffrey Thomas, *Encounters with Enoch Coffin*];
Werewolves and the War on Terror, by Matthew McEver [Benjamin
Percy, *Red Moon*]; Subtlety Scares, by Hank Wagner [John Langan,
The Wide, Carnivorous Sky and Other Monstrous Geographies; Guy N.
Smith, *Deadbeat*]; Klarkash-Ton Revealed, by Darrell Schweitzer
[Steve Behrends, *Clark Ashton Smith: A Critical Guide*]; Recommended
Reading Despite Reservations, by Leigh Blackmore [Danel Olson, ed.,
Exotic Gothic 4]; Brainless Zombies and Horror with a Heart, by
Richard Bleiler [K. Bennett, *Pay Me in Flesh; The Year of Eating Dan-
gerously; I Ate the Sheriff;* Mark Valentine, *Selected Stories*];
Retrospective Review: Remarks on *Frankenstein*, by Sir Walter Scott; The
Weird Scholar, by S. T. Joshi; Strange Days and Stranger Nights, by
John Edgar Browning [Jeffrey Ford, *Crackpot Palace: Stories;* Brian J.
Showers, *Old Albert: An Epilogue*]; Body Horror Squared, by June
Pulliam [Shane Stadler, *Exoskeleton;* Paul Kane and Marie O'Regan,
ed., *The Mammoth Book of Body Horror*]; Driven to Madness with
Fright, by S. T. Joshi [Simon Strantzas, ed., *Shadows Edge;* Joseph S.
Pulver, Sr., ed., *A Season in Carcosa*]; Fangs for Fans, but no Braiiins
for Scholars, by June Pulliam [Joni Richards Bodart, *They Suck, They
Bite, They Eat, They Kill*]; Is This the End of Zombie Shakespeare?, by
June Pulliam [Isaac Marion, *Warm Bodies;* Jonathan Levine, dir.,
Warm Bodies]; Horror, Harmony, and Discord, by Tony Fonseca [Phil-
ip Hayward, *Terror Tracks: Music, Sound and Horror Cinema;* Neil
Lerner, *Music in the Horror Film: Listening to Fear*]; Supernatural
Cliché Powers, by June Pulliam [Libba Bray, *The Diviners*]; Blood
Lust, by Van Viator [Ed Kurtz, *Bleed;* Chuck Wendig, *Double Dead;
Bad Blood*]; See a Zombie; Fuck a Zombie; Repeat . . ., by Tony
Fonseca [Stacey Turner, ed., *Fifty Shades of Decay: Zombie Erotica*];
Dome and Dumber, by June Pulliam [*Under the Dome*, developed by

Stephen King and Brian K. Vaughan]; Don't Touch That Dial!, by June Pulliam [*American Horror Story*, Season 2; *The Walking Dead*, Season 3]; From Heroin to Heroine, by June Pulliam [Fede Alvarez, dir., *Evil Dead*]; Portrait of the Monster as a Young Man, by June Pulliam [Derf Backderf, *My Friend Dahmer*]; Capsule Reviews; Notes on Contributors.

132.   EDITH MINITER. *The Village Green and Other Pieces*. Edited by Kenneth W. Faig, Jr. and Sean Donnelly. 2013. xvii, 363 pp. tpb.

Contents. Introduction; UNFINISHED NOVELS: *Lydia 'n Gerald; The Village Green; Love Without Wings*; SHORT FICTION: Who Brought the Children Home? 'lizbeth Prue; The Woman Over Way; The Other Elizabeth; When the Fog Lifted; For a Big Roll of Money; Overheard on the Beach; Maggie; An Unknown Mystery; Cindy's Child; Bookends; A Rearward Glance; How to Dress on $40 a Year.

Notes. Cover design by Sean Donnelly incorporating a photograph from *Ex-Presidents of the National Amateur Press Association: Sketches* by Wm. C. Ahlhauser (Athol: W. Paul Cook, 1919). Interesting second assemblage of fiction by a close friend of Lovecraft in the realm of amateur journalism, who also published much work professionally.

133.   *Dead Reckonings* No. 14 (Fall 2013). EDITED BY JUNE M. PULLIAM AND TONY FONSECA. 100 pp.

Contents. Wagner and Vincent on Simmons, by Hank Wagner and Bev Vincent [Dan Simmons, *The Abominable*]; Ramsey Campbell, Probably: The Grin Beneath the Flesh; From Horror to Homage, by Richard Bleiler [J. E. Mooney and Bill Fawcett, eds., *Shadows of the New Sun: Stories in Honor of Gene Wolfe*; Joseph S. Pulver, Sr., ed. *The Grimscribe's Puppets*]; Joel Lane: In Memoriam, by Robert Butterfield; Other Realities—Alternate Readings: Two Views on Jason V Brock: Outlier, by Jonathan Johnson; Brock as Intriguing New Voice, by Darrell Schweitzer [Jason V Brock, *Simulacrum and Other Possible Realities*]; Malignant Mothers, by Richard Bleiler [John Boyne, *This House Is Haunted*; Sophie Hannah, *The Orphan Choir*]; What Happens After?, by Sarah Simms [Ellen Datlow and Terri Windling, ed., *After: Nineteen Stories of Apocalypse and Dystopia*]; 571 Forrester Lane Eats Babies, by Matthew McEver [Sonja Condit, *Starter House*]; Triskaidekaphilia, by Jonathan Johnson [Jonathan Thomas, *Thirteen Conjurations*]; Submitted: My Stamp of Approval, by Tony Fonseca [Reba Wissner, *A Dimension of Sound: The Music of The Twilight Zone*]; Religious Fanaticism Run Amok, by Antoinette F. Winstead [L. Andrew Cooper, *Burning* the *Middle Ground*]; Fifty Years of Ramsey Campbell, by S. T. Joshi [Ramsey Campbell, *Holes for Faces; The Kind Folk;* and *The Last Revelation of Gla'aki*]; Two Veteran Storytellers Demonstrate How It Is Done, by Robert Butterfield [Darrell Schweitzer, *The Emperor of the Ancient Word;* Tony Richards, *The Universal and Other Terrors*]; Zombie Scholarship Earns Respect, by June Pulliam [Jennifer Rutherford, *Zombies;* Aalya Ahmad and Sean Moreland, eds., *Fear and Learning: Essays on the Pedagogy of Horror*]; Sequel Deserves to be a Forgotten Chapter, by Braden Dauzat [James Wan, dir., *Insidious: Chapter 2*]; Haunted from Within and Without, by Richard Bleiler [Ellen Datlow, ed. *Hauntings*]; A Darker Piece of Darkness, by John Edgar Browning [Ellen Datlow, ed., *The Best Horror of the Year, Volume 5* and *Blood and Other Cravings;* Laird Barron, *The Beautiful Thing That Awaits Us All and Other Stories*]; The Lovecraftian Magickal Mystery Tour, by Leigh Blackmore [Peter Levenda, *The Dark Lord: H. P. Lovecraft, Kenneth Grant and the Typhonian Tradition in Magic*]; A Smorgasbord of Weird, by S. T. Joshi [Lois H. Gresh, ed., *Dark Fusions: Where Monsters Lurk!*]; Portrait of the Mythos-Maker as a Young Man, by Tony Fonseca [S. T. Joshi, *The Assaults of Chaos: A Novel about H. P. Lovecraft*]; Second Time's the Charm, by Leigh Blackmore [H. P. Lovecraft, *The Ancient Track: The Complete Poetical Works*]; Covens, Witchcraft, and Murder, Oh My!, by Antoinette Winstead [Debbie Viguie, *The Thirteenth Sacrifice: A Witch Hunt Novel*]; Zombies Are People Too, by June Pulliam [Jonny Campbell, dir., *In the Flesh*]; The Weird Scholar, by S. T. Joshi; Notes on Contributors.

134.   H. P. LOVECRAFT. *Letters to Elizabeth Toldridge and Anne Tillery Renshaw.* Edited by David E. Schultz and S. T. Joshi. 2014. 470 pp. tpb.

Contents. Introduction; Letters to Elizabeth Toldridge; Letters to Anne Tillery Renshaw; APPENDIX: *Poems by Elizabeth Toldridge:* Expectancy; I Know a Forest Dark and Deep; Locusts and Wild Honey; Poe; H. P. Lovecraft; Mist; Ephemera; Midnight Sky; Divinity; Toldridge's Poetry Manuscripts at JHL; Contents of *Winnings* (ms., New York Public Library); Letters by Elizabeth Toldridge; Unpublished Parts of *Well-Bred Speech* as written by H. P. Lovecraft; Glossary of Frequently Mentioned Names; Bibliography; Index.

Notes. Cover design by Anastasia Damianakos (uniform with item 13). Meticulously edited volume of Lovecraft's complete surviving letters to two women, the disabled poet Elizabeth Toldridge and the amateur writer Anne Tillery Renshaw, whose elementary treatise *Well Bred Speech* (1936) Lovecraft revised late in life. Several chapters from that treatise that Lovecraft had written for Renshaw, but which were rejected by her, are published here for the first time.

135. SIMON STRANTZAS. *Burnt Black Suns: A Collection of Weird Tales*. 2014. 308 pp. tpb.

Contents. Dig My Grave, by Laird Barron; On Ice; Dwelling on the Past; Strong as a Rock; By Invisible Hands; One Last Bloom; Thistle's Find; Beyond the Banks of the River Seine; Emotional Dues; Burnt Black Suns; Acknowledgments.

Notes. Cover illustration by Santiago Caruso. Strong collection of weird stories by one of the leading contemporary figures in the field. A finalist for the 2014 Shirley Jackson Awards.

136. CLINT SMITH. *Ghouljaw and Other Stories*. 2014. 258 pp. tpb.

Contains. Introduction, by S. T. Joshi; Benthos; Ghouljaw; Dirt on Vicky; Don't Let the Bedbugs Bite; Retrograde; What About the Little One?; Double Back; The Tell-Tale Offal; Like Father, Like . . .; Corbin's Gore; The Hatchet; The Jellyfish; What Happens in Hell Stays in Hell; The Day of the Earwig.

Notes. Cover design and illustration by Jared Boggess. First collection of weird tales by a dynamic young author whose work is bound to be noticed in the years to come. Notably, a "soundtrack" to the collection was issued on audio CD by Kell of Shadowland.

137. *Dead Reckonings* No. 15 (Spring 2014). EDITED BY JUNE M. PULLIAM AND TONY FONSECA. 100 pp.

Contents. HPL³: A Multi-Dimensional View of Lovecraft, by Leigh Blackmore [David Goudsward, *H. P. Lovecraft in the Merrimack Valley*; Kenneth W. Faig, Jr., *Lovecraft's Pillow and Other Strange Stories*; Steven J. Mariconda, *H. P. Lovecraft: Art, Artifact, and Reality*]; Ramsey Campbell, Probably: Here Comes the Code; A Weird Fiction Tour de Force, by Robert Butterfield [Simon Strantzas, *Burnt Black Suns*]; Carnacki Lives Again!, by S. T. Joshi [Sam Gafford, ed. *Carnacki: The New Adventures*]; Holding Up the Undead as a Mirror, by June Pulliam [Rob Kuhns, dir., *Birth of the Living Dead*]; Reading the Impenetrable, by Javier A. Martínez [Luigi Serafini, *Codex Seraphinianus*]; Instant Rarity, by Darrell Schweitzer [John Shire, *Their Hand Is at Your Throats: Stories After Lovecraft*]; The Return of Fedogan & Bremer, by Leigh Blackmore [Scott Nicolay, *Ana Kai Tangata: Tales of the Outer, the Other, the Damned and the Doomed*; S. T. Joshi, ed., *Searchers After Horror: New Tales of the Weird and*

Fantastic]; Robocraftian Myths, by Martin Andersson [Brian M. Sammons and Glynn Owen Barrass, ed., *Eldritch Chrome: Unquiet Tales of a Mythos-Haunted Future*]; This Is the Forest Primeval . . ., by Jim Rockhill [Bernice M. Murphy, *The Rural Gothic in American Popular Culture: Backwoods Horror and Terror in the Wilderness*]; Out of the Distant Dark, by John Edgar Browning [Jeffrey Andrew Weinstock, ed., *The Ashgate Encyclopedia of Literary and Cinematic Monsters*; Steve Rasnic Tem, *Here with the Shadows*]; Portrait of the Gothic Fan as a Young Child, by Sarah Simms [Gert Jan Bekenkamp, *The World of Wonder: On Children's Lust for Terror*]; Spanning the Genres with William F. Nolan, by S. T. Joshi [William F. Nolan. *Like a Dead Man Walking and Other Shadow Tales*]; The Expanding Fictional Universe of the Small Screen, by June Pulliam [*Hannibal,* created by Bryan Fuller; *Fargo,* created by Noah Hawley]; The World Is Beautiful, Dark and Deep, by Richard Bleiler [Bruce Boston, *Dark Roads: Selected Long Poems, 1971–2012*]; From Japan with Love, by June Pulliam [Gareth Edwards, dir., *Godzilla*]; Immorality Story Dead on Arrival, by Richard Bleiler [Walter Jarvis, *The Fleshing*]; Even in Horror, Boys Will Be Boys, by June Pulliam [Andrew Smith, *Grasshopper Jungle: A History*; Geoffrey Girard, *Project Cain and Cain's Blood*]; The Blood Is the Life, by John Edgar Browning [Cole Hadden, creator, *Dracula*]; Zombies as Social (Media) Creatures, by June Pulliam [Murali Balaji, ed. *Thinking Dead: What the Zombie Apocalypse Means*]; A Thoroughly Engaging Collection of Mythos-Inspired Tales, by Robert Butterfield [Don Webb, *Through Dark Angles*]; Unedited and Uneven, by June Pulliam [Willy Adkins, et al., *The Dead Walk*]; No Hollow Praise for The Hollow City, by Van Viator [Ransom Riggs, *The Hollow City: The Second Novel of Miss Peregrine's Peculiar Children*]; Edgar Allan Poe, by Walter de la Mare; Capsule Reviews; Notes on Contributors.

138. DON WEBB. *Through Dark Angles: Works Inspired by H. P. Love-craft.* 2014. 250 pp. tpb.

Contents. The Mythos and I; The Man Who Scared Lovecraft; The Megalith Plague; Lavinia's Lament; The Gold of the Vulgar; The Doom That Came to Devil's Reef; Wilbur's Song; Pages from a Diary; Sanctuary; Wilbur Whatley's Twin; Platinum Hearts; Plush Cthulhu; Emily's Rose Window; A Ship Afar; Looking Glass; To Mars and Providence; After Alhazred; Lovecraft's Pillow; The Codex; Doc Corman's Haunted Palace One Fourth of July; Slowness; Rats; A Game of Nine Pins; Powers of Air and Darkness; Casting Call; Acknowledgments.

Notes. Cover design and illustration by Fergal Fitzpatrick. A volume of the selected Lovecraftian tales by a veteran writer of weird fiction.

139.   *Spectral Realms* No. 1 (Summer 2014). EDITED BY S. T. JOSHI. 138 pp.

Contents. Editorial, by S. T. Joshi; POETRY: Spectral Province, by Wade German; The Laundrymen, by Ann K. Schwader; Seasonal Affective Disorder, by Richard L. Tierney; Nocturnal Poet, by K. A. Opperman; Old Graveyard in the Woods, by Jonathan Thomas; Carathis, by Ashley Dioses; Night Stalker, by Michael Fantina; A Weird Tale, by Charles Lovecraft; The Star's Prisoner, by D. L. Myers; Emeraldesse, by Leigh Blackmore; Black Wings, by Ian Futter; Fortune Teller, by Carole Abourjeili; The Stomach Only Tries, by Marge Simon; Audience at Sunset, by David Barker and W. H. Pugmire; As Told to My Infant Grandchildren, by Phillip A. Ellis; The Hidden God, by Adam Bolivar; Siren of the Dead, by K. A. Opperman; Climate of Fear, by Ann K. Schwader; The Meromylls of Lake Lurd, by Donald R. Broyles; White Chapel, by Kendall Evans; Horror, by Ashley Dioses; Night Visit, by Charles Lovecraft; Fairy Song, by Darrell Schweitzer; Miranda, by Michael Fantina; States, by Ian Futter; In Splendour All Arrayed, by Leigh Blackmore; Dark Mirage, by Fred Phillips; In Cavernous Depths Yawning, by Randall D. Larson; Sea Princess, by Claire Smith; Necromancy, by Kyla Lee Ward; The Asteroid, by Richard L. Tierney; The Thing on the Mountain, by D. L. Myers; Note of the Executioner, by David Schembri; Ex Nihilo, by Daniel Kolbe Strange; The Den, by Chad Hensley; Awakening, by Carole Abourjeili; The Witches' House, by Margaret Curtis; Museum Piece, by Oliver Smith; Kiss the Stars, by Ashley Dioses; Pursuit, by Ian Futter; Afrasiab Down the Oxus, by Charles Lovecraft; Omens from Afar, by Phillip A. Ellis; Titan, by Michael Fantina; Lines on a Drawing by Hannes Bok, by Leigh Blackmore; Beneath the Ferny Trees, by David Schembri; "The Hound", by W. H. Pugmire; The Angels All Are Corpses in the Sky, by K. A. Opperman; A Carcass, Waiting, by Jason V Brock; The Rim, by Chad Hensley; CLASSIC REPRINTS: The Hidden Pool, by George Sterling; Resurrection Night, by Benjamin De Casseres; The Angels, by Théodore de Banville (tr. Stuart Merrill); Three Prose Poems, by Lord Dunsany; A Night with the Boys, by Bruce Boston; REVIEWS: To the Stars and Beyond, by Donald Sidney-Fryer; Ligotti on Sterling; Petrifying Poesy and Shivers in Verse, by Alan Gullette; Notes on Contributors.

Notes. Cover illustration by Eugenio Lucas ("Death Reading from a Human Lectern, Congregation in Background," c. 1850). The first issue of a journal devoted to weird poetry—a literary mode that has clearly experienced a renaissance in recent years. The journal also contains articles and reviews on weird poetry.

140.   S. T. JOSHI. *Lovecraft and a World in Transition: Collected Essays on H. P. Lovecraft.* 2014. 620 pp. hc.

Contents. Introduction; I. BIOGRAPHICAL STUDIES: Lovecraft and *Weird Tales*; Further Notes on Lovecraft and Music; Lovecraft's Library; Lovecraft's Revisions: How Much of Them Did He Write?; Lovecraft and His Wife; Lovecraft and the Films of His Day; The Rationale of Lovecraft's Pseudonyms; Lovecraft and the Munsey Magazines; Barbarism vs. Civilization: Robert E. Howard and H. P. Lovecraft in Their Correspondence; II. PHILOSOPHICAL STUDIES; The Political and Economic Thought of H. P. Lovecraft; "Reality" and Knowledge: Some Notes on Lovecraft's Aesthetic; *In Defence of Dagon* and Lovecraft's Philosophy; Lovecraft's Alien Civilisations: A Political Interpretation; Lovecraft and a World in Transition; Lovecraft and the "Big Issue"; H. P. Lovecraft: The Fiction of Materialism; Lovecraft and Religion; Time, Space, and Natural Law: Science and Pseudo-Science in Lovecraft; III. THEMATIC AND TEXTUAL STUDIES: Autobiography in Lovecraft; Lovecraft's Other Planets; Textual Problems in Lovecraft; The Structure of Lovecraft's Longer Narratives; The Dream World and the Real World in Lovecraft; Topical References in Lovecraft; Humour and Satire in Lovecraft; A Guide to the Lovecraft Fiction Manuscripts at the John Hay Library; IV. STUDIES OF INDIVIDUAL WORKS: Who Wrote "The Mound"?; On "The Book"; On "Polaris"; On "The Tree on the Hill"; Lovecraft and the *Regnum Congo*; The Sources for "From Beyond"; On "The Descendant"; What Happens in "Arthur Jermyn"; "The Tree" and Ancient History; Lovecraft and Dunsany's *Chronicles of Rodriguez*; Some Sources for "The Mound" and *At the Mountains of Madness*; *The Case of Charles Dexter Ward*; Excised Passages from "The Thing on the Doorstep"; V. ON LOVECRAFT'S ESSAYS, POETRY, AND LETTERS: "History of the *Necronomicon*"; "Supernatural Horror in Literature"; Two Spurious Lovecraft Poems; A Look at Lovecraft's Letters; Lovecraft's Fantastic Poetry; Lovecraft, Regner Lodbrog, and Olaus Wormius; Lovecraft's Essays; VI. ON LOVECRAFT'S LEGACY AND INFLUENCE: The Development of Lovecraftian Studies: 1971–1982; R. H. Barlow and the Recognition of H. P. Lovecraft; A Literary Tutelage: Robert Bloch and H. P. Lovecraft; Passing the Torch: H. P. Lovecraft and Fritz Leiber; *Lovecraft at Last*; The Cthulhu Mythos; The Recognition of H. P. Lovecraft, 1937–2013; Sources; Index.

Notes. Cover design by Jessica Forsythe, incorporating a seldom seen photograph of HPL. Enormous volume of Joshi's collected essays on Lovecraft, with some dating to as early as 1979 and others written in 2013. Supersedes such earlier volumes as *Selected Papers on Lovecraft* (Necronomicon Press, 1989) and *Primal Sources* (item 16 above). Printed in a signed, limited hardcover edition (1000 copies) by Covington Group; the paperback edition (see item 149) was released almost simultaneously. A finalist for the 2014 Bram Stoker Award for nonfiction.

141.   S. T. JOSHI. *200 Books by S. T. Joshi: A Comprehensive Bibliography.* 2014. 200 pp. tpb.

Contents. Introduction; I. Books Written; II. Books Edited; III. Editions of Works by H. P. Lovecraft; IV. Books Translated; V. Joshi as Series Editor; VI. Contributions to Books and Periodicals; VII. Journals Edited: VIII. Translations of Works by S. T. Joshi; IX. Forthcoming Books; APPENDIX: Murder; The Writing of *Mystery and Horror Writers of the Twentieth Century*; Books Published by Year.

Notes. Cover illustration by Jason C. Eckhardt. A volume that contains more information than anyone wants to know on Joshi's books, articles, reviews, stories, and other writings. Copies were sent free to advance purchasers of item 140, above; in addition, one hundred complimentary copies were distributed at the 2014 World Fantasy Convention. Joshi has now published an expanded edition, *300 Books by S. T. Joshi* (Sarnath Press, 2020).

142.   WADE GERMAN. *Dreams from a Black Nebula.* 2014. 134 pp. tpb.

Contents. PHANTASMAGORICAL REALMS: Starry Wisdom; New Lost Worlds; The Black Idol; The Witch of Time; The Black Abbess; The Demon Sea; Astral Hierarchy; In Ultima Thule; December in the Druid Woods; Château Nevreant; Swamp Fantasy; Valley of the Sorcerers; Moonflowers; Hendecasyllabics; Walpurgisnacht; Spectral Province; HYPNAGOGIC TERRAIN: Beyond the Wall of Tsang; A Voyage to Carcosa; In Carsultyal; The House of Neptune; Restoration; The Night Forest; Shadow and Silence; Prophecy of the Red Death; Lemurian Night Dive; Oneiromancy; Grimoire; The Necromantic Wine; Night Vigil for the Necromancer; Green Wine of Xei Cambael; Dragon; Barbarian; Black Sabbath Sestina; Trans-Neptunian Shores; Lords of Chaos; Hwamgaarl, the City of Screaming Statues; Dead Meadow; IN SPECTRAL PROVINCES: Plutonian; Event Horizon; Solarized; Return at Evening; Nocturne; Ghost Sonata; Eclogue; Nature

Unveiled; Dreams in the Lich House; The Barrow in the Highlands; Ghost Mountains; Succubus; Night Winds; *"Curst be he yt moves my bones"*; De Vermis Mysteriis; Inscriptions; Necuratul; SONGS FROM THE NAMELESS HERMITAGE: The Eremite; A Vessel for Black Waters; Brotherhood of the Black Waters; Tombs of the Dead Gods; Procession; Dreams from the Black Nebula; Night Songs; In Term; Astronomy Domine; Black Suns; Apparitions of Astral Night; Revelation in Black; ANOMALIES: The Kin Fetch; Supernatural Refugees; The Propagule; Thing of Spring; Mooncalf; Dunwich Pastoral; The Worm Conjurer; Anadromous; Weavers; Old Growth; Golem Variant; From Tindalos; Brood of the Black Goat; Overheard at a Wharfside Tavern; The Necklace; Gothic Blue Book; The Stains; Classical Revenant; Remembrancer of the Bibliognostic Hippocamp; The Sales Pitch; Chimera Park; The Priest of P'rea; Nightfall in Sesqua; Inquisition on the Dunes; Atlach-Nacha; Monastic Ruins; Divine Invasion; 90482 Orcus; Acknowledgments.

Notes. Cover illustration by Dariusz Zawadzki ("Artefact", 2008). A strong collection of weird poetry by one of the leading contemporary practitioners, a Canadian poet who specializes in finely crafted formalist verse, especially in the sonnet form.

143.   BOBBY DERIE. *Sex and the Cthulhu Mythos*. 2014. 314 pp. tpb.

Contents. Introduction; A Note on Sources and Citations; 1. SEX AND LOVECRAFT: Lovecraft and Love; Views on Sex; Views on Love and Relationships; Views on Eroticism and Pornography; The Shadow of Syphilis; Views on Gender and Homosexuality; Views on Miscegenation; Mrs. H. P. Lovecraft; 2. SEX AND THE LOVECRAFT MYTHOS: Precursors and Influences; Analyses; Themes and Parallels; The Role of Women; Asexual Aliens; Homosexual Interpretation; 3. SEX AND THE CTHULHU MYTHOS: New Developments; Family Trees of the Gods; Naming the Unnamable; The *Necronomicon* as Pornography; Body Horror; Alien Heats; Parody; Lovecraft as a Sexual Character; Gender, Sexuality, and Mythos Writers; Key Works and Authors (Robert E. Howard; Clark Ashton Smith; Robert Bloch; August Derleth; Ramsey Campbell; Richard A. Lupoff; Peter H. Cannon; Brian McNaughton; Robert M. Price; W. H. Pugmire; Caitlín R. Kiernan; Edward Lee; Alan Moore; *Cthulhu Sex* Magazine; *Eldritch Blue: Love & Sex in the Cthulhu Mythos*; *Cthulhu-rotica*; *Whispers in Darkness: Lovecraftian Erotica*; Other Authors and Works of Note; Sex and Mythos Poetry; Mythos Ebook Erotica); 4. BEYOND CTHULHUROTICA: Sex and the Lovecraftian Occult; Sex and the Mythos in Art; Sex and the Mythos in Comics; Sex and the Mythos in

Japanese Manga and Anime; Sex and the Mythos Cinema; The Mythos and Rule 34; Afterword; Works Cited; Suggested Further Reading; Index.

Notes. Cover illustration by Gahan Wilson ("Flasher", c. 1973). Learned and comprehensive treatise on the sexual elements in the work of Lovecraft, his contemporaries, and his disciples, including such issues as Lovecraft's own sexuality, homosexuality, rape, and other matters, all treated with delicacy and scholarly rigor.

144.   *Lovecraft Annual* No. 8 (2014). EDITED BY S. T. JOSHI. 222 pp.

Contents. Editorial; Letters to Farnsworth Wright, by H. P. Lovecraft (ed. S. T. Joshi and David E. Schultz); The Night Ocean, by R. H. Barlow and H. P. Lovecraft; Sanity, Subjectivity, and the Supernatural: Dreams of the Devil in Existentialism and the Weird Tale, by Dustin Geeraert; Terror and Terrain: The Environmental Semantics of Lovecraft County, by James O. Butler; Two Poets and Beauty: H. P. Lovecraft and James Elroy Flecker, by Phillip A. Ellis; Lovecraft's Third Meeting with David V. Bush, by Kenneth W. Faig, Jr.; Echoes of a Warrior Poet: The Influence of Alan Seeger on Lovecraft, by J. D. Worthington; Gothic Mythology: "The Moon-Bog" and the Greek Connection, by Juan Luis Pérez de Luque; REVIEWS: [Review of Jack Koblas, *The Lovecraft Circle and Others as I Remember Them*], by S. T. Joshi; [Review of H. P. Lovecraft, *The New Annotated H. P. Lovecraft*, ed. Leslie S. Klinger], by S. T. Joshi; [Review of Gavin Callaghan, *H. P. Lovecraft's Dark Arcadia*], by Michael J. Abolafia.

Notes. The cover in "Pugmire Pink," a color created by Barbara Briggs Silbert, honors our steadfast friend, author W. H. Pugmire.

145.   S. T. JOSHI. *Unutterable Horror: A History of Supernatural Fiction.* 2014. 2 vols. tpb.

Contents. VOLUME 1 (FROM GILGAMESH TO THE END OF THE NINETEENTH CENTURY): Preface; I. Introduction; II. Anticipations; III. The Gothics; IV. Interregnum; V. Edgar Allan Poe; VI. Mid-Victorian Horrors; VII. The Deluge: British and European Branch; VIII. The Deluge: American Branch; Epilogue; Bibliographical Essay; Bibliography; VOLUME 2 (THE TWENTIETH AND TWENTY-FIRST CENTURIES): Preface; IX. The Titans; X. Other Early-Twentieth Century Masters; XI. Novelists, Satirists, and Poets; XII. H. P. Lovecraft and His Influence; XIII. American Pulpsmiths; XIV. Horrors at Midcentury; XV. Anticipations of the Boom; XVI. The Boom: The Blockbusters; XVII. The Boom: The Literati; XVIII. The Contemporary Era; Epilogue; Bibliographical Essay; Bibliography; Index.

Notes. Cover illustrations by Harry Clarke (Vol. 1) and S. H. Sime (Vol. 2). A reprint of Joshi's exhaustive history of supernatural fiction over the millennia; slightly corrected from the original edition (PS Publishing, 2012), which won the World Fantasy Award (special award, non-professional) in 2013.

146.   MASSIMO BERRUTI, S. T. JOSHI, AND SAM GAFFORD, EDITORS. *William Hope Hodgson: Voices from the Borderland: Seven Decades of Criticism on the Master of Cosmic Horror.* 2014. 326 pp. tpb.

Contents. Introduction, by Sam Gafford; I. SOME STUDIES OF HODGSON'S LIFE AND EARLY RECEPTION: Houdini v. Hodgson: The Blackburn Challenge, by Sam Gafford; William Hope Hodgson: In His Own Day, by A. Langley Searles; Pioneering Essays (H. P. Lovecraft, "The Weird Work of William Hope Hodgson"; Clark Ashton Smith, "In Appreciation of William Hope Hodgson"; H. C. Koenig, "William Hope Hodgson: Master of the Weird and Fantastic"; August Derleth, "William Hope Hodgson"; Ellery Queen, "William Hope Hodgson and the Detective Story"; Fritz Leiber, "William Hope Hodgson: Writer of Supernatural Horror"); II. SOME SPECIAL TOPICS: William Hope Hodgson, by Brian Stableford; The Dark Mythos of the Sea: William Hope Hodgson's Transformation of Maritime Legends, by Emily Alder; Things in the Weeds: The Supernatural in Hodgson's Short Stories, by S. T. Joshi; Against the Abyss: Carnacki the Ghost-Finder, Mark Valentine; William Hope Hodgson in the Underworld: Mythic Aspects of the Novels, by Phillip A. Ellis; Decay and Disease in the Fiction of William Hope Hodgson, by Sam Gafford; Hodgson's Women, by Sam Gafford; III. STUDIES OF INDIVIDUAL TALES: Things Invisible: Human and Ab-Human in Two of Hodgson's Carnacki Stories, by Leigh Blackmore; Sexual Symbolism in W. H. Hodgson, Sid Birchby; The "Wonder Unlimited"—The Tales of Captain Gault, Mark Valentine; *The House on the Borderland:* On Humanity and Love, by Henrik Harksen; IV. COMPARATIVE STUDIES; Time Machines Go Both Ways: Past and Future in H. G. Wells and W. H. Hodgson, by Andy Sawyer; The Long Apocalypse: The Experimental Eschatologies of H. G. Wells and William Hope Hodgson, by Brett Davidson; Shadow out of Hodgson, by John D. Haefele; R. H. Barlow's "A Memory" in William Hope Hodgson's *The Night Land*, Marcos Legaria; WILLIAM HOPE HODGSON: A BIBLIOGRAPHY, by S. T. Joshi and Sam Gafford, with Mike Ashley: I. Works by Hodgson in English: A. Books and Pamphlets; B. Contributions to Books and Periodicals; C. Media Adaptations; II. Hodgson in Translation; III. Works about Hodgson; INDEXES: A. Names; B. Works by Hodgson; C. Periodicals; General Index.

Notes. Cover illustration by Daniele Serra. Comprehensive anthology of essays, both new and reprinted, on the master of sea horror and one of the pioneers of the "psychic detective." Concludes with the first exhaustive bibliography of work by and about Hodgson.

147.   RHYS HUGHES. *Bone Idle in the Charnel House: A Collection of Weird Stories.* 2014. 246 pp. tpb.

Contents. Introduction; The Swinger; Bitter in Sour; The Old House Under the Snow; Degrees of Separation; The Warlord; Vampiric Gramps; Bone Idle in the Charnel House; What I Fear Most; Rediffusion; Casimir the Converter; Smuggling Old Nick to Newfoundland; Shelling the Toad; The Hydrothermal Reich; The Spoon; Chameleons; Happiness Leasehold; Life and the Plumbline; The Unsubtle Cages; Sigma Octantis; The Century Just Gone; Acknowledgements.

Notes. Cover illustration by Mike Dubisch. Striking collection of weird and fantastic tales by the popular and critically acclaimed Welsh author, whose work draws upon the tradition of Borges and Calvino.

148.   DONALD TYSON. *The Lovecraft Coven.* 2014. 218 pp. tpb.

Contents. The Lovecraft Coven; Iron Chain.

Notes. Cover illustration by Robert H. Knox. A pair of substantial novellas of Lovecraftian horror.

149.   S. T. JOSHI. *Lovecraft and a World in Transition: Collected Essays on H. P. Lovecraft.* 2014. 620 pp. tpb.

Notes. Paperback edition of item 140.

150.   MICHAEL ARONOVITZ. *The Witch of the Wood.* 2014. 234 pp. tpb.

Notes. Cover illustration by Lyndsay Harper. A vivid short novel of witchcraft, eroticism, and cosmic terror by a rising star in the realm of weird fiction.

151.   *Dead Reckonings* No. 16 (Fall 2014). EDITED BY JUNE M. PULLIAM AND TONY FONSECA. 102 pp.

Contents. Ramsey Campbell, Probably: Four Colour Horror; From Mythos to Icon, by Martin Andersson [S. T. Joshi, ed., *A Mountain Walked*]; Recommended by Stephen King, by Hank Wagner and Bev Vincent [Christopher Golden, *Snowblind;* Nick Cutter, *The Troop*]; Tales of Two (Word)Smiths, by Robert Butterfield [Clint Smith,

Ghouljaw and Other Stories; James Robert Smith, *A Confederacy of Horrors*]; Horror Everlasting, by Jonathan Johnson [Michael Aronovitz, *The Voices in Our Heads*; *Alice Walks*; and *The Witch of the Wood*]; Le Fanu at 200: Dublin Celebrates the Bicentenary of Its "Invisible Prince," by Jim Rockhill; Memories and Ghosts of Ireland, the *Other* Europe, and Beyond, by John Edgar Browning [John Howard, *The Silver Voices*; Jim Rockhill and Brian J. Showers, ed. *Dreams of Shadow and Smoke: Stories for J. S. Le Fanu*]; Uneven But Essential for Researchers, by Richard Bleiler [James Goho, *Journeys into Darkness: Critical Essays on Gothic Horror*; Gary Hoppenstand, ed. *Critical Insights: The American Thriller*]; Why We Need Horror Film Fanzines, by Chris Dallis [John Szpunar, *Xerox Ferox: The Wild World of the Horror Film Fanzine*]; Obscure But Excellent, by Greg Gbur [John Blackburn, *Our Lady of Pain*]; Girls Will Be Ghouls, by Stephanie A. Graves [June Pulliam, *Monstrous Bodies*]; Vampire Classic Back in Print, by Darrell Schweitzer [Michael Talbot, *The Delicate Dependency*]; The Tale Remains Untold, by Tony Fonseca [Robin Spriggs, *The Untold Tales of Ozman Droom*]; Old Ghouls Gone Wild, by Martin Andersson [Ellen Datlow, ed. *Lovecraft's Monsters*]; Scholar Alert!, by June Pulliam [Alexandra Heller-Nicholas, *Found Footage Horror Films*; Katarzyna Marak, *Japanese and American Horror*; Shaka McGlotten and Steve Jones, ed. *Zombies and Sexuality*; William Schoell. *The Horror Comics—1940s–1980s*; and Jon Towelson, *Subversive Horror Cinema*]; Chambers, Lovecraft, and Pastiche, by S. T. Joshi [Glynn Owen Barrass, ed. *In the Court of the Yellow King* and Jesse Bullington, ed. *Letters to Lovecraft*]; A Fate Worse Than Death, by Hank Wagner and Bev Vincent [Stephen King, *Mr. Mercedes*, and *Revival*]; Idle Minds and Literary Playthings, by Richard Bleiler [Rhys Hughes, *Bone Idle in the Charnel House*]; A Fine and Diverse New Horror Anthology, by Robert Butterfield [Ellen Datlow, ed. *The Best Horror of the Year: Volume Six*]; Doomed to Fail, by Tony Fonseca [Daryl Gregory, *We Are All Completely Fine*]; Victorian, Verbose, and Never Picks Up Steam, by Leigh Blackmore [K. W. Jeter, *Fiendish Schemes*]; Kamog! Kamog!, by S. T. Joshi [David Barker and W. H. Pugmire, *The Revenant of Rebecca Pascal*]; A Dark Shadow from the Past, by Darrell Schweitzer [Evangeline Walton, *She Walks in Darkness*]; The Mystery Man of Weird Fiction, by S. T. Joshi [Matt Cardin, ed. *Born to Fear: Interviews with Thomas Ligotti*; Thomas Ligotti, *The Spectral Link*]; Eeking Out a Passable Adult Novel, or Not, by Richard Bleiler [Greg van Eekhout, *California Bones*]; The *Schauerroman* in Its Proper Context . . ., by Jim Rockhill [Andrew Cusack and Barry Murnane, ed. *Popular Revenants*]; Supernatural

Senility, by June Pulliam [*The Taking of Deborah Logan*, dir. Adam Robitel]; Capsule Reviews; Notes on Contributors.

152.   JOSH KENT. *The Witch at Sparrow Creek: A Jim Falk Novel.* 2015. 356 pp. tpb.

Notes. Cover illustration by Jason C. Eckhardt. A gripping first novel of witchcraft set in rural Appalachia, evoking echoes of Manly Wade Wellman's John the Balladeer novels but with an atmosphere and richly textured characterization that are the author's own. The first of an expected series of novels featuring the central character, Jim Falk.

153.   JAMES ROBERT SMITH. *A Confederacy of Horrors.* 2015. 232 pp. tpb.

Contents. A CONFEDERACY OF GHOSTS: Listen; Through Becky's Eyes; Of Rodents and Sinking Vessels; Toke Ghost; Tommy; Moving; The Pool; A CONFEDERACY OF VENGEANCE: On the First Day; The Jawbone of an Ass; Dope; Translator; Love & Magick; A CONFEDERACY OF OBSESSION: NUMHED; A Last, Longing Look; Symptom; Wet; One of Those Days; The Call; Just Like Jesus, He Said; A CONFEDERACY OF BLOOD: It's Not a Blessing, She Said; Just a Gigolo; The Old Man's Final Visit; Ice Bounty; The Reliable Vacuum Company; Pure Southern; Afterword, by Stephen Mark Rainey; Acknowledgments.

Notes. Cover illustration by Pete Von Sholly. The first short story collection by a noted and popular horror novelist and editor.

154.   *Spectral Realms* No. 2 (Winter 2015). EDITED BY S. T. JOSHI. 2015. 160 pp.

Contents. POETRY: A Spectral Realm Mystery, by Donald Sidney-Fryer; At the Last of Carcosa, by Ann K. Schwader; The Spire, by Chad Hensley; Fallen: A Lament and Affirmation, by Jason V Brock; The Dark Road from Yorehaven, by D. L. Myers; Mummify Me, by Jonathan Thomas; The Apple, by Claire Smith; Conundrum, by Fred Phillips; The Song of the Unformed, by Gemma Files; Occult Agency, by Wade German; The Promise, by Darrell Schweitzer; Witch's Love, by Ashley Dioses; The Lamp: A Fable, by John C. Tibbetts; When Rose Petals Fall, by John Shirley; Haunted, by William F. Nolan; Among the Ghouls, by K. A. Opperman; Incantations, by Michael Fantina; Revenant, by F. J. Bergmann; Another Knife-Grey Day, by Michael Kelly; Song for Naughty Children, by David Barker; Rock On, by Marge Simon; The Ballad of Jack Keeper, by Adam Bolivar; The Desolate Kirkyard, by Liam Garriock; The Realm of Angels, by

David Schembri; Invocation to Dispel Loneliness on Insomniac Nights, by Dan Clore; The Final Conversation, by Ian Futter; Robert Nelson: An Invitation, by Charles D. O'Connor III; The Sire, by Chad Hensley; Foiled Design, by Fred Phillips; "The Outsider", by W. H. Pugmire; Calving, by Gemma Files; Girls and Their Balloons, by Stephanie M. Wytovich; Barn, by Jonathan Thomas; The Night Is Black and White, by Leigh Blackmore; Harrow, by D. L. Myers; Mother Killer, by Melissa Frederick; Void Music, by Ann K. Schwader; Lavinia Whateley, by Darrell Schweitzer; Lines on Reading A. Merritt, by John C. Tibbetts; The Mood of the Moon, by Wade German; The Keeper of the Innsmouth Light, by M. F. Webb; The Cobbled Trail, by Michael Fantina; The Depths of Enlightenment, by Sean Elliot Martin; A Billion Souls Gaze West, by David Barker; The Bone Bird, by Mike Allen; Furaq, by Carole Abourjeili; The Blood Garden, by K. A. Opperman; Tricks, by Ian Futter; Legacy, by Fred Phillips; Ligeia, by Ashley Dioses; Hungry, the Rain-God Wakens, by Michael Kelly; A Search for Light in Night; A Search for Dark in Day, by John Shirley; Palimpsest, by F. J. Bergmann; Kiosk to Kadath, by Chad Hensley; The Nightmare-Monger, by Dan Clore; A Devil's Nursery Book, by Adam Bolivar; Swampsong, by Oliver Smith; Beauty and Oblivion, by K. A. Opperman and Charles D. O'Connor III; Head Ornaments, by Stephanie M. Wytovich; The Dream Sorceress, by Michael Fantina; My Ashen Heart, by Leigh Blackmore; Oblivion's Daughter, by David Barker; Vexteria, by Ashley Dioses; The Writer, by Ian Futter; Purloined, by Mike Allen; CLASSIC REPRINTS: The Skeleton Sexton, by Francis S. Saltus; The Ballad of Dead Men's Bay, by Algernon Charles Swinburne; The Cathedral of Lost Faces, by Bruce Boston; ARTICLES: "Figures in a Nightmare"—The Poetry of Leah Bodine Drake: Part 1, by Leigh Blackmore; REVIEWS: Some Hits, Some Misses, by Sunni K Brock; Notes on Contributors.

Notes. Cover illustration by Charles E. Burchfield ("Childhood's Garden," 1917).

155.   WILLIAM F. NOLAN AND JASON V BROCK, EDITORS. *The Bleeding Edge: Dark Barriers, Dark Frontiers.* 2015. 318 pp. tpb.

Contents. Foreword, by S. T. Joshi; Welcome to the Dark Side, by William F. Nolan and Jason V Brock; "Some of My Best Friends Are Martians . . .," by Ray Bradbury; Just a Suggestion, by John Shirley; Love & Magick, by James Robert Smith; MADRI-Gall: A Short Skit for the Stage, by Richard Matheson and Richard Christian Matheson, Hope and the Maiden, by Nancy Kilpatrick; The Death and Life of Caesar LaRue, by Earl Hamner, Jr.; A Certain Disquieting Darkness, by Gary

A. Braunbeck; The Boy Who Became Invisible, by Joe R. Lansdale; Getting Along Just Fine, by William F. Nolan; The Grandfather Clock: A Teleplay for *The Twilight Zone*, by George Clayton Johnson; Triptych: Three Bon-Bons, by Christopher Conlon; The Hand That Feeds, by Kurt Newton; The Central Coast, by Jason V Brock; Omnivore: An Illustrated Screenplay Excerpt, by Dan O'Bannon; De Mortuis, by John Tomerlin; I, My Father, and Weird Tales, by Frank M. Robinson; Silk City, by Lisa Morton; Red Light, by Steve Rasnic Tem; How it Feels to Murder: A Teleplay, by Norman Corwin; At the Riding School, by Cody Goodfellow; Notes on Contributors.

Notes. Cover illustration by Kris Kuksi ("Ode to Decadence [detail]", 2009). Interior illustrations by Dan O'Bannon. First paperback edition of an acclaimed anthology of original tales, teleplays, and other matter, first published by Cycatrix Press in 2009.

156.   JOSEPH S. PULVER, SR. *A House of Hollow Wounds.* Edited by Jeffrey Thomas. 2015. 316 pp. tpb.

Contents. On the Embankment of Tangibility: An Introduction, by Jeffrey Thomas; A Thousand Injuries—; A (~BIG~) Fishy Menu; and the bass keeps thumpin'; (he) Dreams of Lovecraftian Horror . . .; Saturday Night . . . With a Dead Girl in It; Doom . . . & Sigh; into the world; A Night of Moon & Blood,   Then   Holstenwall; she sings. I sob......; The Golem; The Ozymandias Display; under stars with no desire to flee; no one ever talks about there will come a day these days; "c"-O[lLi(S)I;o!N,S   iN tHE word   box or   (i)'s Disintegration; On a Faraway Beach . . .; Down . . . and down we go; The Pencil; Tender. Sins.; Movietime . . . with popcorn and . . .; Caroline No. Bleue; Brick. By . . Brick; A House of Hollow Wounds; Desert Highway Motel; One Window, Two Hearts; The Sommerset Tales; Aubade in a Graveyard; I once possessed a fragile blue vase; Twilight Sonatas; Tears & the stars fall; Certain Sunday Evenings in Summer; A Traveler Came with Gifts; In a Raven's Eye; She Comes in Blood; Words Touching; Under June; I'll simply call her V; Sarah smile; In the spaces in between; The blood of a damsel's breast on the green door of the forest; I once possessed little other than a fragile blue vase; wind. ardent. circular, back on itself as if in dismay.; Being Led by Pictures . . .; The Ground She Sleeps upon Is a Clue . . . and a Mystery; 8mm . . . soil; a stained translation [in 2 acts]; In a Black Studio No. 76; Vase; A Cold Yellow Moon; Acknowledgments.

Notes. Cover illustration by Daniele Serra. Pulver's fourth collection of stories, prose-poems, and vignettes.

157.   PARK BARNITZ. *The Book of Jade: A New Critical Edition.* Compiled by David E. Schultz and Michael J. Abolafia. 2015. 324 pp. tpb.

Contents. THE BOOK OF JADE: Prelude; PART ONE: Ashtoreth; Parfait Amour; Opium; Sombre Sonnet; Languor; Ennui; Litany; Harvard; Pride; Song of Golden Youth; Mais Moi Je Vis la Vie en Rouge; Louanges d'Elle; Hélas; Sonnet; Sonnet; Rondeau; Autumn Song; Ballad; Changelessness; Madonna; Poppy Song; Consolation; Liebes-Tod; Evening Song; Song of the Stars in Praise of Her; Aubade; Remember; Song; Song; Constancy; Requiem; Autumn Burial; Sonnet of Burial; Nocturne; PART TWO: Mad Sonnet; The House of Youth; De Profundis; Prayer; Sestettes; Sonnet of the Instruments of Death; Truth; Hegel; Monotony; Sepulture; Miserrimus; Scorn; The Grave; Mummy; Sepulchral Life; Corpse; Mankind; The Defilers; The Grotesques; Dead Dialogue; Fragments; Envoi; Postlude; Song of India; Dedication; UNCOLLECTED WRITINGS: After-Life; Danse Macabre; [Letter to Doxey's, 1901]; The Truth about Rudyard Kipling; The Art of the Future; [Review]; Bibliography; PARK BARNITZ: A BIOGRAPHY, by Gavin Callaghan; CRITICISM: Contemporary Reviews; The Promise of Contemporary Art; Two American Poets: A Study in Possibilities, by Floyd Dell; We (Almost) Die for Art, by Floyd Dell; The Poet of Montsalvat, by Carey McWilliams; A Land of Poets, by Carey McWilliams; America's "Yellow Nineties" Poet, by Joseph Payne Brennan; Renaissance, by David E. Schultz; The Perfection of the Corpse: Necrophilia in The Book of Jade by K. A. Opperman; The Grotesques: Sins against the Afterlife, by Ashley Dioses; Barnitz and Pessimism, by Matt Sarraf; "I Am Weary of That Lidless Eye": Gazing into the Hegelian Abyss of Subjectivity in the Mad Sonnets of Park Barnitz, by Chuck Caruso, Ph.D. Two Dead Men: Park Barnitz and Rudyard Kipling, by Gavin Callaghan; Afterword, by Michael J. Abolafia; Index of Titles and First Lines.

Notes. Cover artist (from original edition) unknown. A reprint of the fabulously rare poetry volume first issued in 1901, with additional uncollected and unpublished material. Barnitz (1878–1901) was rumored to have committed suicide shortly after the book appeared. Thanks in part to the interest of Donald Wandrei and H. P. Lovecraft, the volume has become a choice acquisition for the weird collector. This edition includes a substantial biography of Barnitz by Gavin Callaghan, who has spent years researching the poet's life and work.

158.   JONATHAN THOMAS. *Dreams of Ys and Other Invisible Worlds.*
        2015. 268 pp. tpb.

Contents. Three Dreams of Ys; Down the Hatch; We Are Made of
Stars; Pests: A Provisional Translation; A Quirk of the Mistral;
Welcome Back; Houdini Fish; Girl on a Swing; Sinister Illuminator;
DEAD CITY SUITE: Introduction: Some Homebrew from a Haunted
Cellar; Integrity; The Immortality Sequence; A Light in the
Wilderness; Watcher of the Invisible World; Acknowledgments.

Notes. Cover illustration by David C. Verba. Thomas's fourth story
collection, containing not only several vivid Lovecraftian tales but also
some previously unpublished stories written as part of his M.A. thesis
at Brown University in the 1980s.

159.   *Dead Reckonings* No. 17 (Spring 2015). EDITED BY JUNE M.
        PULLIAM AND TONY FONSECA. 94 pp.

Contents. Hidden City Deserves Discovery, by Chris Dallis [Robert
Butterfield, *The Hidden City: Van Ark I*]; Ramsey Campbell, Probably;
Excursions into the Imagination: Report on ICFA 36, by Simone
Caroti; The Variegated World of Ray Bradbury, by S. T. Joshi [Jona-
than R. Eller, *Ray Bradbury Unbound*]; Elementary, My Dear James, by
Bev Vincent [Dan Simmons, *The Fifth Heart*]; The Poetry of
Darkness, by Greg Gbur [David E. Cowen, *The Madness of Empty
Spaces*]; Darker Than Any Earth-Bound Sea, by Jeremy Cavaterra
[Scott Thomas, *The Sea of Ash*]; Terror in a Sentence, by S. T. Joshi
[Ramsey Campbell, *Think Yourself Lucky*]; Book of Fiction of the
Month!, by Chris Dallis [Michael Loughrey, *The Parallax Groove*]; Of
Poetry and Corpses, by Leigh Blackmore [Stephanie M. Wytovich,
Mourning Jewelry]; The Weird Is Alive and All Too Real, by Chris
Dallis [M. A. Katz-Savoy, *The Place Where Nothing Is Real*]; Life in the
Urban Gothic: One Big Ghost Rope, by June Pulliam [David Robert
Mitchell, dir., *It Follows*]; H. P. Lovecraft and Subtle Realms of Dark
Matter, by John Edgar Browning [S. T. Joshi, ed., *Black Wings III: New
Tales of Lovecraftian Horror*]; Silence Is Deadly, by Hank Wagner
[Tim Lebbon, *The Silence*]; Creepy Stories That Send Shivers, by Beth
Younger [Jeani Rector, ed., *Shrieks and Shivers from The Horror Zine*];
For the Vintage Paperback Nostalgia Market, by Darrell Schweitzer
[Gregory Luce, ed., *Horror Gems, Vol 7*]; Dig Wide, Dig Deep: The
Need for Better Research, by Tony Fonseca [Patrick McAleer and
Michael A. Perry, ed. *Stephen King's Modern Macabre: Essays on the
Later Works*]; Keeping the Undead Fascinating, by Chris Dallis [June
Michele Pulliam, and Anthony J. Fonseca, *Encyclopedia of the Zombie:
The Walking Dead in Popular Culture and Myth*]; Mangling Brothers

and Burn'em and Burry: The Circus Is in Town, by Danel Olson [Ellen Datlow, ed. *Nightmare Carnival*]; Burrage: Back in Print, by Greg Gbur [A. M. Burrage, *The Waxwork and Other Stories*]; For Horror Fans, It's a Small, Weird World, by June Pulliam [Jennifer Kent, dir., *The Babadook*; Gerard Johnstone, dir., *Housebound*; Tommy Wirkola, dir., *Dead Snø II: Red vs. Dead*]; Fantasy, or Disneyfied Horror?, by Tony Fonseca [Greg van Eekhout, *Pacific Fire*]; One Mother of a TV Series, by June Pulliam [Carlton Cuse, Kerry Ehrin, and Anthony Cipriano, creators, *Bates Motel*]; All You Ever Wanted to Know about Vampires, by June Pulliam [Margot Adler. *Vampires Are Us: Understand Our Love Affair with the Immortal Dark Side*]; Retrospective Review: The Woods of Weir, by Allan Nevins [Leonard Cline, *The Dark Chamber*]; Notes on Contributors.

160.   ANN K. SCHWADER. *Dark Equinox and Other Tales of Lovecraftian Horror.* 2015. 259 pp. tpb.

Contents. Dark Equinox; The Sweetness of Your Heart; When the Stars Run Away; Wings of Memory; Her Beloved Son; Custom Order; Desert Mystery! Gas & Go!; Rehab; Scream Saver; The Water Lily Room; The Death Verses of Yian-Ho; Twenty Mile; Experiencing the Other; Paradigm Wash; Night of the Piper; The Wind-Caller; Acknowledgments.

Notes. Cover illustration and frontispiece by Lyndsay Harper. Generous selection of the Lovecraftian tales of one of the leading weird poets and fiction writers of our time, timed for her appearance as Poet Laureate at the NecronomiCon II convention. Many of the tales are set in or around the author's native Wyoming and draw deeply upon her knowledge of the area and of the Native American traditions that linger there.

161.   ROBERT H. WAUGH. *The Bloody Tugboat and Other Witcheries.* 2015. 268 pp. tpb.

Contents. The Portrait of Miss Constance; Iceboy; In Her Eye; The Hot Tub Horror; The Bloody Tugboat; The Bright Thin Room; Yet Here's a Spot; The Churches on the Hill; The *Narcissus* Anchors in the Caribees; The Puzzle in the Cellar Pantry; The Black Plastic Rag; Alice by the Beautiful Sea; Mr. Hoffmann's Cat; Playing with Fire; Punch Stands Alone; The Broker and His Pet; Down by the Alyscamps, Up on the Hill; The Violinist; Johnny's Tin Toy; Her Crooked Mouth; The Wind of His Passing; Nancy's Dreams; The Infected Land; The Creature from the Zodiacal Crab; Click.

Notes. Cover illustration by Mike Dubisch. Engaging and diverse collection of stories by a leading critic of weird, fantasy, and science fiction.

162. LOIS H. GRESH. *Cult of the Dead and Other Weird and Lovecraftian Tales.* 2015. 238 pp. tpb.

Contents. Introduction, by S. T. Joshi; Cult of the Dead; Devil's Bathtub; Dreams of Death; Necrotic Cove; Old Enough to Drink; Death Doll; Willie the Protector; Wee Sweet Girlies; Debutante Ball; Let Me Make You Suffer; Where I Go, Mi-Go; The Lagoon of Insane Plants; Soleman; Snip My Suckers; Psychomildew Love; Digital Pistil; Algorithms and Nasal Structures; Little Whorehouse of Horrors; Showdown at Red Hook; Mandelbrot Moldrot; Acknowledgments.

Notes. Cover illustration by Robert H. Knox. Rich collection of stories by a leading contemporary practitioner of Lovecraftian fiction, timed for her appearance as a Guest of Honor at the NecronomiCon II convention.

163. W. H. PUGMIRE. *Monstrous Aftermath: Stories in the Lovecraftian Tradition.* 2015. 266 pp. tpb.

Contents. Within Your Unholy Pit of Shoggoths; Your Weighing of My Heart; The Tomb of Oscar Wilde; These Harpies of Carcosa; An Ecstasy of Fear; Darkness Dancing in Your Eyes; Beyond the Wakeful Senses; Ye Unkempt Thing; Half Lost in Shadow; Circular Bone; Jester of Yellow Day; This Splendor of the Goat; Monstrous Aftermath; An Element of Nightmare; Some Unknown Gulf of Night; *Fungi from Yuggoth,* by H. P. Lovecraft; Acknowledgments.

Notes. Cover illustration and interior illustrations by Matthew Jaffe. New collection of tales by one of our leading contemporary Lovecraftians, gifted with a prose style of unexcelled fluency and poetic lyricism.

164. H. P. LOVECRAFT. *Letters to Robert Bloch and Others.* Edited by David E. Schultz and S. T. Joshi. 2015. 548 pp. tpb.

Contents. Introduction; LETTERS: To Robert Bloch; To Natalie H. Wooley; To Robert and Mrs. Elmer Nelson; To William Frederick Anger; To Kenneth Sterling; To Donald A. Wollheim; To Wilson Shepherd; To Willis Conover; APPENDIX: *Robert Bloch:* A Visit with H. P. Lovecraft; Lilies; The Black Lotus; How I Get My Inspiration; [*unsigned*] Milwaukee Youth Writes Horror Tales, Sells 'Em; *Natalie H. Wooley:* Admonition; Dream Fantasy; Antares; Avatar; The Alien; Flight; A Heavenly Tragedy; Lines to Cleopatra; Coward; Sailor's

Child; Western Night; Mountain Trail; End of the Trail; Mountain Pool; Sanctuary; Dream Tryst; The Adventure Story; Is Criticism Necessary?; Have You a Hobby?; "Tillicum"; The Dance; Reminiscense; Spurs of Death; *Robert Nelson:* Night of Unrest; Fragment; The Unremembered Realm; Below the Phosphor; Dream-Stair; Jorgas; Sable Revelry; Under the Tomb; Lost Excerpts; Trilogy of Death; The Weird Tale (A Dialogue); *Fred Anger:* Fantastic Bread & Butter; or, the Mystery of the Missing Authors [and An Answer to Mr. Anger, by Farnsworth Wright; A Writer Comments on the Anger–Wright Controversy, by Anonymous]; An Interview with E. Hoffmann Price, with Louis C. Smith; *Donald A. Wollheim:* Review of THE NECRONOMICON; Allalieor; Umbriel; Pure Fantasy; Howard Phillips Lovecraft; Editor's Preface [to "The Shadow out of Time"]; The Future of Publishing; *Kenneth Sterling;* The Horror Element in Poe; *Wilson Shepherd:* Death; *Willis Conover, Jr.:* Observations and Otherwise; The Lost Chord; The Spirits Mourn. Chronology; Glossary of Frequently Mentioned Names; Bibliography; Index.

Notes. Cover design by Anastasia Damianakos (uniform with item 13). Another volume of the *Collected Letters* project, printing the complete extant letters to Robert Bloch (first published in an edition by Necronomicon Press, 1993) and other related correspondents of the 1930s, with substantial ancillary material and exhaustive annotations by the editors.

165. S. T. JOSHI. *The Rise, Fall, and Rise of the Cthulhu Mythos.* 2015. 412 pp. tpb.

Contents. Preface; Introduction; I. Anticipations; II. The Lovecraft Mythos: Emergence; III. The Lovecraft Mythos: Expansion; IV. Contemporaries: Peers; V. Contemporaries: Scions; VI. The Derleth Mythos; VII. Interregnum; VIII. The Scholarly Revolution; IX. Recrudescence; X. Resurgence; Epilogue; Notes; Index.

Notes. Cover illustration by Jason C. Eckhardt. Exhaustively revised edition of a book first published (as *The Rise and Fall of the Cthulhu Mythos*) by Mythos Books in 2008, containing extensive discussion of work written by leading Lovecraftian writers (Caitlín R. Kiernan, Donald Tyson, Jonathan Thomas, W. H. Pugmire, and others) in the years since the book's first appearance.

166.   *Spectral Realms* No. 3 (Summer 2015). EDITED BY S. T. JOSHI.
155 pp.

Contents. POETRY: Song of the Rushes, by M. F. Webb; In Fits of
Wildest Dreaming, by K. A. Opperman; Inheritance, by Christina
Sng; Rune, by Wade German; Preserves, by G. O. Clark; Barley
Night, by Jonathan Thomas; Ode to Hecate, by Liam Garriock; A
Shuddery Tale, by Charles Lovecraft; Arcane Stars, by DJ Tyrer;
Northern Lights, by Mary Krawczak Wilson; Always Look under the
Bed, by Mark McLaughlin; The Cave of Ebon Boughs, by D. L. Myers;
The Empty Room, by Darrell Schweitzer; Dolls, by Jason V Brock;
Painted Ladies, by David Barker; Brownfields, by John Mundy; Even
Madness Cannot Hide, by Ashley Dioses; Revelation, by Fred Phillips;
Daemon Insectarium, by Chad Hensley; Sorcerers in Love, by Don
Webb; Moonrise, by Christina Sng; The Game of Cat and Dragon, by
Pat Calhoun; Lovers' Wine, by Stanley Gemmell; Childe Jackson
Drake, by Adam Bolivar; Zann, by Ian Futter; The Golden Diadem,
by Leigh Blackmore; To See or Not to See?, by Nicole Cushing; The
Dark at the Top of the Stairs, by Jonathan Thomas; Butterfly, by
Carole Abourjeili; Carcosa in Mind, by DJ Tyrer; The Death of Twi-
light, by D. L. Myers; Tragic, Trembling Giant, by Linda D. Addison;
Witches at the Switches, by David Barker; My Heart's Thin Veil, by
Margi Curtis; Clarethea, by K. A. Opperman; Ghoul of the Enamel,
by Jason Sturner; A Queen in Hell, by Ashley Dioses; Azathoth, by
Charles Lovecraft; Waking, by Ian Futter; Spinal Piano, by Reiss
McGuinness; The Thirst of Sekhmet, by Ann K. Schwader; The
Shadow within Darkness, by Randall Larson; Guardians of the Seven
Gates, by Chad Hensley; Schadenfreude, by John Mundy; Dead Pale
Moon, by Leigh Blackmore; To Reach Carcosa, by Mark McLaughlin;
Sand Bar, by Jonathan Thomas; Toujours Il Coûte Trop Cher, by
Mike Allen and C. S. E. Cooney; Alone in the Desert, by Mary Kraw-
czak Wilson; Mother, by Christina Sng; The Perfect Rose, by Ashley
Dioses; End Times, by DJ Tyrer; The Lich's Last Laugh, by Dan Clore;
A Garden of Unearthly Delights, by Marge Simon; Masque Macabre,
by K. A. Opperman; Gorgoneion, by Oliver Smith; Unexpected Meet-
ings, by Ian Futter; Black Panther, by David Barker; CLASSIC RE-
PRINTS: Old Trinity Churchard, by A. Merritt; Illumination in the
Mutant Rain Forest, by Bruce Boston; Three Songs from Nosferatu,
by Dana Gioia; ARTICLES: "Figures in a Nightmare"—The Poetry of
Leah Bodine Drake: Part 2, by Leigh Blackmore; REVIEWS: Studies of
Death, by Michael Dirda; Two from Eldritch, by D. L. Myers; Notes
on Contributors.

Notes. Cover illustration by Rabban.

167.	H. P. LOVECRAFT. *Collected Fiction: A Variorum Edition, Volume 1: 1905–1925*. Edited by S. T. Joshi. 2015. 530 pp. hc.

Contents. Introduction; The Beast in the Cave; The Alchemist; The Tomb; Dagon; A Reminiscence of Dr. Samuel Johnson; Polaris; Beyond the Wall of Sleep; Memory; Old Bugs; The Transition of Juan Romero; The White Ship; The Street; The Doom That Came to Sarnath; The Statement of Randolph Carter; The Terrible Old Man; The Tree; The Cats of Ulthar; The Temple; Facts concerning the Late Arthur Jermyn and His Family; Celephaïs; From Beyond; Nyarlathotep; The Picture in the House; Ex Oblivione; Sweet Ermengarde; or, The Heart of a Country Girl; The Nameless City; The Quest of Iranon; The Moon-Bog; The Outsider; The Other Gods; The Music of Erich Zann; Herbert West—Reanimator; Hypnos; What the Moon Brings; Azathoth; The Hound; The Lurking Fear; The Rats in the Walls; The Unnamable; The Festival; Under the Pyramids; The Shunned House; The Horror at Red Hook; He; In the Vault.

168.	H. P. LOVECRAFT. *Collected Fiction: A Variorum Edition, Volume 2: 1926–1930*. Edited by S. T. Joshi. 2015. 538 pp. hc.

Contents. Introduction; Cool Air; The Call of Cthulhu; Pickman's Model; The Silver Key; The Strange High House in the Mist; *The Dream-Quest of Unknown Kadath; The Case of Charles Dexter Ward*; The Colour out of Space; The Descendant; History of the "Necronomicon"; Ibid; The Dunwich Horror; The Whisperer in Darkness.

169.	H. P. LOVECRAFT. *Collected Fiction: A Variorum Edition, Volume 3: 1931–1936*. Edited by S. T. Joshi. 2015. 520 pp. hc.

Contents. Introduction; *At the Mountains of Madness*; The Shadow over Innsmouth; The Dreams in the Witch House; Through the Gates of the Silver Key; The Thing on the Doorstep; The Book; The Shadow out of Time; The Haunter of the Dark; APPENDIX: Juvenilia (The Little Glass Bottle; The Secret Cave; The Mystery of the Grave-Yard; The Mysteriovs Ship [short version]; The Mysterious Ship [long version]); The Very Old Folk; Discarded Draft of "The Shadow over Innsmouth"; The Evil Clergyman; [Cigarette Characterizations]; Of Evil Sorceries done in New England, of Daemons in No Humane Shape; Bibliography.

Notes. Cover design and illustrations by Fergal Fitzpatrick. The three cover illustrations represent Lovecraft's famous description of his own nature as "tripartite" (in item 25, p. 184). The facsimile signature of Lovecraft stamped in foil on the front cover of each volume was offset from his ownership signature in a book of stories by M. R. James. These three volumes contain roughly 10,300 footnotes.

A new edition of Lovecraft that draws upon decades of research by the editor. It is the first edition that prints textual variants for all relevant publications of Lovecraft's stories from their first publication to recent editions. The stories are printed in chronological order, and Joshi has made slight revisions from his earlier corrected editions based on new information and a refined awareness of Lovecraft's stylistic and punctuational preferences. This should become the definitive text of Lovecraft's fiction for decades to come.

170.   K. A. OPPERMAN. *The Crimson Tome.* 2015. 181 pp. tpb.

Contents. Preface: Opperman's Opus, by Dr. W. C. Farmer. Introduction: Crimson Pages from the Future Perfect Past, by Donald Sidney-Fryer; THE NIGHTMARE MUSE: *The Land of Darkest Dreams:* I. The Nightmare Muse; II. Yorehaven; III. Tavern Rumors; IV. A Daemon Impulse; V. The Witch-Light; VI. The Trail Between Two Trees; VII. The Pumpkin King; VIII. The Wood of Hissing Shadows; IX. The Cemetery of Dead Dreamers; X. The Muttering Mushroom; XI. The Windows; XII. The Shadow of Yorehaven; XIII. The Bookshop; XIV. Transformation; XV. A Mirror Image; XVI. The Beckoning Hand; XVII. Necromancy; XVIII. Initiation; XIX. The Black Kiss; XX. Dream Decay; UNPLEASANT DREAMS: Nocturnal Poet; The Crimson Tome; The Chimeras of Midnight; Unpleasant Dreams; Halloween; Mandrake; The Fatal Flower; Soul Rot; The Darkness Within; What the Moon Saw; The Treachery of the Stars; Sirius; And They Took Her Away; Corpse Moon; The Crimson Unicorn; The Thirst of Count Aster; A Vampire Fear; The Scarlet Font; Vampiric Roses; Blood; Bathory; Siren of the Dead; My Darling Bride; NOCTURNAL LOVERS PART I: Succubus; Nocturnal Lover; Dark Poetry; Witch's Charms; A Heart Defiled; O Pale Temptress; Ashiel; Ashiel's Gem; Ashiel's Mirror; Ashiel's Prisoner; Ashiel's Diary; Ashiel's Ritual; *Three Poems After* Venus in Furs: Severin's Venus; Wanda von Dunajew; Venus in Furs; Mistress of Torture; Priestess of Pleasure; The Demon and the Vampiress; NOCTURNAL LOVERS PART II: Dark Star of My Desire; Dark Poetess of My Heart; Sorcerer's Lament; A Secret Sorcery; Sorcerous Bond; The Scarlet Seal; Lunar Love; Dark Valentine; Love Atlantean; To an Unknown Enchantress; Beneath the Cold, Cold Stars; The Perishing Rose; Decapitated Kiss; Love Beyond the Grave; Graveyard Promise; THE PALACE OF PHANTASIES; Cemetery of Broken Hearts; The Corpse of Beauty; Moonrise; The Moonward Trail; Possibilities; Faerie Song; The Faerie Moon; Duel with the Dark Double; Nocturnal Flowers; The Well of

Purple Wine; Zeriatis; The Dreamer; Writing Shrine; Oracle of the Black Pool; The Wrath of Xyre; The Wizard; Khayyam's Wine; Lord of Illusion; The Palace of Phantasies; TWILIGHT SORROWS: The Tree; Autumn Hearts; Toadstools; October; All Hallow's Eve; Jack-o'-Lanterns; The Wraith; Thin Grows the Veil; November; Funereal Sun; Winter Crow; Twilight Sorrows; The Angels All Are Corpses in the Sky; The Mascaron; The Gargoyle; Shattered Hopes; Ancientness; In Mortal Dream; The Doom of Words; TRIBUTES: Twisted Trails of Thought, by Ashley Dioses; A Sorcerous Tome, by Ashley Dioses; The Crimson Kist, by D. L. Myers; The Sorcerous Scribe, by D. L. Myers. ACKNOWLEDGMENTS.

Notes. Cover and interior art by Steve Lines. Cover design by Barbara Briggs Silbert. A scintillating book of mostly formalist verse by a young California poet who has drawn deeply from the work of Edgar Allan Poe, George Sterling, Clark Ashton Smith, and other weird poets.

171.   *Lovecraft Annual* No. 9 (2015). EDITED BY S. T. JOSHI. 231 pp.

Contents. Letters to Marian F. Bonner, by H. P. Lovecraft (ed. David E. Schultz and S. T. Joshi); Miscellaneous Impressions of H.P.L., by Marian F. Bonner; Can You Direct Me to Ely Court?: Some Notes on 66 College Street, by Kenneth W. Faig, Jr.; 66 College Street, by David E. Schultz; The Thing (Flung Daily) on the Doorstep: Lovecraft in the Antipodean Press, 1803–2007, by Brendan Whyte; The Search for Joseph Curwen's Town Home, by Donovan K. Loucks; Charles Baxter on Lovecraft, by S. T. Joshi; Six Degrees of Lovecraft: Henry Miller, by Bobby Derie; Cassie Symmes: Inadvertent Lovecraftian, by David Goudsward; Clergymen among Lovecraft's Paternal Ancestors, by Kenneth W. Faig, Jr.; Lovecraft and Houellebecq: Two Against the World, by Todd Spaulding; Donald A. Wollheim's Hoax Review of the Necronomicon, by Donovan K. Loucks; REVIEWS: [Review of H. P. Lovecraft, *Collected Fiction: A Variorum Edition*, ed. by S. T. Joshi], by Steven J. Mariconda; [Review of Paul Roland, *The Curious Case of H. P. Lovecraft*], by Darrell Schweitzer; Briefly Noted.

172.   JOHN MICHAEL SEFEL AND NIELS-VIGGO S. HOBBS, EDITORS. *Lovecraftian Proceedings: Papers from NecronomiCon Providence: 2013.* 2015. 264 pp. tpb.

Contents. Preface, by John Michael Sefel; Introduction, by Niels-Viggo S. Hobbs; Poe, Lovecraft, and "the Uncanny": The Horror of the Self, by Anthony Conrad Chieffalo; "A Stalking Monster": The Influence of Radiation Poisoning on H. P. Lovecraft's "The Colour out of Space", by Andy Troy; Dead Lies Dreaming: H. P. Lovecraft and the

Other Side of Modernity, by Andrew Lenoir; Lovecraftian Milton: Prophetic Certainties, Romantic Rebellions, and Horrific Imaginings in the Weird Worlds of Milton and Lovecraft, by Marcello C. Ricciardi; The Failed Promises of Rationality: Sam J. Lundwall on the Individual Lost in an Uncaring and Soulless World, by Lars G. E. Backstrom; New England's Curator: Colonial Revival in the Travelogue and Fiction of H. P. Lovecraft, by Kenneth W. Lai; Lovecraft, Fear, and the Medieval Body Frame, by Perry Neil Harrison; Attempting to "Untangle" the Mind, Body, and Phallus in Lovecraft's "The Thing on the Doorstep," by Zack Rearick; The Shadow of His Smile: Humor in H. P. Lovecraft's Fiction, by Stephen Walker; Monstrous Modernism: H. P. Lovecraft's Theory of the Aesthetic in Modernity, by Jason Ray Carney; Dagon and Derrida: The Modern and Post-Modern in Dialogue in the Cthulhu Mythos, by Lyle Enright; I and Cthulhu: Using Martin Buber's Ontology of Dialogue to Examine H. P. Lovecraft's Cosmic Dread, by Daniel Holmes; Thinking Ecocritically: A Look at Embodiment and Nature in the Fiction of H. P. Lovecraft, by Cory Willard; Genuine Pagans: A Foray into Lovecraftian Religions, by Dennis P. Quinn; Appendix: Abstracts of Papers Presented at NecronomiCon Providence—2013 Emerging Scholarship Symposium, by John Michael Sefel; Index.

Notes. Cover illustration by Pete Von Sholly. A collection of papers presented at the "Emerging Scholarship Symposium" at NecronomiCon Providence (August 20–23, 2013), containing a variety of subtle and innovative analyses of Lovecraft the man, writer, and thinker.

173.   DONALD R. BURLESON. *Lovecraft—An American Allegory: Selected Essays on H. P. Lovecraft.* 2015. 259 pp. tpb.

Contents. Abbreviations; Darkness and Light: Lovecraft's Impact on My Life; THEMATIC STUDIES: Zen and the Art of Lovecraft; A Note on Lovecraft, Mathematics, and the Outer Spheres; Lovecraft and Chiasmus, Chiasmus and Lovecraft; Lovecraft and the World as Cryptogram; Lovecraft and the Death of Tragedy; Lovecraft and Romanticism; Lovecraft: An American Allegory; Lovecraft and Adjectivitis: A Deconstructionist View; Lovecraft and Chaos; Lovecraft and Interstitiality; Lovecraft and Gender; H. P. Lovecraft: Textual Keys; SOURCES AND INFLUENCES: H. P. Lovecraft: The Hawthorne Influence; Strange High Houses: Lovecraft and Melville; Ambrose Bierce and H. P. Lovecraft; A Note on Lovecraft and Rupert Brooke; STUDIES OF INDIVIDUAL TALES: Iranon and Kuranes: An Intertextual Gloss; On Lovecraft's Fragment "Azathoth"; Aporia and Paradox in

"The Outsider"; Is Lovecraft's "Ph'nglui mglw'nafh . . ." a Cryptogram?; *The Dream-Quest of Unknown Kadath*; The Mythic Hero Archetype in "The Dunwich Horror"; Prismatic Heroes: The Colour out of Dunwich; Humour beneath Horror: Some Sources for "The Dunwich Horror" and "The Whisperer in Darkness"; The Thing: On the Doorstep; LOVECRAFT'S POETRY" Lovecraft's "The Unknown": A Sort of Runic Rhyme; On Lovecraft's "Nemesis"; On Lovecraft's "The Ancient Track"; Scansion Problems in Lovecraft's "Mirage"; Lovecraft's Cheshire Cat; Lines of Verse Evoking Close Reading: Acrostic-Formulated Text. Works Cited; Works about Lovecraft by Donald R. Burleson; Index.

Notes. Cover design (incorporating a photograph of Lovecraft) by Barbara Briggs Silbert. The collected Lovecraftian papers of one of the pioneering scholars of recent decades, whose work since the late 1970s has revolutionized our understanding of the dreamer from Providence.

174. DERRICK HUSSEY, S. T. JOSHI, AND DAVID E. SCHULTZ. *Fifteen Years of Hippocampus Press: 2000–2015.* 2015. 148 pp. tpb.

Contents. Foreword, by Derrick Hussey; My Years with Hippocampus Press, by S. T. Joshi; Publications of Hippocampus Press: 2000–2015; Index of Authors, Editors, and Artists.

Notes. Cover design by Barbara Briggs Silbert, featuring the distinctive spiderweb logo designed by Anastasia Damianakos. In the grand tradition of August Derleth and Arkham House, the leading figures behind Hippocampus Press provide a history and bibliography of the firm's publications during its first fifteen years of existence.

175. ANTONIS ANTONIADES. *Necronomicon: The Manuscript of the Dead.* Translated from the Greek by Maria Mountokalaki and Elizabeth Georgiades. 2015. 357 pp. tpb.

Notes. Cover illustration and design by Fotis Papadopoulos. A compelling historical novel, focusing on Theodorus Philetas, the putative Greek translator of the *Necronomicon.*

176. *Dead Reckonings* No. 18 (Fall 2015). EDITED BY JUNE M. PULLIAM AND TONY FONSECA. 105 pp.

Contents. Of Revenants and Seedy Taverns, by S. T. Joshi [Reggie Oliver, *The Sea of Blood*]; *The Blue Light:* An Aickman Favourite, by Ramsey Campbell [Leni Riefenstahl, dir., *The Blue Light*]; Flawed but Worthwhile, by Richard Bleiler [Clark Ashton Smith, *The End of the Story: The Collected Fantasies* and David Riley and Linden Riley, ed.,

Kitchen Sink Gothic]; You Just Fucked with the Wrong Virgin: Third Wave Feminist Slasher Films, by June Pulliam [Tom DeNucci, dir., *Almost Mercy*; Todd Strauss-Schulson, dir., *The Final Girls*]; Ravenous Unravelings, by Simone Caroti [Alicia Cole, *Darkly Told: An Audio Chapbook*; China Miéville, *Three Moments of an Explosion: Stories*]; Another Year, Another Banner Volume, by Greg Gbur [Ellen Datlow, ed., *The Best Horror of the Year: Volume 7*]; Book of the Month!, by Chris Dallis [Danel Olson, Justin Bozung, Catriona McAvoy, and Lee Unkrich, ed., *Stanley Kubrick's The Shining*]; Time to Think, by Tony Fonseca [s. j. bagley, with Simon Strantzas, ed., *Thinking Horror: A Journal of Horror Philosophy*]; A World out of Darkness, by Jason V Brock [Belinda Sallin, dir., *Dark Star: H. R. Giger's World*]; Hail Daoloth and Y'golonac!, by S. T. Joshi [Ramsey Campbell, *Visions from Brichester*; Steve Rasnic Tem, *In the Lovecraft Museum*]; Anger, Appropriately Focused, by June Pulliam [Shane Stadler, *Exoskeleton II: Tympanum*]; Your Mournful Psyche, by Jim Rockhill [Christina Morin and Niall Gillespie, ed., *Irish Gothics: Genres, Forms, Modes, and Traditions, 1760–1890*; Dara Downey, *American Women's Ghost Stories in the Gilded Age*]; The Weird Scholar, by S. T. Joshi [On Thomas Burke (1886–1945)]; The Stream of Collective Consciousness, by Alexander Lugo [Joseph S. Pulver, Sr., *A House of Hollow Wounds*]; Trembling with Tremblay, by Hank Wagner [Paul Tremblay, *A Head Full of Ghosts*]; Familiar, but Fantastic, by June Pulliam [Ellen Datlow, ed., *The Monstrous*]; A Quaint and Curious (but Excellent) Volume, by Greg Gbur [Nancy Kilpatrick and Carol Soles, ed., *nEvermore! Tales of Murder, Mystery and the Macabre: Neo-Gothic Fiction Inspired by Edgar Allan Poe*]; Beware of Geeks Bearing Gifts, by June Pulliam [Joel Edgerton, dir., *The Gift*]; Working Together, by S. T. Joshi [David Barker and W. H. Pugmire, *In the Gulfs of Dream and Other Lovecraftian Tales*]; Ramsey Campbell: My Nightmare Man, by Greg Gbur; Playing with the Reel/Real, in Real Time, by June Pulliam [Ivan Kavanagh, dir., *The Canal*; Levan Gabriadze, dir., *Unfriended*]; Editor Unhinged, by Richard Bleiler [Joshua Viola, ed., *Nightmares Unhinged: Twenty Tales of Terror*]; The End of an Era, by Greg Gbur [Clive Barker, *The Scarlet Gospels*]; A Zombie Walks into a Bar . . ., by Tony Fonseca [Scott Kenemore, *The Zen of Zombie* and *The Ultimate Book of Zombie Warfare and Survival: A Combat Guide to the Walking Dead*]; Horror Television: The Good, the Bad, the Downright Ugly, by June Pulliam [*American Horror Story: Season Five* and *The Walking Dead: Season Six*]; Notes on Contributors.

177.   *Spectral Realms* No. 4 (Winter 2016). EDITED BY S. T. JOSHI. 144 pp.

Contents. POEMS: The Phosphorescent Fungi, by D. L. Myers; Bone Fences, by Christina Sng; The Stain, by John Mundy; Relative Dark, by M. F. Webb; The Merlin of the Suns, by Liam Garriock; Who Knocks?, by Scott Thomas; The Flower Maidens, by David Barker; The Ghosts of Hyperborea, by Wade German; The Moon-Gate, by Ann K. Schwader; Machen Spoke the Hidden Thing, by John Shirley; Deeper Flowers Thrive, by Oliver Smith; With a Love So Vile, by Ashley Dioses; A Lone Figure, by Mary Krawczak Wilson; The Adverse Star, by Leigh Blackmore; The Vipers' Lament, by Jeff Burnett; Divine Marriage Comedy, by Alan Gullette; And Only Then I Saw, by Charles Lovecraft; Up the Stairs, by Alicia Cole; A Witch She Is, by William F. Nolan and Jason V Brock; The Stone of Sacrifice, by Kyla Lee Ward; Metamorphosis, by Christina Sng; Phantom, by Claire Smith; The Question, by Ian Futter; Someone Coming, by F. J. Bergmann; Absinthia, by K. A. Opperman; Lucinda the Killed, by Reiss McGuinness; The Yellow Jester, by John Thomas Allen; The Witch's Cat, by Pat Calhoun; Fiddler Jack, by Adam Bolivar; Caressa's Song, by David Barker; The Procession, by M. F. Webb; The Lovely Place, by John Mundy; Gargoyles for the Cathedral, by Kendall Evans; Flyover States, by Steven Withrow; Bedtime Story, by Chad Hensley; Zombification, by Alicia Cole; Souls of Samhain, by Leigh Blackmore; Ilvaa, by Ashley Dioses; We Who Have Encountered Monsters, by Darrell Schweitzer; Missed Horizons, by Ann K. Schwader; The Ghost of Samhain Past, by Margaret Curtis; The Poetry of Evil Must Never Be Shouted, by Darrell Schweitzer; The Rise of Set, by Liam Garriock; The Living Dead, by Ian Futter; To My Goddess, Nicnevin, by Liam Garriock; Deacon Mercer, by Jonathan Thomas; Alastor, by Wade German; Weird Tale, by Charles Lovecraft; Among the Gargoyles, by K. A. Opperman; The Girl with Pennies on Her Eyes, by Scott Thomas; The Reunited, by Oliver Smith; Graveyard Circumspect, by Alan Gullette; Fog of War, by Christina Sng; Two Fates, by John Mundy; Alchemy, by Ian Futter; Werewolf, by K. A. Opperman; Panos, by Fred Phillips; Water Tears, by Mary Krawczak Wilson; The Summons, by David Barker; The Witching Hour, by Alicia Cole; CLASSIC REPRINTS: St. Irvyne's Tower, by Percy Bysshe Shelley; His Dream, by W. B. Yeats; Cthulhu, by David E. Schultz; ARTICLES: The Poets of *Weird Tales:* Part 1, by Frank Coffman; REVIEWS: In the Court of Hades, by Adam Bolivar [K. A. Opperman, *The Crimson Tome*]; Enlightenment from the Outer Dark, by Donald Sidney-Fryer [Wade German, *Dreams from a Black Nebula*]; Two Centuries of Pleasing Terrors, by Steven J. Mariconda [Brett Rutherford, ed., *Tales of Terror: The Supernatural Poem Since 1800, Volume 1*]; Notes on Contributors.

Notes. Cover illustration by Botond Reszegh.

178.   DON SWAIM. *The Assassination of Ambrose Bierce: A Love Story.* 2016. 391 pp. tpb.

Notes. Cover illustration and design by Jared Boggess. This historical novel, written some twenty-five years before it saw publication, is a vivid portrayal of Bierce's later life, when he becomes involved in a complex romance with Elizabeth Dumont, with flashbacks to earlier episodes in Bierce's earlier years. The cover painting was selected for the Society of Illustrators 59th Annual of Illustration.

179.   CODY GOODFELLOW. *The Rapture of the Deep and Other Lovecraftian Tales.* 2016. 308 pp. tpb.

Contents. Introduction; The Anatomy Lesson; König Feurio; To Skin a Corpse; In the Shadow of Swords; Garden of the Gods; Grinding Rock; Rapture of the Deep; Inside Uncle Sid; Archons; Broken Sleep; Cahokia; Swinging; Acknowledgments.

Notes. Cover illustration by Rob Winfield. Cover design by Cody Goodfellow. A collection of Goodfellow's numerous Lovecraftian tales, enlivened by vibrant prose and chilling weird scenarios.

180.   H. P. LOVECRAFT. *Letters to J. Vernon Shea, Carl F. Strauch, and Lee McBride White.* Edited by S. T. Joshi and David E. Schultz. 2016. 435 pp. tpb.

Contents. Introduction; Letters to J. Vernon Shea; Letters to Carl Ferdinand Strauch; Letters to Lee McBride White; APPENDIX: *J. Vernon Shea, Jr.*: On Writing in Bed; Four Playwrights; *Carl F. Strauch:* The Beauty of Decay; The White Fiend Death; A Library Goes Regionalist; *Lee McBride White:* For Aldous Huxley; Out of Sorrow; Look at Your Thumb. Glossary of Frequently Mentioned Names; Bibliography; Index.

Notes. Cover design by Anastasia Damianakos. A volume that prints the complete available letters to Shea for the first time, along with the letters to two other colleagues from the 1930s.

181.   H. P. LOVECRAFT. *Letters to F. Lee Baldwin, Duane W. Rimel, and Nils Frome*. Edited by David E. Schultz and S. T. Joshi. 2016. 443 pp. tpb.

Contents. Introduction; Letters to F. Lee Baldwin; Letters to Duane W. Rimel; Letters to Nils Frome; APPENDIX: *F. Lee Baldwin*: Writings in The Fantasy Fan; H. P. Lovecraft: A Biographical Sketch; Preface to the Fantasy Fan Index; *Duane W. Rimel*: H. P. Lovecraft As I Knew Him; A Fan Looks Back; Lee Baldwin—A Fan's Fan; Weird Music (with Emil Petaja); The Forbidden Room; The Sorcery of Aphlar; Dreams of Yid; Dreams of Yith; The Ship; Late Revenge; The Snake; Its Prayer. Chronology; Glossary of Frequently Mentioned Names; Bibliography; Index.

Notes. Cover design by Anastasia Damianakos. Collection of letters to two young fans living in the Pacific Northwest, along with a few letters to a Canadian fantasy fan.

182.   *Lovecraft Annual* No. 10 (2016). EDITED BY S. T. JOSHI. 239 pp.

Contents. Lovecraft and Egypt: A Closer Examination, by Duncan Norris; Forgotten Influence: A. Merritt's "The Face in the Abyss" and H. P. Lovecraft's "The Mound," by Peter Levi; Essential Saltes: Lovecraft's Witchcraft, by John Salonia; H. P. Lovecraft's Weird Body, by Alison Sperling; Queer Geometry and Higher Dimensions: Mathematics in the Fiction of H. P. Lovecraft, by Daniel M. Look; Postcards to Jonathan E. Hoag, by H. P. Lovecraft; The Mouse in the Walls: Disney, Lovecraft, and *Gravity Falls*, by Tom Miller; Lovecraft Quoted in Support of David V. Bush, by Kenneth W. Faig, Jr.; Pieces of Reality: Lovecraft's Innovative Depiction of Music and Relativity, by Tristan Zaba; Fragments from the Lost Letters of H. P. Lovecraft to Robert E. Howard, by Bobby Derie; Pop Cultural Assimilation of the Lovecraftian Worldview through the Lens of *Rick and Morty*, by Duncan Norris; REVIEWS: [Review of H. P. Lovecraft, *Fungi from Yuggoth: An Annotated Edition*, ed. David E. Schultz], by Steven J. Mariconda; [Review of Charlotte Montague, *H. P. Lovecraft: The Mysterious Man Behind the Darkness*], by Darrell Schweitzer; [Review of Victor LaValle, *The Ballad of Black Tom*], by S. T. Joshi; Index to *The Lovecraft Annual* 1–10.

183.   DONALD SIDNEY-FRYER. *Hobgoblin Apollo: Hobgoblin Run Away with the Wreath of Apollo—A Life of My Own: The Autobiography of Donald Sidney-Fryer*. 2016. 382 pp. tpb.

Contents. HOBGOBLIN APOLLO: Induction; I. I Enter a New Dimension; II. Childhood and Family Background; III. Schooling and Adolescence; IV. Early Sexual Experience; V. Further Schooling and Adolescence; VI. Military Service and Young Adulthood; VII. U.C.L.A. and Odd Jobs; VIII. Later Life and Sexual Experience; IX. Northern California: Auburn and San Francisco; X. Sacramento and Beyond; XI. Westchester and Back; XII. Catching Up; Afterword. ODDS AND ENDS: A Spectral Realm Nearby; Solomon Kane Surveys the Vestiges of Empire; To Do Gone Like the Doe; Villanelle; "Authentic Irishman for Hire"; Almost As If; Pohnpei and Kosrae, Micronesia; Hawaii, the Big Island; Pool Sweep, Hollywood Hills; Just a Thought; A Bit of Doggerel; A Rendezvous with Poedelaire; Preliminary Note; Correspondences; The Enemy; Bad Luck; Anterior Life; "I Love You the Same"; De Profundis Clamavi; Duellum; "I Give You These Verses"; "What Will You Say Tonight?"; The Cats; The Broken Bell; Spleen; Destruction; Epigraph to a Book Condemned; Contemplation; The Abyss; The Complaints of an Icarus; Consolation; Nenuphar; A Third Pilgrimage to Buddha-Land; Speech of Love; A Far-off Memory of Notre-Dame; On Going Past a Curio Shop Deep in Bangrak; Fragmentary; Baan Shadis, Koh Samui; Baan Shadis, the Swimming Pool; Quietude; Geometry for Picnic Time; On Walking All Around the Old Grand Palace in Bangkok; Aftermath; A Meeting with Rimbaudelaire; The Intoxicated Steamboat; Goodbye, Brother William; The Lighthouse Above the Cemetery; Undersea Tableau; Notes, by Dlanod Yendis; About the Poet.

Notes. Cover illustration and design by Jared Boggess, incorporating a line drawing by Norman Lindsay. Interior art by Norman Lindsay. Exhaustive account of Sidney-Fryer's long and rich life, from his years in San Francisco during the 1960s to his life as an elder statesman in the fantasy field. The book focuses on his research on Clark Ashton Smith and other writers and concludes with some 100 pages of the author's recent poetry.

184.   MICHAEL CISCO. *The Wretch of the Sun*. 2016. 272 pp. tpb.

Notes. Cover illustration by Harry O. Morris. Dense, complex novel by one of the most scintillating writers in contemporary weird fiction.

185.   JOHN SHIRLEY. *Lovecraft Alive! A Collection of Lovecraftian Stories.* 2016. 253 pp. tpb.

   Contents. Preface; When Death Wakes Me to Myself; Those Who Come to Dagon; The Rime of the Cosmic Mariner; The Witness in Darkness; How Deep the Taste of Love; Buried in the Sky; Windows Underwater; At Home with Azathoth; The Holy Grace of Cthulhu; Broken on the Wheel of Time; Acknowledgments.

   Notes. Cover illustration by Harry O. Morris. Substantial collection of Shirley's Lovecraftian tales, combining cosmicism with deft character portrayal and richly textured prose.

186.   LINDA SHEA AND S. T. JOSHI, EDITORS. *And Death Shall Have No Dominion: A Tribute to Michael Shea.* 2016. 277 pp. tpb.

   Contents. Editor's Note, by Linda Shea; Salutation to the World as Beheld at Dawn from Atop Mount Eburon; Foreword: Michael Shea Remembered, by Dan Temianka; FICTION: Credit Card; The Growlimb; In Memory Drive Slow; King Gil Gomez and Monkey-Do; VERSE: The Younger Shea; The Greek Plowman; Two Nights; From the Novels: From *A Quest for Simbilis:* Though now you face a cheerless waste; From *Nifft the Lean:* Your sons have fattened in my rule; Man, for the million million years; What man in wealth excels my lover's state?; And that Neverquit Bird, though small and weak; From *In Yana, the Touch of Undying:* Advance, great Shlubb, both Dam and Sire; Oh cease to dissemble! Thou loves't me not!; All day in fragrant toil we've filled; I'm each salt ocean's other shore; Curse you, Kagag Hounderpound!; From *The Mines of Behemoth:* Mines of Behemoth in Heroic Couplets; What dread being dares to farm; The Apotheosis of Scroffle Smalls; Hermaphrod's Vow; Heliomphalodon Incarnadine; Hymn to Having Had; Introductory Stanzas to Selected Chapters; From *The A'Rak:* A'Rak-on-Epos; Let the A'Rak's web be woven; Something Unspeakable Followeth Me; Galactivore Imperator; Pompilla's Taunt; From *Epistle to Lebanoi:* She swung her staff against the stone; The flagship's a galleon of seventy sail; Father who art sunk in sleep; From *Mr. Cannyharme:* In Netherlands did old Van Haarme; My ancient lust was to enslave the dead; Where the lich in the loam has lain mouldering long; Through all the human stockyards you have trod; From the Short Stories: From "The Angel of Death": Those sniggering bitches; From "Fat Face": Shun the gulf beneath the peaks; Epithalamion; From "The Recruiter": A series of small poems making up a narrative of Chester's reanimation; From "Beneath the Beardmore": Excerpt from "The Old One's Story"; Life is pretty fucking complicated; TRIBUTES: Shine On, Dark Star, by Laird Barron; A

Memory of Michael Shea, by Cody Goodfellow; How I Met Michael Shea, by Sam Hamm; "Grab the Morning, You'll Have the Day": An Elegy for Michael Shea, by Maya Khosla; Memories of Michael Shea, by Marc Laidlaw; Read More Michael Shea, by John O'Neill; Remembering Michael, by W. H. Pugmire; Abysses, Mountains, and Skies; or, How My Vision Was Enlarged, by Jessica Amanda Salmonson; My Memories of Michael, by Jerad Walters; Michael Shea, by Jason V Brock. Images; Afterword, by Michael Shea; A Michael Shea Bibliography; Notes on Contributors.

Notes. Cover illustration by Michael Whelan. A volume to commemorate the life and work of Michael Shea (d. 2014), featuring several unpublished stories, an extensive collection of his poetry (some taken from his published fantasy novels), memoirs and assessments by friends and colleagues, and a comprehensive bibliography.

187. *Spectral Realms* No. 5 (Summer 2016). EDITED BY S. T. JOSHI. 144 pp.

Contents. POEMS: Borean Soul, by Jeff Burnett; Sin Eater, by Jennifer Ruth Jackson; The First Haunting, by M. F. Webb; The Second Haunting, by M. F. Webb; The Serpent Borne of Helios, by Nathaniel Reed; Coda, by Joseph S. Pulver, Sr.; Grin, by John J. Mundy; Graveyards of the Living, by G. O. Clark; Only in Dreams, by Darrell Schweitzer; The Forest of Horror, by Frank Coffman; The Egregious Error of Werner Witherbye, by John Shirley; Angry Gods, by Mary Krawczak Wilson; All Masks Are Mirrors, by Ann K. Schwader; The Rime of the Eldritch Mariner, by Adam Bolivar; Dark Poet of My Heart, by Ashley Dioses; Dark House of Hunger, by D. L. Myers; The Ghoul's Dilemma, by W. H. Pugmire; The City of Dreadful Life, by Richard L. Tierney; The Resurrection of Death, by Gregory MacDonald; The Waves of Fear, by Leigh Blackmore; Underwater, by Ian Futter; Sylvan Blood, by Jeff Burnett; Myths and Legends, by Charles D. O'Connor III; Beyond the Stones, by Liam Garriock; Cast Away, by Oliver Smith; Me, by Ross Balcom; Dies Irae, by Carole Abourjeili; The Alchemist's Disease, by Nathaniel Reed; Transylvanian Darkness, by K. A. Opperman; Temple of the Flame, by David Barker; The Sayings of the Seers, by Wade German; Antagonist, by F. J. Bergmann; Heaven in Your Arms, by Jennifer Ruth Jackson; Season Spirits, by Juan J. Gutiérrez; Fallow Fields, by Mary Krawczak Wilson; Redux, by John J. Mundy; Death and a Locket, by Jonathan Thomas; The Endless Night, by Christina Sng; An Existence, by Ian Futter; The Cold Fog of Regret, by John Shirley; Postcard from the Night Desert, by G. O. Clark; Other Humans, by Gregory MacDonald; The Festival, by Chad Hensley;

The Summons, by D. L. Myers; A Traveler to the City, by Frank Coffman; Fallen Atlantis, by Ashley Dioses; Mari Lwyd, by Liam Garriock; In Nether Pits, by David Barker; Yesterdawn, by Jeff Burnett; Dancer, by Christina Sng; Alive, by Joseph S. Pulver, Sr.; Origins, by Nathaniel Reed; Atu II: The High Priestess, by Leigh Blackmore; Visitor, by Fred Phillips; The Fetch, by John J. Mundy; R'lyeh, by F. J. Bergmann; Whisper, by Oliver Smith; Beauty's Veil, by Gregory MacDonald; Ever Fair, by Ashley Dioses; Agents of Dread, by David Barker; CLASSIC REPRINTS: The Song of the Sea, by Edgar Saltus; Voodoo, by Annice Calland; ARTICLES: The Poets of *Weird Tales:* Part 2, by Frank Coffman; REVIEWS: The Generalist and the Specialist, by S. T. Joshi; Leaves Grown Heavy with Omens, by Wade German; Sex and Sin, by Sunni K Brock; Notes on Contributors.

Notes. Cover illustration by Harry Clarke.

188. *Dead Reckonings* Nos. 19/20 (Spring 2016). EDITED BY JUNE M. PULLIAM AND TONY FONSECA. 137 pp.

Contents. Once upon a Midnight Dreary, by Leigh Blackmore [Ann K. Schwader, *Dark Energies*]; Life Is More Horrible Than Death, by S. T. Joshi [Jacqueline Baker, *The Broken Hours: A Novel of H. P. Lovecraft*]; Rotten Tomatoes? How about Rotten Reviews?, by June Pulliam [Mike Flanegan, dir., *Hush*; Jordan Galland, dir. *Ava's Possessions*]; A Geriatric Anti-Hero, Splatstick, and Retro Rock, by Chris Dallis [Craig Digregorio, Bruce Campbell, Ivan Raimi, Sam Raimi, and Rob Tapert, executive producers, *Ash vs. Evil Dead*]; Famous Men of Filmland, by Tony Fonseca [Jason V and Sunni K Brock, director/producers. *Charles Beaumont: The Short Life of Twilight Zone's Magic Man* and *The Ackermonster Chronicles*]; Of Old Ones and Zombies, by Richard Bleiler [Charles Black, *Black Ceremonies*; Phil Smith, *The Footbook of Zombie Walking*]; Not for the Faint of Heart, by Greg Gbur [Livia Llewellyn, *Furnace*]; The Killer and the Killed, June Pulliam [Michael Aronovitz, *Phantom Effect*]; Is the Well Running Dry?, by S. T. Joshi [Ross E. Lockhart, ed., *Cthulhu Fhtagn! Weird Tales Inspired by H. P. Lovecraft*]; A Love/Hate Relationship, by Tony Fonseca [Nicole Cushing, *The Mirrors*]; Revisionist Indigenous Horror, by Chris Dallis [Adam Cesare, *Tribesmen*]; Just Like the Movies, by S. T. Joshi [Orrin Grey, *Painted Monsters & Other Strange Beasts*]; Lovecraftianism as Contagion, by Darrell Schweitzer [Steve Rasnic Tem, *In the Lovecraft Museum*]; Ramsey Campbell, Probably; The Mummy Walks, Again. And Again. And Again, by Greg Gbur [Riccardo Stephens, *The Mummy*]; Lively and Engaging Take on the Legend, by Richard Bleiler [June Pulliam and Anthony J. Fonseca, *Richard Matheson's Monsters: Gender* in the Stories, Scripts, Novels, and Twilight Zone Episodes]; Forget the Butler: The Mafia Did It, by June Pulliam [Todd C. Elliott, *Axes of Evil: The True Story of the Ax-Man Murders*]; What's Lost Is Lost, by Michael J. Abolafia [John Langan, *The Fisherman*]; Horrors in Winnipeg, by S. T. Joshi [Keith Cadieux and Dustin Geeraert, ed., *The Shadow over Portage & Main: Weird Fictions*]; Bierce and "The Damned Thing," by David Goudsward [Don Swaim, *The Assassination of Ambrose Bierce: A Love Story*]; Who's the Psycho Now?, by Chris Dallis [Chet Williamson and Robert Bloch, *Psycho: Sanitarium*]; An Interview with Chet Williamson, by Chris Dallis; Ghosts as Linguistic Processes, by Alexander Lugo [Michael Cisco, *The Wretch of the Sun*]; The Time Is Here for Iron Man to Spread Fear, by June Pulliam [Shin'ya Tsukamoto, dir., *Tetsuo: The Iron Man*]; What Makes a Lovecraftian Story?, by S. T. Joshi [Ellen Datlow, ed., *Children of Lovecraft*]; The Genius of Guillermo del Toro, by Richard Bleiler [Danel Olson, ed., *Guillermo del Toro's* The Devil's Backbone *and* Pan's Labyrinth]; A Modern Master, by David Goudsward [Chet Williamson, *The Night Listener and Others*]; Editor's Column, by Tony Fonseca; Five Decades of Labyrinthine, Blood-Spattered Gialli!, by Chris Dallis [Troy Howarth, *So Deadly, So Perverse: 50 Years of Italian Giallo Films*]; A Promising Start, by S. T. Joshi [Michael Griffin, *The Lure of Devouring Light*]; Capsule Reviews; Notes on Contributors; Index to *Dead Reckonings* 11–20.

189.   *Spectral Realms* No. 6 (Winter 2017). EDITED BY S. T. JOSHI. 161 pp.

Contents. POEMS: Spider Eggs by John Shirley; Edgar A. Poe (1809–1849) by W. H. Pugmire; Finite by Ian Futter; Oracle by Wade German; Next by John J. Mundy The Fateful Flower by Frank Coffman; Vul Ravin by D. L. Myers; Transfiguration by Ronald Terry; Mistress of the Dark Fortress by K. A. Opperman and Leigh Blackmore; Un-Hallowed E'en by Richard L. Tierney; Diluvian Night Out by Jessica Amanda Salmonson; Chrysalides in the Cromlech by Jeff Burnett; When the Stars Are Right by Oliver B. Harris; The Dust That Was You by Mary Krawczak Wilson; Hunted by Claire Smith; The Spell by Liam Garriock; Moonlight in the Playground by Christina Sng; An Unimaginable Horror by Norbert Gora; The Fugitives by Manuel Pérez-Campos; Under the Tuscan Moon by Leigh Blackmore; Kappa Alpha Tau by Josh Medsker; Yes, There Are Wonders Beyond Death by Darrell Schweitzer; rUBBLE ®ubbLe by Jason V Brock; Desolation by M. F. Webb; The Cosmic Women by Pat Calhoun; Descent by Ian Futter; The God-Builders by Nathaniel Reed; Sighting by Ross Balcom; Falling for You by John J. Mundy; Icons by Ronald Terry; The

Sword by Chad Hensley; Dual Purpose by Kyla Lee Ward; A Dream from R'lyeh by Charles Lovecraft; The Witch of the Woods by Frank Coffman; Fallen by Claire Smith; The Germ of the Earth by Farah Rose Smith; The Road to Long-Ago by Ruth Berman; Spawn of the Wicked Hive by Jeff Burnett; Night Play by Ashley Dioses; The Prey by Mary Krawczak Wilson; A Return by Benjamin Blake; When the Earth Was Young by Christina Sng; The House of Gloom by Adam Bolivar; Elder Beings by Leigh Blackmore; Reunion by Manuel Pérez-Campos; The Awen by Michelle Claire White; Ghosts of 1816 by Clay F. Johnson; Quetzalcoatl by Kendall Evans; Relic by Nathaniel Reed; Admonishments for the Incautious by David Barker; Yaga by Oliver Smith; The Demon Corn by D. L. Myers; Timeless Ghosts by Liam Garriock; Clearing Sky by Ronald Terry; The Door by Christina Sng; Tending the Grave by Ian Futter; Woodsmoke: A Folk Song That Never Was by John Shirley; The Wolf's Last Words by Claire Smith; Dark Solstice Cold and Deathly by Richard L. Tierney; The Rainy Season by John J. Mundy; Siren's Song by Ashley Dioses; The Mask of Leprous Light by Jeff Burnett; Of Rippers, Psychos, and Scarves by Randall D. Larson and Charles Lovecraft; Dark Shuttle by Ruth Berman; Downstream by Oliver Smith; The War of Dragons by Christina Sng; Temple of the Plumed Serpent by Ann K. Schwader; Those by David Barker; Samhain Redivivus by Frank Coffman; CLASSIC RE-PRINTS: The Old Ghost by Thomas Lovell Beddoes; Red Ghosts in Kentucky by Leah Bodine Drake; ARTICLES: In Pursuit of the Transcendent: The Weird Verse of Walter de la Mare by Leigh Blackmore; REVIEWS: A Dreamer's Rimes by J.-M. Rajala; The Ghostly Verses of the Science Fiction Poetry Association by Michael J. Abolafia. Notes on Contributors.

Notes. Cover illustration by Dugald Stewart Walker.

190.   H. P. LOVECRAFT. *Fungi from Yuggoth: An Annotated Edition.* Edited by David E. Schultz. 2017. 287 pp. hc.

Contents. FUNGI FROM YUGGOTH: I. The Book; II. Pursuit; III. The Key; IV. Recognition; V. Homecoming; VI. The Lamp; VII. Zaman's Hill; VIII. The Port; IX. The Courtyard; X. The Pigeon-Flyers; XI. The Well; XII. The Howler; XIII. Hesperia; XIV. Star-Winds; XV. Antarktos; XVI. The Window; XVII. A Memory; XVIII. The Gardens of Yin; XIX. The Bells; XX. Night-Gaunts; XXI. Nyarlathotep; XXII. Azathoth; XXIII. Mirage; XXIV. The Canal; XXV. St Toad's; XXVI. The Familiars; XXVII. The Elder Pharos; XXVIII. Expectancy; XXIX. Nostalgia; XXX. Background; XXXI. The Dweller; XXXII. Alienation; XXXIII. Harbour Whistles; XXXIV. Recapture; XXXV. Evening Star;

XXXVI. Continuity; Fungi from Yuggoth: The Manuscript; Dim Essences: The Origins of Fungi from Yuggoth; Notes; APPENDIXES: A. Notes for Additional Sonnets; B. [The Book]; C. Chronology of Appearances of Fungi from Yuggoth; D. Textual Variants; E. The Musical Compositions of Harold S. Farnese. Bibliography; Index of Titles and First Lines; Acknowledgments.

Notes. Cover and interior art by Jason Eckhardt. A landmark of scholarship, embodying decades of research by Schultz. The text consists of the text of the 36 sonnets of the *Fungi* (with an illustration by Eckhardt facing each poem), a reproduction of the autograph manuscript, an exhaustive analysis and commentary on the cycle, and much other interesting matter. Printed in dark green ink in a limited hardcover edition (300 copies) by Covington Group.

191.   S. T. JOSHI. *Varieties of the Weird Tale.* 2017. 350 pp. tpb.

Contents. Introduction: Establishing the Canon of Weird Fiction; I. THE GOLDEN AGE: Some Notes on Ambrose Bierce—I. Bierce as Political Satirist; II. Bierce as Fabulist; III. What Happens in "The Death of Halpin Frayser"; A Triumvirate of Fantastic Poets: Ambrose Bierce, George Sterling, and Clark Ashton Smith; Gertrude Atherton: Death and Women; Bram Stoker: Dracula and Others; Mary E. Wilkins Freeman: The Domestic Ghost; E. Nesbit: Lying Awake in the Dark; Edna W. Underwood: Dear Dead Women; Things in the Weeds: The Supernatural in Hodgson's Short Stories; II. THE ERA OF LOVECRAFT: M. R. James and the Classic Ghost Story; Some Notes on Lord Dunsany—I. The Pegāna Mythos; II. Jorkens; III. Christianity and Paganism in Two Dunsany Novels; Sax Rohmer: The Popular Weird Tale; Maurice Level and the Grand Guignol; Irvin S. Cobb and Gouverneur Morris: A Taste for the Weird; Bran Mak Morn and History; The Novels of Donald Wandrei; III. SOME CONTEMPORARIES: Science and Superstition: Fritz Leiber's Modernization of Gothic; Master and Pupil: August Derleth and Ramsey Campbell's First Book; Thomas Ligotti's *The Nightmare Factory*; Caitlín R. Kiernan and Sensuous Prose. Acknowledgments; Index.

Notes. Cover illustration by Wallace Smith for *The Shadow-Eater* by Benjamin De Casseres (1923). Cover design by Kevin Slaughter of Underworld Amusements, a press specializing in De Casseres. Slaughter later designed covers for numerous Hippocampus titles. Another collection of Joshi's miscellaneous articles on weird fiction old and new.

192.   LORD DUNSANY. *The Ghost in the Corner and Other Stories.* Edited by S. T. Joshi and Martin Andersson. 2017. 264 pp. tpb.

Contents. Introduction; TALES AND SKETCHES, 1931–1957: The Use of Man; The Ghost in the Corner; Very Secret; Tales for the Dark Continent; Advance Regulations; A Modern Portrait; The Rations of Murdoch Finucan; A Day on the Bog; Little Tim Brannehan; The Burrahoola; Kind Pagan Lights; A Witch in the Balkans; A Talk in the Dark; Mid Snow and Ice; A Treasure of India; Two Young Officers; The Unforgivable Choice; The Old Detective's Story; TALES FROM THE 1956 COLLECTION: Helping the Fairies; The Story of Tse Gah; The Dwarf Holóbolos and the Sword Hogbiter; Progress; One Night in Eldorado; The Traveller to Thundercliff; The Lucky Escape; How Mickey Paid His Debt; Lost Lyrics; The Dance at Weirdmoor Castle; As It Seems to the Blackbird; The Haunting of Whitebeams; The Romance of His Life; A Theory of Evolution; The Stolen Power; The Cook of Santamaria; The Awakening; A Goat in Trousers; A Breeze at Rest; A Channel Rescue; In the Governor's Palace; Hard Horses; The Blundering Curate; A Tale of the Irish Countryside; The Price of the World; When Mrs. Fynn Was Young; At the Scene of the Crime; A Tale of Bad Luck; In a Hotel Lounge; The Chambermaid of the Splendide; The Motive; The Quiet Laugh; Bibliography.

Notes. Cover illustration from *Queen of the Secret City* by Joseph J. Doke (1916); artist unknown. Cover design by Kevin Slaughter, who also fully redrew the illustration as a vector graphic due to quality issues with the source image. Originally announced under the title *A Walk in the Wastes of Time,* the book was recast due to the unavailability of several tales. Nevertheless, a rich collection of many of Dunsany's uncollected and unpublished stories, including the late tales that he assembled in 1956 for an untitled story collection but never arranged for publication. Also included are a number of Dunsany's essays, many of which are tantamount to prose-poems.

193.   JASON V BROCK. *The Dark Sea Within: Tales and Poems.* 2017. 351 pp. tpb.

Contents. Preface; The Dark Sea Within; The Man with the Horn; Memento Mori; Transposition; A Carcass, Waiting; The Shadow of Heaven; Fallen: A Lament and Affirmation; Brood; Verlassen; Key; A Darke Phantastique; Chrysalis; Dolls; Afterlife (with Sunni K Brock and William F. Nolan); Windows, Mirrors, Doors; Colossi; Double Feature; Unity of Affect; Epistles from Dis; Out of Their Heads; Notes; Acknowledgments.

Notes. Cover illustration by Samuel Araya. Cover design by Jason V Brock. Map for "Brood" by Jason C. Eckhardt; all other interior illustrations by Jason V Brock. A second collection of Brock's weird fiction, featuring mellifluous prose, highly original weird conceptions, and a wide diversity of theme and motif.

194.   MIKE FANTINA. *Alchemy of Dreams and Other Poems.* 2017. 343 pp. tpb.

Contents. VANISHED REALMS AND LOST WORLDS: A Dream of the Minotaur; Genius Loci; Spirits; Roc; Cecily; The Haunted Inn; Stone Pillars; The Haunted Archipelago; When Wizards Meet; Lyonnesse; A Careless Kiss; A Dream of Gold; A Centauress; On Wings of Steel; The Dawn; The Return; Angels of Ice; Cockaigne; The Pale Château; Nymphs; I Circle Methane Seas; The Lover's Curse; I Wander; The Satrap; My Dreams Take Me; The Ghost Army; Ride the Night Wind; Dispatched; Out of the Mountain Pool; The Call of Orion; Like a Stone; Girl from Altair; Like Solomon; Ghost of the Fen; Haunted; Among the Stars; In Nan Modal; The Dream Rider; Ghost Kings of Mu; Atlantis; Strange Harbor; The Nymph's Prayer; The Temptress; A Traveler through Time; Strange Stars; In Isfahan; Ganymede; Ulysses; Intruder; Castles in the Air; Only an Evil Wind Went Roaring; Spirit Cave; Vengeful Vipers Vex All This; A Vision; The Fatal Shore; Ur; Cold Is the River; In Castles of Steel; Realm of Dreams; Argosy of Dreams; Centaur Love; Barge; Lost World; The Glen; The Harpy; Elemental; I Have Danced with Princesses; The Haunted Temple; The Sorceress at the End of Space-Time; The Seneschal; The Singing Sword; The Witches' Château; 1934; The Forsaken City; I Sigh to Orion; In Upland Fields; The Ghost, the Gold, and the Dark; DOWN TO THE SEA IN SHIPS: Secluded Bays; These Haunted Hills I Roam; The Drowning; Under an Iron Moon; The Viking Horn; Rendezvous; Song of the Sea Dog's Ghost; One Misty Morn; Beguiled; In the Moonlight; Iron and Silver; Sea Shanty; Harold Owen Confronts His Brother's Ghost; Leviathan; The Matilda; Bethany; Xardoc Ibrahim; A Dark Dream of the Sea; Sea Magic; The Ferryman; The Schooner; The Vanished Sea; Above the Bay in Rajapore; Sea Ghosts and Shipwrecks; Mount Carmel by the Sea; A Shipman's Dream; The Witch of the West; Calypso; The Dark Girl; The Ship; Six Days out of Zanzibar; Conversion; A Dream of Leviathan; Bell Isle; By the Haunted Sea; I Heard Swift Ghostly Fingers; The Trysting Place; Windward and Lee; Seven Sisters; Love Uncanny; The Sea King's Daughter; Arcanum; Vengeance for Io; The Legs of Leviathan Loop; Fugue; The Flying Dutchman; Flight 19; The Merman Tempts a Girl; Lovesick; Call of the Restless Sea; I Wander;

Sea Dream; Merlin's Daughter; Veronique; A Sea Change; A Sea Spell in Winter; Lure of the Siren; LOVERS, GHOSTS, AND MONSTERS: Vengeance; Death on the Moor; Stars That Sunder; The Wizard Makes a Girl; The Lover; Idol Found in the Woods; The Constant Lover; I Ride the Nightmare; The Fell at Twilight; A Midnight Tryst; Wizard Love; The Necromancer; In Amber; The Abandoned Lover; Dark Machinations; Rolling the Bones; Tan Girl; She-Wolf; Night of the Banshee; She Soared Upon the Wind; Illicit Rendezvous; The Madness of the Moon; Withered Roses; Forlorn; Lycanthropy at Dusk; Purchased Love; Fable; Under These Stars; Girl in the Dunes; She; The Black Comet; Ghost Poet; Regret; Clarice; The Love Potion; The Princess of Grant Street; The Spire and the Ghost; Warlocks and Mages; Sower of Discord; Moon Prayer; The Wind; Zahlore; Ingénue; The Muse; The Upper Air; The Inconstant Lover; The Sorcerer Fashions a Lover for Himself; The Offering; The Pretty Jinn; An Encounter at Dusk; Three Kisses; Sarah Jane; Above the Fallen Gate; Where Shadows Weave; The Ghost of Guinevere; Cold Love; Haunted Château; To Wake the Dead; Raquel; Moon Love; The Ghost Train; Aphasia; The Fire Fairy; All Hallows Eve; Phantom Wife; Bewitched and Beguiled; Gray Eyes; Street Walker; The Silver Pin; The Wicked Girl; The Ghost Bell; An Iron Gong; Dark Paramour; Una Sandoval; Frankenstein; Ghost Rider; A Nightmare; Selene; Lamentation; Alchemy of Dreams; The Lover Despairs; Duplicity; The Girl; I Dream of Her; Sylph; Like Queen Mab; The Awful Dream; Ghost Wife; Jocelyn; Under the Pole Star; A WELLSPRING OF ARCANA: The Centauress; One Misty Morn; The Ale; Daydream at Dusk; The Stuff of Dreams; The Abbey Bells; Moonlight; Vespers; Time and Space; Spoons; The Sunken Road; New Love for Old; Isfahan; Remembrance; Serenity; Scryer; The Glory Hand; The Old Shop; Winter Spells; Girl with a Crystal Ball; Give Me a Brand; The Bell; The Riven Oak; The Rescue; Ransom; Hammer; The End of the Wizards; A Spell in Measure; Magics; Winter; Harpies and Ravens; Love Is Cruel; The Pond; Lover of the Moon; A Ghost; Ghost in the Mirror; Wind-Blown Dream; The Dusk; The Glue; The Haunted Clock; Nocturnal; Of Fairy Rings and Cedar Chests; The Woodland Nymph; Pursued by the Jinn; The Gander; An Elixir of Love; The Ghostly Monarch; The Forsaken City; The Moon Riders; I Remember; With a Vengeance; Wizard; Men; The Harpy Queen; A Fragment from a Dream; I Dream; A Ghost Girl from 1918; The Caliph's Lover; Pursuit of the Belovèd.

Notes. Cover painting and interior artwork by Steve Lines. Cover design by Kevin Slaughter. A bountiful selection of the thousands of poems that Fantina (d. 2018) wrote in the years before his death. The poems are distinguished by metrical precision, chilling weird conceptions, and a mingling of supernaturalism and eroticism.

195. *Dead Reckonings* No. 21 (Spring 2017). EDITED BY ALEX HOUSTOUN AND MICHAEL J. ABOLAFIA. 111 pp.

Contents. Bestarred with Fainting Flowers: Symbolism and Myth in the Work of R. Murray Gilchrist, by Daniel Pietersen; The "V" Word, by Jose Cruz [T. E. Grau, *They Don't Come Home Anymore*]; Shadows with Teeth, by Darrell Schweitzer [Ellen Datlow, ed. *The Best Horror of the Year, Volume 8*]; Existential and Ontological Horror, by S. T. Joshi [Joel Lane, *This Spectacular Darkness: Critical Essays*, ed. Mark Valentine and John Howard]; In the Heliotherapy Ward, by Amber Doll Diaz [David F. Sandberg, *Lights Out*]; The Horror in the Card Catalog, by S. T. Joshi [Darrell Schweitzer and John Ashmead, ed., *Tales from the Miskatonic University Library*]; Southern Discomfort and the Ubiquitous Undead, by Stephanie Graves [Eric Gary Anderson, Taylor Hagood, and Daniel Cross Turner, ed., *Undead Souths: The Gothic and Beyond in Southern Literature and Culture*]; Forever I'm Alone with You, by Jose Cruz [Lynda E. Rucker, *You'll Know When You Get There*]; Stranger Things: A Conversation between Bev Vincent and Hank Wagner; Terrors of the Natural World, by S. T. Joshi [Richard Gavin, *Sylvan Dread: Tales of Pastoral Darkness*]; Ramsey's Rant: Remembering Kirby, by Ramsey Campbell; Psychosexual Syzygy: Checking in at the Bates Motel, by Gavin Callaghan [*Bates Motel*, Seasons 1 through 5]; Terror for Children, by Taij Devon [Aric Cushing, *Vampire Boy*]; The Homely Commonplace and the Unimaginably Deranged: J. G. Ballard's *High Rise*, by Alexander Lugo; The Resurgence of Weird Magazines, by Ashley Dioses; The Final Work of Mark Fisher, by James Machin [Mark Fisher, *The Weird and the Eerie*]; SMASH EVERYTHING! Bobby Rhodes and His *Demons*, by Nathan Chazan; THINKING HORROR: An Exchange with s. j. bagley, by Alex Houstoun; Pastiches of Pastiches, by S. T. Joshi [Brian M. Sammons and Glynn Owen Barrass, ed., *The Children of Gla'aki: A Tribute to Ramsey Campbell's Great Old One*]; About the Contributors.

Notes. The first issue edited by Abolafia and Houston, and introducing a slightly different take on content.

196. JONATHAN THOMAS. *Naked Revenants and Other Fables of Old and New England.* 2017. 264 pp. tpb.

Contents. Plenty of Irem; Ritual Damage; Old Graveyard in the Woods; Gone to Doggerland; The Poor in Spirit; The Dark at the

Top of the Stairs; Naked Revenants; Sand Bar; Vade Mecum; Old Goodman Brown; Barn; Purging Mom; Death and a Locket; Shed a Tear for Asenath; The Demon Thought; Barley Night; Rat Letters; The Sarsen in the Ditch; Deacon Mercer; Cups of Memory; Mummify Me; Acknowledgements.

Notes. Cover photo by John Seeley. Cover design by John Seeley and Shonna Dowers. Thomas's fifth short story collection, featuring his usual entertaining mix of Lovecraftian tales and general weird fiction, all enlivened by pungently satirical prose and shrewd portrayals of character.

197.   SAM GAFFORD. *The Dreamer in Fire and Other Stories.* 2017. 242 pp. tpb.

Contents. Casting Fractals; Showtime; The Adventure of the Prometheus Calculation; Homecoming; The Gathering Daemonica; Static; Sunspots; My Brother's Keeper; "How Does That Make You Feel?"; What Was That?; "The Dreamer in Fire": Notes on Robert Winslow's "Sutter's Corners"; He Whose Feet Trod the Lost Aeons; "Good Morning, Innsmouth!"; Weltschmerz; Hellhounds on the Trail; The Land of Lonesomeness; Passing Spirits; Acknowledgments.

Notes. Cover illustration and design by Jared Boggess. Gafford's first short story collection, comprising tales (many of them inspired by Lovecraft or William Hope Hodgson) written over the past two decades.

198.   JEFFREY THOMAS. *Haunted Worlds.* 2017. 249 pp. tpb.

Contents. Introduction, *by Ian Rogers*; PART ONE: OUR WORLD: Carrion; Spider Gates; Feeding Oblivion; Mr. Faun; The Left-Hand Pool; riaH gnoL; The Toll; Saigon Dep Lam; The Green Hands; PART TWO: OTHER WORLDS: The Green Hands; Good Will toward Men; The Temple of Ugghiutu; Drawing No. 8; Redemption Express; Story Notes; Acknowledgments.

Notes. Cover and interior illustrations by Kim Bo Yung. Cover design by Kevin Slaughter. Strong story collection by Thomas, one of the leading figures in contemporary weird fiction.

199.   *Spectral Realms* No. 7 (Summer 2017). EDITED BY S. T. JOSHI. 125 pp.

Contents. POEMS: This Mountain of Skulls, by John Shirley; Lightless Oceans, by Ann K. Schwader; The Dream-Wife, by Adam Bolivar; More Than the Shark, by M. F. Webb; The Embrace, by Jessica Amanda Salmonson; A Rude Awakening, by Ian Futter; For Sale, by

Deborah L. Davitt; Invocation to the Daemon for Modern Times, by Liam Garriock; Aenid's Dream, by Christina Sng; The God Within, by Ronald Terry; The Dark Pharaoh, by Richard L. Tierney; Ave Augustissime: An Acrostic Sonnet on H. P. Lovecraft, Esq., by Manuel Pérez-Campos; Portrait of H. P. Lovecraft, Esq.: A Scrambled Acrostic Sonnet, by Manuel Pérez-Campos; Dracul's Demesne, by Frank Coffman; The Reaper's Garden, by Ashley Dioses; Testament of the Scribe, by David Barker; The Graveyard Knows My Name, by Ross Balcom; Teratology, by F. J. Bergmann; Repoman Homunculus, by Chad Hensley; Imprisoned, by Mary Krawczak Wilson; His Voice in the Whisper of Waves, by Deborah L. Davitt and Kendall Evans; Mary of the Rosy Grave, by K. A. Opperman; Things Come out of the Fog, by G. O. Clark; Moment, by Nathaniel Reed; Ad'Naigon, by Maxwell I. Gold; Doll in the Wall, by Jessica Amanda Salmonson; From the Yellow Text of Thanos Khan, by Don Webb; Angry Sun/Bloated Moon, by Claire Smith; Secret Tree, by John Shirley; Only 13, by Ian Futter; Expanding Universe, by Ronald Terry; The Final Turn, by Ann K. Schwader; Arrival, by M. F. Webb; He Dreams of Beauty, by Liam Garriock; Pull, by Christina Sng; Innsmouth Shanty, by David Barker; Metamorphosis, by Frank Coffman; The Wyrde of the Bibliognost; or, Another Solitude, by Manuel Pérez-Campos; Silent Songs, by Deborah L. Davitt; The Ballad of the de la Poers, by Adam Bolivar; Corridors Enough, by Ann K. Schwader; The Daughter of Death, by Charles D. O'Connor III; Under the Blood Moon, by Sunni K Brock; Her Skull and the Sea, by Mary Krawczak Wilson; What It Means When You Dream of Swords, by F. J. Bergmann; My Beloved Bones, by Jessica Amanda Salmonson; Rising Damp, by M. F. Webb; Night Terrors, by Ian Futter; David Lynch, by Liam Garriock; It's Hell Being Your Guardian Angel, by John Shirley; The Spiders of Kepler 452B, by Kendall Evans; CLASSIC REPRINTS: Amenophra, by Ernest A. Edkins; Faces and Souls, by Paul Eldridge; ARTICLES: On "A Wine of Wizardry," by S. T. Joshi; REVIEWS: Tim Powers, Poet, by John Shirley; The Virtues and Drawbacks of Free Verse, by Leigh Blackmore; Notes on Contributors.

Notes. Cover illustration by Gustave Doré.

200.   H. P. LOVECRAFT. *Letters to C. L. Moore and Others.* Edited by David E. Schultz and S. T. Joshi. 2017. 411 pp. tpb.

Contents. Introduction; LETTERS: H. P. Lovecraft and C. L. Moore; To Henry Kuttner; To Fritz and Jonquil Leiber; To Harry O. Fischer; To Frederic Jay Pabody; APPENDIX: Verse by C. L. Moore; For H. P. Lovecraft, by Henry Kuttner; My Correspondence with Lovecraft, by

Fritz Leiber. Glossary of Frequently Mentioned Names; Bibliography; Index.

Notes. Cover design by Anastasia Damianakos. A volume distinguished by the publication of Moore's voluminous letters to Lovecraft (his letters to her survive only in fragments).

201.   DENNIS QUINN, EDITOR. *Lovecraftian Proceedings 2: Select Papers from the Dr. Henry Armitage Memorial Scholarship Symposium, NecronomiCon Providence, 2015.* 2017. 275 pp. tpb.

Contents. Introduction: From Armitage Symposium to *Lovecraftian Proceedings,* by Dennis Quinn; Dreams of Antiquity: H. P. Lovecraft's Great Roman Dream of 1927, by Byron Nakamura; The Poet's Nightmare: The Nature of Things According to Lovecraft, by Sean Moreland; Reordering the Universe: H. P. Lovecraft's Subversion of the Biblical Divine, by René J. Weise; Resisting Cthulhu: Milton and Lovecraft's Errand in the Wilderness, by Marcello Ricciardi; "The Discriminating Urban Landscapist": Tradition and Innovation in the Architectural Writings of H. P. Lovecraft, by Connor Pitetti; Tentacles in the Madhouse: The Role of the Asylum in the Fiction of H. P. Lovecraft, by Troy Rondinone; Unspeakable Languages: Lovecraft Editions in Spanish, by Juan L. Pérez-de-Luque; Color out of Mind: Correlating the Cthulhu Mythos Universe to the Autism Disorder Spectrum, by Lars G. Backstrom; Darwin and the Deep Ones: Anthropological Anxiety in "The Shadow over Innsmouth" and Other Stories, by Jeffrey Shanks; The "Inside" of H. P. Lovecraft's Supernatural Horror in the Visual Arts, by Nathaniel R. Wallace, H. P. Lovecraft's Optimism, by Matthew Beach; Insider, Outsider: From the Commonplace to the Uncanny in H. P. Lovecraft's Narration and Descriptions, by Daphnée Tasia Bourdages-Athanassiou; H. P. Lovecraft, Georges Bataille, and the Fascination of the Formless: One Crawling Chaos Seen Emerging from Opposite Shores, by Christian Roy; Ripples from Carcosa: H. P. Lovecraft, *True Detective,* and the Artist-Investigator, by Heather Poirier; Lovecraft for the Little Ones: *Para-Norman,* Plushies, and More, by Faye Ringel and Jenna Randall; Contributors; Appendix: Abstracts of Papers Presented at the Dr. Henry Armitage Memorial Scholarship Symposium, NecronomiCon Providence 20–23 August 2015; Index.

Notes. Cover illustration by Pete Von Sholly. Another solid collection of academic papers, dealing with a wide range of subjects relating to Lovecraft and his influence.

202.	H. P. LOVECRAFT AND CLARK ASHTON SMITH. *Dawnward Spire, Lonely Hill: The Letters of H. P. Lovecraft and Clark Ashton Smith.* Edited by David E. Schultz and S. T. Joshi. 2017. 799 pp. hc.

Contents. Introduction; Letters; APPENDIX: Annie E. P. Gamwell, Postcard to Clark Ashton Smith; H. P. Lovecraft, [Review of *Ebony and Crystal*]; From "Supernatural Horror in Literature"; Clark Ashton Smith, [Fantasy and Human Experience]; C. A. Smith on "Garbage-Mongering"; [Realism and Fantasy]; [On the Forbidden Books]; The Tale of Macrocosmic Horror; [Crossword Puzzles]; Clifford Gessler, Treader of Obscure Stars; Various, In re exhibitions of Smith's artwork; The Boiling Point; Chronology; Glossary of Frequently Mentioned Names; Bibliography; Index.

Notes. Cover illustration and frontispiece by David C. Verba. Another work decades in the making, as the editors were tasked with securing the hundreds of letters between the two writers from a multiplicity of sources, both institutional and private. The letters have been exhaustively annotated. Printed in a limited hardcover edition (500 copies) by Covington Group. The paperback reprint (2020, in two volumes) contains text for a few postcards discovered after publication of the first edition.

203.	DONALD SIDNEY-FRYER. *Aesthetics, Ho! Essays on Art, Literature, and Theatre.* 2017. 209 pp. tpb.

Contents. AESTHETICS HO!; Introduction; Jesse Allen's First Mural; A Defense and Illustration of One Poetic Method; San Francisco, by G. Sutton Breiding; A Note on History and/or Historiography; Old versus New; Poetry and Poetry Again; Perfect Form, Perfect Shape; Atlantis; One Poetic Practice; H. P. Lovecraft—A Belated Homage; Flickering Shadows on a Lighted Screen; Intangibility; That's Hollywood? That's Hollywood!; Farewell to All That; Appendix; ENDS AND ODDS: A POETIC MISCELLANY IN VERSE AND PROSE: St. Ichabod; The Conquistadors; A Modest Breviary; A Labyrinth of Caverns; Swimming Somewhere in the Antillias; A Modest Beastiary; A Colonnade out of Time; Temporal Enigma; On the Death Mask of J. Sheridan Le Fanu; The Crippled Octopus; To a Professor of Professors; Puzzlement; Isca Silurum; The Capricorn; The Key; Brave Ocean Cavaliers; Queen Elizabeth II: 2016; What's in a Name? Indeed, Just What Lies in a Name?; Where Now the Towns of Legend and of Myth?; And Have You Seen a Peacock as of Late?; Retrospective; Have You Viewed the Big Five? Are They All still Extant?; Enigma; The Bird of Indigo and Verde; The Transcendence of King Bhumibol; "Yea, Though I Walk through the Valley of the Numen of Light. . . ."; Another Forsaken Garden; The Forsaken Garden Again; Some Holy Grail; Another Grail Re-found`; An Obvious Announcement; Artorius, Arthurius, or Arthur Rex?; The Lyre-Bird; Upon a Maya Pyramid in El Salvador; The Nonsense Eater; A King out of Macedonia; Alexandros Megalos; Fountains; Katnyptian; A Song in Reverse; A Sunday Noontide Ritual; Mouse in Boots; The "X"—The Unknown Quantity; By the Light of Flambeaux; The Grove of Ceiba Trees along the Stream; Those Giant Ceiba Trees Again; From Script to Script, From Crypt to Crypt; On Jesse Allen's Biggest African Tableau; "The Girl with the Ice Cream Tits"; The New Conquistadors; Lo Ordinario; A Maya Pyramid Revisited; The Cup from Otherwhere; Divertissement I; Divertissement II; Transition; To H. P. L.—A Tribute out of Time; A Bit of Nostalgia; The Hunting of the Ampersand; Notes by Dlanod Yendis.

Notes. The cover illustration, "Prelude to an Orgy," by Hannes Bok; also known as "Prelude to the Afternoon of a Faun." A richly diverse array of Sidney-Fryer's essays, as well as an assemblage of his recent poetry and prose-poetry. Released to coincide with Sidney-Fryer's appearance as Poet Laureate of NecronomiCon Providence.

204. H. P. LOVECRAFT. *Collected Fiction: A Variorum Edition, Volume 4: Revisions and Collaborations.* Edited by S. T. Joshi. 2017. 717 pp. tpb.

Contents. Introduction, by S. T. Joshi; The Green Meadow, by Elizabeth Neville Berkeley [i.e., Winifred Virginia Jackson] and Lewis Theobald, Jun.; Poetry and the Gods, by Anna Helen Crofts and Henry Paget-Lowe; The Crawling Chaos, by Elizabeth Berkeley [i.e., Winifred Virginia Jackson] and Lewis Theobald, Jun.; The Horror at Martin's Beach, by Sonia H. Greene; Two Black Bottles, by Wilfred Blanch Talman; The Last Test, by Adolphe de Castro; The Curse of Yig, by Zealia Bishop; The Electric Executioner, by Adolphe de Castro; The Mound, by Zealia Bishop; Medusa's Coil, by Zealia Bishop; The Trap, by Henry S. Whitehead; The Man of Stone, by Hazel Heald; Winged Death, by Hazel Heald; The Horror in the Museum, by Hazel Heald; Out of the Aeons, by Hazel Heald; The Horror in the Burying-Ground, by Hazel Heald; The Slaying of the Monster, by R. H. Barlow; The Hoard of the Wizard-Beast, by R. H. Barlow; The Tree on the Hill, by Duane W. Rimel; The Battle That Ended the Century, with R. H. Barlow; The Disinterment, by Duane W. Rimel; "Till A' the Seas," by R. H. Barlow; Collapsing Cosmoses, with R. H. Barlow; The Challenge from Beyond, with C. L. Moore, A. Merritt, Robert E.; Howard, and Frank Belknap Long; The Diary of Alonzo

Typer, by William Lumley; In the Walls of Eryx, with Kenneth Sterling; The Night Ocean, by R. H. Barlow; APPENDIX: Four O'Clock, by Sonia H. Greene; A Sacrifice to Science, by Gustav Adolphe Danziger; The Automatic Executioner, by Gustav Adolphe Danziger; [Fragment], by J. Vernon Shea; The Sorcery of Aphlar, by Duane W. Rimel; The Diary of Alonzo Typer, by William Lumley; Bibliography; Index.

Notes. Cover design and illustrations by Fergal Fitzpatrick. An extensive collection of Lovecraft's revisions and collaborations, with textual variants. The appendix prints the original versions of some of the tales Lovecraft revised.

205.   KENNETH W. FAIG, JR. *Lovecraftian Voyages.* Edited by Christopher M. O'Brien and J.-M. Rajala. 2017. 352 pp. tpb.

Contents. Foreword, by S. T. Joshi; Preface; LOVECRAFTIAN VOYAGES: 1. Lovecraft's family and childhood; 2. Grandfather Whipple and the collapse of the Phillips household; 3. Lovecraft's literary executor and the John Hay Library collection; 4. Some Lovecraftiana; bibliographical research and amateur press work; 5. The ultra-collectables; planned edition of the *Fungi from Yuggoth*; 6. *The Shunned House* book; 7. The rarest Lovecraft editions; 8. Some additions to the Lovecraft bibliography; 9. The "Lost Lovecrafts"; 10. Lovecraft in Rhode Island newspapers; 11. Lovecraft's destroyed and abandoned fiction; 12. Lovecraft's use of dreams and newspaper clippings in his fiction; 13. Lovecraft's planned novels; 14. Lovecraft's revisory work; a few miscellaneous observations; 15. Lovecraft's financial affairs; 16. Notes on the education of Lovecraft's family; 17. Lovecraft's travelogues; the Arkham country; 18. Real New England locales in Lovecraft's fiction; 19. Who Ate Roger Williams?; 20. Searching for the Dark Swamp; 21. Lovecraft's pseudonyms; 22. The Kalem Club; Lovecraft's correspondence with his wife; 23. About the pronunciation of Cthulhu; 24. Of the Commonplace Book; 25. Lovecraft's Providence; APPENDIX: Calculations of Lovecraft's earnings; Notes; Bibliography; Index.

Notes. First publication in its entirety, some 45 years after Faig wrote the monograph. The editors provided the section titles, notes, and back matter.

206.   *Lovecraft Annual* No. 11 (2017). EDITED BY S. T. JOSHI. 178 pp.

Contents. Personal Tragedy in "The Thing on the Doorstep," by W. H. Pugmire; Lovecraft's Greek Tragedy, by Duncan Norris; On Lovecraft's Lifelong Relationship with Wonder, by Jan B. W. Pedersen; Some Philological Observations on "The Horror at Red Hook," by

Armen Alexanyan; New York, Culture Shock, and a Glimpse of the Future in "He," by Cecelia Drewer; H. P. Lovecraft in "The Sideshow," ed. S. T. Joshi; Lovecraft and the *Argosy*, by David E. Schultz; H. P. Lovecraft's Determinism and Atomism: Evidence in R. H. Barlow's "The Summons," by Marcos Legaria; Lovecraft and *Arrival:* The Quiet Apocalypse, by Duncan Norris; Letters to the Coryciani, by H. P. Lovecraft (ed. S. T. Joshi and David E. Schultz); Aristeas and Lovecraft, by Claudio Foti; Sinister Showmen and H. P. Lovecraft, by Gavin Callaghan; REVIEWS: [Review of Kenneth W. Faig, Jr., *Lovecraftian Voyages*], by S. T. Joshi; [Review of W. Scott Poole, *In the Mountains of Madness: The Life and Extraordinary Afterlife of H. P. Lovecraft*], by Darrell Schweitzer; [Review of H. P. Lovecraft, *Letters to C. L. Moore and Others*], by Stefan Dziemianowicz; Briefly Noted.

207.   ADAM BOLIVAR. *The Lay of Old Hex: Spectral Ballads & Weird Jack Tales.* 2017. 327 pp. tpb.

Contents. Preface; Introduction: The Lay of Adam Bolivar, by K. A. Opperman; I. The Ballad of Jack Keeper; II. The Black Cup; III. The Lay of Jackson Drake; IV. The Dream Emerald; V. The Broken Promise; VI. Gooseberry Tea; VII. Jack the Hunter; VIII. Fiddler Jack; IX. Jack, a Key, and Dreame; X. Jack in Ye Dreame; XI. Death Came to Hexham; XII. Ye Yellow'd Reed; XIII. Jack and the Devil; XIV. The Lay of Old Hex; XV. The Ineffable Journey of Jasper Drake; XVI. Jack in the Witch House; XVII. Jack and the Giants; XVIII. The Hexham Horror; XIX. The Ballad of Harold Gloom; XX. The Devil's Lanthorn; XXI. The Ballad of Jack Drake; XXII. The Grimalkin's Curse; XXIII. The Black Tree; XXIV. The Death of Arthur Drake; XXV. Scarlett Cloake; XXVI. The Pixy-Wife; XXVII. The Lay of King Marock; XXVIII. The Unquiet Grave; XXIX. Black Star; XXX. The Dream-Quest of Unknown Jack; XXXI. The Rime of the Eldritch Mariner; XXXII. An Ancient Tomb A-Yonder Lies; XXXIII. Ye Jack of War; Acknowledgments.

Notes. Cover design and restoration of vintage interior illustrations by Daniel V. Sauer. Sauer later designed covers and provided artwork for numerous Hippocampus titles. A compelling collection of poetry, fiction, and vignettes by one of the leading contemporary exponents of weird poetry. Bolivar has developed a remarkable facility at old-time ballad poetry.

208.   ASHLEY DIOSES. *Diary of a Sorceress.* 2017. 170 pp. tpb.

Contents. Introduction, by Donald Sidney-Fryer; Prelude: My Dark Diary; Entry One: Atop the Crystal Moon; Diary of a Sorceress; A

Sorcerous Tome; The Glass Vial; Witch Lord of the Hunt; Labyrinthine King; Midnight Strides; Night Play; Moon Enchantress; Atop the Crystal Moon; Dragonspeak; Scarlet Autumn Aurora; Fire Sprite; Lord of the Deep; Selkie; Fallen Atlantis; Medusa's Mirror; Morning's Moon; Lady Death; ENTRY TWO: KISS THE STARS; A Sea of Snow and Frost; The Abandoned Garden; Graveyard Blossom; Under the Chrysanthemums; Calla Lilies; Black-Veined Whites; Vapors; The Perfect Rose; The Dwelling Place; The Moon; Kiss the Stars; Celestial Mysteries; The Hands of Chaos; ENTRY THREE: STAR LIGHTING; One Winter Eve; To an Unknown Mistress; A Queen in Hell; Ever Fair; Star Lighting; Lover's Witch; Witch's Love; Enchantress; Dark Poet of My Heart; Dark Valentine; Dark Valentine II; My Dark Valentine; The Celebration of Dreams; The Fires of Summer; Rondel to My Love; Sky Fallen Maiden; A Sorceress's Love; A Lover's Sorceress; Panic; Maenads; They Sing in Whispers; A Glamorous Touch; Prisoner of Love; On Amaranthine Lips; Sweet Renegade; Siren's Song; Sephora; Can I Stop Your Heart?; ENTRY FOUR: ON A DREAMLAND'S MOON; Daemonolatry; Goetia; The Black Goddess; Ligeia; Ghoul Mistress; My Corpse, My Groom; A Valkyrie's Vendetta; The Rotting Goddess; Nyarlathotep; On a Dreamland's Moon; Nitokris; Winter Witch; The Necro-Conjuring Sorceress; Narda the Czarina; Castle Csejthe; Painted in Blood; Bathory in Red; I. Nadia; II. Bat in the Boiler Room; III. Black Orchid; IV. The Power of the Sun; Blood Siren's Alcove; Anthropomancy; Carathis; Twisted Trails of Thought; Lady in Black Velvet; Mircalla; With a Love So Vile; The Easter Lily; Even Madness Cannot Hide; Horror; The Medallion; Ilvaa; Saturn; Vexteria; A Sorceress's Final Vision; TRIBUTES; A Page From Jack's Diary, by Adam Bolivar; My Lady of the Nightshade Flower, by K. A. Opperman; Upon Reading Diary of a Sorceress, by Michael Fantina; Ashiel's Garden, by D. L. Myers. Afterword; Acknowledgments.

Notes. Cover and interior illustrations by Steve Santiago. The first poetry collection by a dynamic young poet whose metrical precision and ability to enliven classic weird tropes are enviable.

209.   FRED PHILLIPS. *Winds from Sheol.* 2017. 138 pp. tpb.

Contents. Introduction, by Ann K. Schwader; Shadow over Arkham; By the Book; Song of October; Saruman; Grandsire's Tomes; Jehan; Ballade de Guerre Pennsique Troixieme; In Elder Days; Arboreal Conclave; The Worms Forget; Cronesong; A Dirge at Autumn; Fafia; The Gathering of the Storm; Inn of Memories; A Limerick; To Serve the King at Gondor; A Link; Sita of Oudh; Myn Lyst; The Homeward Pilgrim: A Legend of the Yule; Roads; A Hand Stronger Than Steel;

Blade of Barmuzil; Persistence; Summation; Au Revoir; An Answer to J. W. Riley's "When the Frost Is on the Pumpkin"; Hymn to Thanatos; Abandoned Church: Arkham; Strangers in a Strange Land; Night Hobbies; Pay Attention, Jon; Eomer's Song; The Celeano Fragments, LXII:3; Hallowe'en; For Permanent Residents of Middle-Earth; Autumn Song; In the Pavilion of Iskander; Guruji Aesclapion; The Tale of Muharlal Mun; Visitor; A Sequel to "Old Christmas" by H. P. Lovecraft; The Final Word; The Lay of the Last Bard; Shadow of the North; Faerie Song; Conundrum; Tribute; Legacy of Goldstadt; The Ballad of the Snow-Elves; Secret Passage; Master and Pupil; Paean to Duchess Ysabeau; Der Brüder Unbekennt; There and Home Again; Omnes Spectatores Assentiant; Judgment; Elrond and Celeglas: A Chance Meeting between Two Theoretically Opposed Elvish Heralds; Misty Hills; Then and Now; The Visitors; Second Thoughts; Homage; Tom Byro; Poojaree and Sheir-Khan: The Tale of the Priest and the Tiger; Many Happy Returns; Pivrarcha; Rendezvous; Hymn to Odin; The Song of the Haqqim; Reminiscence; A Dream of Faerie; Orison to Ra; Bedmates; Reward; Meditation; Ostrgard; The Wanderer's Lay; Magister; To Jon Singer; On Returning from a Pennsic War; To Derrick Hussey; Frederic the Silent Held in Durance Vile by His Lady; Looking Backwards; A Maiden's Song; The Voyage of Randolph Carter; Again a Quest; A Song of Fall; The Launching of the Glen Carrig; Dim Horizon; From the Uncollected "Tales of an Old Tavern"; Solitude.

Notes. Cover illustration by William Blake, "The Whirlwind of Lovers" (c. 1826). Interior art by the poet. A second poetry collection by the venerable New York poet, fully equal to its predecessor (see item 84).

210.   *Dead Reckonings* No. 22 (Fall 2017). EDITED BY ALEX HOUSTOUN AND MICHAEL J. ABOLAFIA. 116 pp.

Contents. Hallowed Readings for Hallowe'en, by Greg Gbur [Ellen Datlow and Lisa Morton, ed. *Haunted Nights*]; A Few Reflections, by Martin Andersson; The Creature That Lives in the Dark, by S. T. Joshi [Ramsey Campbell, *Born to the Dark*]; Worthy Wordsmithery, by Tony Fonseca [Jason V Brock, *The Dark Sea Within: Tales & Poems*]; A Visitor to Arkham, by Ramsey Campbell; A Journey Beyond All Journeys, by Donald Sidney-Fryer; Curating Ars Necronomica 2017, by Brian L. Mullen III; The Wonders of the Visible Weird: Ars Necronomica 2017 and Guest of Honor, John Jude Palencar, by Dave Felton; An Artist's Dreamworld Incantation: The Work of John Jude Palencar, by Michelle Y. Souliere; FOREVER and a Day, by Jason V Brock [Darrell Schweitzer, *The Threshold of Forever: Essays and Reviews*]; The History of the Horror Fiction Boom in the 1970s and '80s, by Stephanie Graves [Grady Hendrix, *Paperbacks from Hell: The Twisted History of '70s and '80s Horror Fiction*]; Musings: NecronomiCon 2017, by Alex Smith; In the Wild Beast Wood: The Triad of Mystery in the Artwork of Sidney H. Sime, by Daniel Pietersen; Horrors of the Everyday Life, by June Pulliam [Jordan Peele, dir., *Get Out*; Brian Falchuck and Ryan Murphy, FX *AHS: Cult*]; A Century Too Late, by Tony Fonseca [Sam Gafford, *The Dreamer in Fire and Other Stories*]; Standing Behind the Curtains: A Conversation with T. E. D. Klein, by Barry Lee Dejasu; Uncanny Age: Joachim Kalka's Gaslight, by James Machin [Joachim Kalka (tr. Isabel Fargo Cole), *Gaslight: Lantern Slides from the Nineteenth Century*]; A Mixed Bag, by S. T. Joshi [Justin Steele and Sam Cowan, ed., *Looming Low, Volume 1*]; The Art of NecronomiCon, by Dean Kuhta; Ghosts, Beyond Metaphor and Psychopathology, by Jim Rockhill [Zöe Lehmann Imfield, *The Victorian Ghost Story and Theology*]; The Weird and Eerie in Finest Form, by Daniel Pietersen [Jeffrey Thomas, *Haunted Worlds*]; Panels of People Screaming: An Interview with Sarah Horrocks, by Nathan Chazan; Vibrant and Vivid: NecronomiCon 2017, by Elena Tchougounova-Paulson; Nevertheless, She Persisted, by Bev Vincent [Stephen King and Owen King, *Sleeping Beauties*]; Thinking Visually: Comments on Comics, by Alex Houstoun; Revisiting the Dreamlands, by Darrell Schweitzer [Kij Johnson, *The Dream-Quest of Vellitt Boe*]; A Reflection: NecronomiCon 2017, by Dr. Géza A. G. Reilly; About the Contributors.

211. S. T. JOSHI AND DAVID E. SCHULTZ. *Lovecraft's Library: A Catalogue.* 4th rev. ed. 2017. 201 pp. tpb.

Contents. Introduction; Explanatory Notes; Lovecraft's Library [1085 titles]; Weird &c. Items in Library of H. P. Lovecraft; INDICES: A. Names; B. Titles; C. Works by Lovecraft; D. Publishers; E. Subjects.

Notes. Another edition of this important reference work, adding dozens of titles not previously known to be part of Lovecraft's library.

212. *Spectral Realms* No. 8 (Winter 2018). EDITED BY S. T. JOSHI. 128 pp.

Contents. POEMS: Through Druid Oaks, by Leigh Blackmore; Belladonna, by Abigail Wildes; The Flitter-Bird and the Bloom of Doom, by Richard L. Tierney; Dr. Cat Tree, by Jessica Amanda Salmonson; The Nightmares, by Wade German; The Voice of the *Mary Celeste*, by M. F. Webb; A Longer Winter, by Benjamin Blake; Succubus Waltz, by Joshua Gage; A Witch's Memoir, by Ashley Dioses; A Frenzy of Witches, by David Barker; The Girl and Her Wolf Dog, by Christina

Sng; The Vortex That Ate Poseidonis, by Manuel Pérez-Campos; Fleeting Existence, by J. T. Edwards; Terrarium, by Oliver Smith; The Return, by Ian Futter; Gas Giant, by F. J. Bergmann; The Spirit of the Place, by Liam Garriock; Red, by Mary Krawczak Wilson; The Old Courthouse, by Don Webb; The Black Hunt, by Adam Bolivar; Forever the Covens Break Us, by Claire Smith; Lycanthrope Moon, by Frank Coffman; Look Beyond, by Darrell Schweitzer; Pumpkin, Oh Pumpkin!, by Will Hart; The World Turns, by Kendall Evans; Looking After Death, by John Reinhart; The King of Horrors, Howard Phillips Lovecraft, by Charles Lovecraft; The Scrying Mirror, by Chelsea Arrington; Desert Witch, by Rob Matheny; The Milk Hare, by David Barker; The Fetch, by K. A. Opperman; Nosferatu, by David Schembri; Hiding the Corpse, by Shawn Ramsey; The Final Masquerade, by Alan Gullette; A Modern Exorcism, by Ian Futter; The Vellum of the Damned, by Joshua Gage; Berserker, by Benjamin Blake; When We Fall, by Christina Sng; Mama Drool, by Ross Balcom; Germina Amoris, by Oliver Smith; The Ballad of 3 A.M., by M. F. Webb; Past, Present, and Future, by Liam Garriock; Odd Todd, by Jessica Amanda Salmonson; The Waning Hours of Woe, by J. T. Edwards; Sea Creatures, by Mary Krawczak Wilson; Stanzas of the Metaphysical Student Found in a Notebook, by Manuel Pérez-Campos; The Sudden Raving of a Quiet One, by John Shirley; Procession of the Expendable, by David Barker; The Stalking Horror, by Frank Coffman; Memoirs in the Dark, by Christina Sng; Facing the Demon, by Ian Futter; Volunteers, by Ann K. Schwader; Hollow of the Night, by F. J. Bergmann; CLASSIC REPRINTS: The Death Angel, by Farnsworth Wright; To a Young Murderess, by Arthur O'Shaughnessy; ARTICLES: Verse vs. Free Verse, by Frank Coffman; REVIEWS: The Exquisite Nightmares of Christina Sng, by Sunni K Brock [Christina Sng, *A Collection of Nightmares*]; Of Femmes Fatales and Lost Worlds, by Leigh Blackmore [Michael Fantina, *Alchemy of Dreams and Other Poems*]; Notes on Contributors.

Notes. Cover illustration by Mutartis Boswell.

213.   E. NESBIT. *From the Dead: The Complete Weird Stories of E. Nesbit.* Edited by S. T. Joshi. 2018. 263 pp. tpb.

Contents. Introduction, by S. T. Joshi; FROM THE DEAD: John Charrington's Wedding; The Ebony Frame; The Mass for the Dead; From the Dead; Uncle Abraham's Romance; The Mystery of the Semi-Detached; Man-Size in Marble; Hurst of Hurstcote; The Power of Darkness; The Shadow; The Head; The Three Drugs; In the Dark; The New Samson; Number 17; The Five Senses; The Violet Car;

The Haunted House; The Pavilion; APPENDIX: From *My School-Days*; Part IV: In the Dark; Part V. The Mummies at Bordeaux. Bibliography.

Notes. Cover illustration by Aeron Alfrey. Cover design and custom title font by Daniel V. Sauer. The first volume of a new series, Classics of Gothic Horror. The first eight volumes were compiled for Joe Morey's Dark Renaissance Books, but his retirement from publishing derailed the series. The editor is grateful to Derrick Hussey for picking it up.

214.   MARY E. WILKINS FREEMAN. *Lost Ghosts: The Complete Weird Stories of Mary E. Wilkins Freeman.* Edited by S. T. Joshi. 2018. 355 pp. tpb.

Contents. Introduction, by S. T. Joshi; A Symphony in Lavender; A Far-Away Melody; A Gentle Ghost; The Twelfth Guest; The Little Maid at the Door; Silence; The White Witch; The School-Teacher's Story; The Prism; The Wind in the Rose-Bush; The Vacant Lot; Luella Miller; The Shadows on the Wall; The Hall Bedroom; The Southwest Chamber; The Lost Ghost; The Witch's Daughter; The Jade Bracelet; Giles Corey, Yeoman; Bibliography.

Notes. Cover illustration by Aeron Alfrey. Cover design and custom title font by Daniel V. Sauer. The second volume in the Classics of Gothic Horror series. It contains a play about the Salem witch trials, *Giles Corey, Yeoman,* which is not supernatural but is of interest in any event. Due to a fortuitous mischance, the book's cover was printed with a matte (rather than glossy) finish; subsequently, all even-numbered books in the series followed suit.

215.   *Dead Reckonings* No. 23 (Spring 2018). EDITED BY ALEX HOUSTOUN AND MICHAEL J. ABOLAFIA. 134 pp.

Contents. Introduction to Japanese Vampire Fiction, by Darrell Schweitzer, [Kazuki Sakuraba, *A Small Charred Face*]; The Coming Singer: Early Critical Responses to Clark Ashton Smith, by Scott Connors; Who Is Dr. Prozess?, by S. T. Joshi [Mark Samuels, *The Prozess Manifestations*]; Dreams of a Particular Place: Karin Tidbeck's *Jagannath*, by Dr. Géza A. G. Reilly; Dreams of the House of the Worm: Gary Myers's Debut Dreamlands Story, by Nicholas Diak; Ramsey's Rant: Honoured by Horror, by Ramsey Campbell; Undertow Publications: An Interview with Michael Kelly, by Daniel Pietersen; Ghosts and Critics Hand in Hand, by Jim Rockhill [Scott Brewster and Luke Thurston, ed., *The Routledge Handbook to the Ghost Story*]; Spoken Art: Cadabra Record's "The Bungalow House" LP, by Sam

Cowan; Justified Obscurity, by Ryne Davis [Seabury Quinn, *The Complete Tales of Jules De Grandin: The Horror on the Links—Volume 1*]; "I'm sorry. You ate my cat": A Fond Look at *Stranger Things 2*, by Hank Wagner and Bev Vincent; James Ulmer: An Exponent of Quiet Horror, by S. T. Joshi [James Ulmer, *The Fire Doll: Stories*]; Visions of the Abyss, by Christopher Ropes [Matthew M. Bartlett, *The Stay-Awake Men*]; *Mantid*: An Interview with Farah Rose Smith, by Alex Houstoun; Considering an Overlooked Jewel, by Jason V Brock [Darrell Schweitzer. *Awaiting Strange Gods: Weird and Lovecraftian Fiction*]; Drabbles of Dread, by Dave Felton [Brandy Yassa, ed., *100 Word Horrors: An Anthology of Horror Drabbles*]; The Theory and Practice of Satirical Criticism, by S. T. Joshi; Clive Barker: A Boy & His Rawhead, An Analysis of the Story and the Film, by Randall D. Larson; A Letter Concerning Things Past, by Acep Hale [*Der Orchideengarten*, ed. Alf Von Czibulka, tr. Helen Grant]; Tested Patience, by June Pulliam [Duane Pesice, ed., *Test Patterns*, Volume 1]; The Banality of Our Bureaucracies, by Javier Martinez [Bentley Little, *The Handyman*]; A Dark, Intense, Fantastic Debut, by Greg Gbur [Nadia Bulkin, *She Said Destroy: Stories*]; About the Contributors.

216.   S. T. JOSHI. *What Is Anything? Memoirs of a Life in Lovecraft.* 2018. 346 pp. hc + 6 pp. of photographs.

Contents. Preface; 1. From India to Illinois (1958–68); 2. Indiana I (1968–72); 3. Indiana II (1972–76); 4. Brown (1976–80); 5. Brown and Princeton (1980–84); 6. Chelsea House I (1984–90); 7. Chelsea House II (1990–95); 8. New York (1995–2001); 9. Seattle I (2001–05); 10. Moravia (2005–08); 11. Seattle II (2008–12); 12. Seattle III (2012–18); Epilogue; Index.

Notes. Cover illustration by Jason C. Eckhardt. A volume written to commemorate Joshi's sixtieth birthday on June 22, 2018, and officially released on that date, at a star-studded Manhattan event dubbed JoshiCon. The book focuses on Joshi's literary career and only treats sporadically of his personal life. Printed in a limited edition (250 copies) by Covington Group.

217.   THOMAS BURKE. *Johnson Looked Back: The Collected Weird Stories of Thomas Burke.* Edited by S. T. Joshi. 2018. 292 pp. tpb.

Contents. Introduction, by S. T. Joshi; The Bird; The Tablets of the House of Li; The Bloomsbury Wonder; The Hands of Mr. Ottermole; Desirable Villa; The Secret of Francesco Shedd; The Yellow Imps; Miracle in Suburbia; Yesterday Street; Funspot; Uncle Ezekiel's Long Sight; The Horrible God; Father and Son; Johnson Looked Back; Two

Gentlemen; The Black Courtyard; The Gracious Ghosts; Jack Wapping; One Hundred Pounds; The Man Who Lost His Head; Murder under the Crooked Spire; The Lonely Inn; The Watcher; Events at Wayless-Wagtail; The Hollow Man; The Golden Gong; Bibliography.

Notes. Cover illustration by Aeron Alfrey. Cover design and custom title font by Daniel V. Sauer. The third volume in the Classics of Gothic Horror series, reprinting the tales from Burke's rare volume *Night-Pieces* (1935) along with much other work.

218.   W. W. JACOBS. *Twin Spirits: The Complete Weird Stories of W. W. Jacobs.* Edited by S. T. Joshi. 2018. 268 pp. tpb.

Contents. Introduction, by S. T. Joshi; A Strange Compact; The Lost Ship; In Mid-Atlantic; The Rival Beauties; The Brown Man's Servant; Over the Side; Jerry Bundler; Three at Table; The Well; Twin Spirits; Captain Rogers; In the Library; The Monkey's Paw; The Castaway; The Toll-House; The Vigil; The Three Sisters; Sam's Ghost; His Brother's Keeper; The Interruption; APPENDIX: The Ghost of Jerry Bundler, by W. W. Jacobs and Charles Rock; In the Library, by W. W. Jacobs and Herbert C. Sargent; The Monkey's Paw: A Story in Three Scenes, by Louis N. Parker; Bibliography.

Notes. Cover illustration by Aeron Alfrey. Cover design and custom title font by Daniel V. Sauer. The fourth volume in the Classics of Gothic Horror series. The editor canvassed the entirety of Jacobs's work, since many of his short story collections contained one or two weird specimens, well beyond the familiar anthology chestnut "The Monkey's Paw."

219.   JAMES CHAMBERS, APRIL GREY, AND ROBERT MASTERSON, EDITORS. *A New York State of Fright: Horror Stories from the Empire State.* 2018. 334 pp. tpb.

Contents. Introduction, by James Chambers; Heels, by Alp Beck; East Side Devil, by John C. Foster; Loathsome in New York, by Monica O'Rourke; The Chosen Place, by Patrick Freivald; The Hunting of the Kipsy: A Cryptozoological Report, by Hal Johnson; A Few Leaves from the Travelogue of Doctor Julius Jonsson, Cryptobotanist and Hylesoprotolist: Bay Ridge, or, The Belief in the Undead Still Exists in New York, by Erik T. Johnson; A Nightmare on 34th Street, by Steven Van Patten; Hurricane Zelda, Part IV, by Kathleen Scheiner; Shoal, by Trevor Firetog; The Insects of Seneca Village, by Jeff C. Stevenson; The Grim, by Allan Burd; In A Pig's Eye, by Teel James Glenn; Welcome to Brooklyn, Gabe, by Marc Abbott; Machine

Gun/Latté, by Amy Grech; The Spouting Devil, by Meghan Arcuri; Rescue Shelter, by David Sakmyster; Blood Will Tell, by JG Faherty; The Lady in the Sideshow: A Circuspunk Story, by Charie D. La Marr; Pink Elephants: A Murphy's Lore Tale, by Patrick Thomas; Everybody Wins, by Lisa Mannetti; Edna's Soul Kitchen, by Elizabeth Crowens; Eyes Left, by Jack Ketchum and Edward Lee; Tales of the White Street Society: The Hairy Ghost, by Grady Hendrix; The Long Lost and Forgotten, by J. Daniel Stone; About the Authors.

Notes. Cover illustration and design by Joseph Sigillo. A charity volume compiled by members of the New York chapter of the Horror Writers Association to support New York City's Girls Write Now non-profit organization. Many contributors attended the release party in Manhattan, held as part of Necropolis, a monthly event.

220. *Lovecraft Annual* No. 12 (2018). EDITED BY S. T. JOSHI. 197 pp.

Contents. The Melancholia of H. P. Lovecraft's "The Music of Erich Zann," by James Goho; Feminine Powerlessness and Deference in *The Case of Charles Dexter Ward*, by Cecelia Hopkins-Drewer; Ravening for Delight: Unusual Descriptions in Lovecraft, by Duncan Norris; Where Lovecraft Lost His Telescope: His Kingston and the Towns around It, by Robert H. Waugh; Why Michel Houellebecq Is Wrong about Lovecraft's Racism, by S. T. Joshi; "Whaddya Make Them Eyes at Me For?": Lovecraft and Book Publishers, by David E. Schultz; Two Centenaries: H. P. Lovecraft and Elsa Gidlow, by Kenneth W. Faig, Jr.; *2001: A Lovecraftian Odyssey*, by Michael D. Miller; That Fool Olson, by Bobby Derie; A Placid Island: H. P. Lovecraft's "Ibid," by Francesco Borri; Lovecraft, Aristeas, Dunsany, and the Dream Journey, by Darrell Schweitzer; H. P. Lovecraft—Beacon and Gateway, by Donald Sidney-Fryer; *The Void:* A Lovecraftian Analysis, by Duncan Norris; Howard Phillips Lovecraft: Romantic on the Nightside, by Jan B. W. Pedersen; How to Read Lovecraft: A Column, by Steven J. Mariconda; REVIEWS: [Review of H. P. Lovecraft, *Letters to Maurice W. Moe and Others* and H. P. Lovecraft and Clark Ashton Smith, *Dawnward Spire, Lonely Hill: The Letters of H. P. Lovecraft and Clark Ashton Smith*], by Steveven j. Mariconda; [Review of Scott Cutler Shershow and Scott Michaelsen, *The Love of Ruins: Letters on Lovecraft*], by S. T. Joshi; Briefly Noted.

221. W. H. PUGMIRE AND DAVID BARKER. *Witches in Dreamland.* 2018. 190 pp. tpb.

Notes. Cover design by Daniel V. Sauer, incorporating a 19th century illustration by Berry F. Berry. A short novel set in Lovecraft's Dreamlands by a pair of authors who had done considerable collaborative work in recent years. Both authors attended the book launch, held at the H. P. Lovecraft Film Festival in Portland, OR.

222.   *Spectral Realms* No. 9 (Summer 2018). EDITED BY S. T. JOSHI. 136 pp.

Contents. POEMS: The Visionary, by Ian Futter; Final Library, by Ann K. Schwader; Flesh Flowers, by John Shirley; Forty Years in Innsmouth, by M. F. Webb; A Dream of Vengeance, by Michael Fantina; The Thing in the Forest, by Frank Coffman; The Urge to Write, by Liam Garriock; The Sorceress's Lament, by Ashley Dioses; Cornflower Valley, by Christina Sng; The Willful Child, by Fred Chappell; Cat Girl Cantata, by Michael D. Miller; A Voyage Too Far, by J. T. Edwards; Are We Not Beautiful in Our Decay?, by Allan Rozinski; The Song of the Siren, by Chelsea Arrington; Acrostic Sonnet in Memory of Providence, R.I., 8 August 1936, by Charles Lovecraft; A Bloodless Man, by Mary Krawczak Wilson; Great Mother, by David B. Harrington; Three Witches, by David Barker; Angry in His Grave, by Darrell Schweitzer; Toads, by Wade German; The Witch's Son, by Adam Bolivar; Halloween Reverie, by K. A. Opperman; Contemplate the Alchemy of Dancing Quantum Particles, by Kendall Evans; Rek-Cocci Stirs, by Scott J. Couturier; The Loved, by Ian Futter; Antarktos Sequence, by Manuel Pérez-Campos; On a Poet's 80th Birthday, by Leigh Blackmore; *Spectral Realms:* An Homage, by Frank Coffman; The Angel's Pen, by Charles D. O'Connor III; Gautier Ghost Story, by Chad Hensley; Lucifer Romantico, by Tatiana; We Are the Owls, by Jessica Amanda Salmonson; Thalía, by Manuel Arenas; The Wendigo, by Michelle Jeffrey; She's a Legend: A Song Sung by the Unsung, by John Shirley; Elegy for Futurism, by Liam Garriock; Spectral Noir, by Deborah L. Davitt; Graveyard Feline Morning, by Benjamin Blake; The Vampire's Mother, by Christina Sng; The Dark Reclaims Us, by Ann K. Schwader; The Unseen, by Mary Krawczak Wilson; The Last God, by David Barker; Night Thoughts of a Nonentity, by Manuel Pérez-Campos; When Black Tom Came, by Scott J. Couturier; Scholar and Sorcerer: For S. T. Joshi, on His 60th Birthday (22 June 2018), by Michael Fantina; Flowers from Another World, by Kendall Evans; Dark Entry IV, by Chad Hensley; The Last Illusion of Robert Houdin, by Jessica Amanda Salmonson; On Wings of Fire, by David B. Harrington; The Merman, by Tatiana; Of Hooves and Horns, by Michelle Jeffrey; *Weird Tales,* the First Run: An Homage, by Frank Coffman; In Ligno, by Deborah L. Davitt; When Nightfall Comes to Ooth-Nargai, by Manuel Pérez-Campos; The Mermaid, by Christina Sng; The Autumn

Sphinx, by Liam Garriock; CLASSIC REPRINTS: The Creaking Door, by Madison Cawein; The Fairy Changeling, by Dora Sigerson Shorter; ARTICLES: Clark Ashton Smith and Robert Nelson: Master and Apprentice (Part 1), by Marcos Legaria; REVIEWS: In the Footsteps of the Masters, by Donald Sidney-Fryer [Henry J, Vester III, *Of Mist and Crystal: Selected Poetry*]; A New Formalist, by Frank Coffman [Ashley Dioses, *Diary of a Sorceress*]; Drowning in Delicious Weird, by Russ Parkhurst [Adam Bolivar, *The Lay of Old Hex*]; Musings Philosophical and Religious, by Donald Sidney-Fryer [Alan Gullette, *Reviving a Dead Priest*]; Notes on Contributors.

Notes. Cover illustration and design by Daniel V. Sauer.

223.   H. P. LOVECRAFT. *Letters to Maurice W. Moe and Others*. Edited by David E. Schultz and S. T. Joshi. 2018. 622 pp. tpb.

Contents. Introduction; LETTERS: To Maurice W. Moe; To Robert E. Moe; To Bernard Austin Dwyer; To Samuel Loveman; To Vincent Starrett; APPENDIX: *Maurice W. Moe:* Why I Am Not a Freethinker; The Church and the World; Life for God's Sake; Looking Backward; "Once an Amateur, Always an Amateur"; First Steps in the Appreciation of Poetry; Maurice W. Moe on Amateur Criticism; Through the Eyes of the Poet; Imagism; Literary Appreciation; From Poem Comments; From Imagery Aids; Introduction to Poetry; In a Sequestered Churchyard Where Once Poe Walked; Edwin and the Red Knight; Seven O'Clock; *Bernard Austin Dwyer:* Ol' Black Sarah; Beautiful Night; Fairies; The Snake-God; Letters to Weird Tales; Quinn's Masterpiece; A de Grandin Movie; Who Is This Gal?; Letter to Strange Tales; "Oy! Oy! Oy!"; *Samuel Loveman:* Collecting Curious Books; A Conversation with Ambrose Bierce; A Holiday Post-Card; The Coast of Bohemia; A Whittier Discovery; [Untitled]; *Vincent Starrett:* [a letter to Samuel Loveman]. Glossary of Frequently Mentioned Names; Bibliography; Index.

Notes. Cover design by Anastasia Damianakos. Complete publication, for the first time, of the letters to Moe and Dwyer, with exhaustive annotations and ancillary material. The Three Stooges font used on the cover was chosen as an in-joke related to MWM's distinctive last name.

224.   THÉOPHILE GAUTIER. *The Mummy's Foot and Other Fantastic Tales*. Edited by S. T. Joshi. 2018. 419 pp. tpb.

Contents. Introduction, by S. T. Joshi; Omphale: A Rococo Story; Clarimonde; One of Cleopatra's Nights; The Mummy's Foot; Arria

Marcella: A Souvenir of Pompeii; Avatar; Jettatura; Spirite: A Fantastic Tale.

Notes. Cover illustration by Aeron Alfrey. Cover design and custom title font by Daniel V. Sauer. The fifth volume in the Classics of Gothic Horror series, containing Lafcadio Hearn's translation of *One of Cleopatra's Nights and Other Fantastic Romances* (1882), Edgar Saltus's translation of *Avatar,* and other works.

225.   MARY SHELLEY. *Frankenstein and Others: The Complete Weird Fiction of Mary Shelley.* Edited by S. T. Joshi. 2018. 281 pp. tpb.

Contents. Introduction, by S. T. Joshi; *Frankenstein; or, The Modern Prometheus;* Valerius: The Reanimated Roman; Roger Dodsworth: The Reanimated Englishman; Transformation; The Invisible Girl; The Mortal Immortal; Bibliography.

Notes. Cover illustration by Aeron Alfrey. Cover design and custom title font by Daniel V. Sauer. The sixth volume in the Classics of Gothic Horror series, timed for the 200th anniversary of the publication of *Frankenstein.*

226.   *Dead Reckonings* No. 24 (Fall 2018). EDITED BY ALEX HOUSTOUN AND MICHAEL J. ABOLAFIA. 99 pp.

Contents. A Feast in Small Bites, by Géza A. G. Reilly [Robert Aickman, *Compulsory Games*]; Alive with Darkness, by S. T. Joshi [Ramsey Campbell, *By the Light of My Skull* and *The Way of the Worm*]; God Is a Disease: The Mystic Exile of Andrzej Zulawski's *Possession,* by Nathan Chazan; Full House, by Hank Wagner [Darrell Schweitzer, *The Dragon House*]; Ringing in Apocalypse, by Christopher Ropes [David Peak, *Corpsepaint*]; Reflections on ICFA 39, by J. T. Glover; Ramsey's Rant: A Modicum of Blood, by Ramsey Campbell; What Is Anything When Considered Twice?: Existential Remembrance, by Donald Sidney-Fryer, and All He Cared to Tell, by Géza A. G. Reilly [S. T. Joshi, *What Is Anything?: Memoirs of a Life in Lovecraft*]; The Case for *Weird Tales* Replicas, by Ryne Davis; Transformative Visions, by Acep Hale [Priya Sharma, *All the Fabulous Beasts*]; A Visionary Work Renew'd, by Sam Gafford and The joey Zone [William Hope Hodgson, *The House on the Borderland,* illustrated by John Coulthart]; Adam Nevill: The Sense of Dread, by S. T. Joshi; Horrifying Abnormality of the Mundane, by Fiona Maeve Geist [Tim Waggoner, *Dark and Distant Voices: A Story Collection*]; Stephen King: Fast Food or Five Star?, by James Arthur Anderson; Signs of a Young Horror Master, by Leigh Blackmore [Josh Malerman, *Goblin: A Novel in Six Novellas*]; When Unreality Becomes Too Unreal, by Darrell Schweitzer [Josh Malerman, *Unbury Carol*]; The Beauty and Horror of Home, by Javier Martinez [Andrew Michael Hurley, *Devil's Day*]; Realities Other Than the Ordinary, by Peter Cannon [Henry Wessells, *A Conversation Larger than the Universe: Readings in Science Fiction and the Fantastic 1762–2017*]; About the Contributors.

227.   *Clark Ashton Smith: The Emperor of Dreams.* Directed by Darin Coelho Spring. Ur Films, 2018. 110 min + special features (7 min). DVD and BluRay; streaming platforms.

Contents. [Prologue]; The Star-Treader: 1893–1926; Hyperborea Beyond Hyperborea: 1927–1937; The Sorcerer Departs: 1938–1961. Special features.

Notes. Cover illustration by Skinner. Cover and insert card design by Daniel V. Sauer. A feature-length documentary focusing on the life and work of the Bard of Auburn, and containing interviews with Harlan Ellison, Cody Goodfellow, S. T. Joshi, Donald Sidney-Fryer, Skinner, W. H. Pugmire, and others. Special features included readings of Smith's poems by Ashley Dioses, K. A. Opperman, and Charles Schneider. The film premiered at the H. P. Lovecraft Film Festival, Portland, OR, with regional premieres in New York City, Providence, RI, Auburn, CA, and Stockholm, Sweden. The soundtrack, featuring music composed by Jacob Mingle, Peter Scartabello, and others, was released by Cadabra Records.

228.   *Spectral Realms* No. 10 (Winter 2019). EDITED BY S. T. JOSHI. 151 pp.

Contents. POEMS: The Name on the Grave, by Thomas Tyrrell; Eurynomos, by Wade German; Winter, by Charles D. O'Connor III; Conjuring in Cupid's Garden, by Claire Smith; The Haunting Bones, by Adam Bolivar; The Island, by Christina Sng; The Promise of Eternity, by Kurt Newton; Salem Liberation, by Manuel Pérez-Campos; Herpetology, by F. J. Bergmann; The Witches' Rite at Beltane, by Frank Coffman; The Old Ones: A Ghazal, by Joshua Gage; Last Ascent, by Ann K. Schwader; Morbidezza, by Manuel Arenas; Life Decayed, by Ashley Dioses; Lord of Pumpkins, by Scott J. Couturier; Nighttime Visitor Where Cats Prowl, by Randall D. Larson; Unnatural Man, by Mary Krawczak Wilson; One Who Walks Alone, by Carl E. Reed; When the Nightwind Howls, by Leigh Blackmore; Going Forth by Night, by Margi Curtis; After the Cryptozoic, by Kendall Evans; The Assignment, by Liam Garriock; A Ride in Hilo, by Chad Hensley; Supernumerary, by Mike Allen and S. Brackett Robertson; Bathysphere, by Oliver Smith;

The Forsaken Idol, by David Barker; In the Garden of Thasaidon, by Jeff Hall; The Dark King, by Allan Rozinski; The Offspring, by Barbara Barrett; The Mirror of Arkham Woe, by Manuel Pérez-Campos; The Driver of the Dragon's Coach, by Wade German; Mad Jack-a-Lee, by Adam Bolivar; The Dutchman, by Frank Coffman; The Light at the End of the Tunnel, by Christina Sng; Gargoyle, by Manuel Arenas; To a Black Hole, by Charles Lovecraft; All Will Taste Death, by Ross Balcom; The Birth of Brahma, by Rich Catalano; The Frightful Ballad of the Third Lord Boyce, by Thomas Tyrrell; Maculation, by F. J. Bergmann; Bone Riders, by Kurt Newton; From Spectral Realms, by Leigh Blackmore; Inescapable Horror, by Liam Garriock; Forbidden Fruit, by Scott J. Couturier; Factotum of the Underworld, by David Barker; The Witches' Bower, by Leigh Blackmore; Warnings to the Curious, by Frank Coffman; Winter, by Ian Futter; Chronoscape Advisory, by Manuel Pérez-Campos; Lazarus Laments, by Allan Rozinski; CLASSIC REPRINTS: The Deserted House, by Lizette Woodworth Reese; The Dark House, by Edwin Arlington Robinson; ARTICLES: Clark Ashton Smith and Robert Nelson: Master and Apprentice (Part 2), by Marcos Legaria; REVIEWS: Witches, Traditional and Otherwise, by Leigh Blackmore [Ashley Dioses, ed., *Eye to the Telescope* No. 30]; A Poetic Original, by Donald Sidney-Fryer [G. Sutton breiding, *Ill Desperado, 2013/2014*]; Notes on Contributors; Index to *Spectral Realms* 1–10.

Notes. Cover illustration by Kim Bo Yung.

229. *Dead Reckonings* No. 25 (Spring 2019). EDITED BY ALEX HOUSTOUN AND MICHAEL J. ABOLAFIA. 97 pp.

Contents. A Look Behind "The Challenge from Beyond," by Michael D. Miller; Finding the Everything in Nothing, by Christopher Ropes [Simon Strantzas, *Nothing Is Everything*]; Weird Fiction and Decadence, by S. T. Joshi [James Machin, *Weird Fiction in Britain 1880–1939*]; That Is Not How the Story Goes, by Bev Vincent [Theodora Goss, *Snow White Learns Witchcraft: Stories and Poems*]; Sesqua Valley's Weirdest Inhabitant, Wilum Pugmire, by David Barker; Ramsey's Rant: Horror versus Horror, by Ramsey Campbell; Marvelous Milicent: The Rise and Removal of a Monster-Artist Maven, by Danel Olson [Mallory O'Meara, *The Lady from the Black Lagoon: Hollywood Monsters and the Lost Legacy of Milicent Patrick*]; Maybe Johnny Is an Old One? *The Room* as Lovecraftian Pastiche, by Edward Guimont; Weird Fiction in the 21st Century: A Conversation with S. T. Joshi, by Alex Houstoun; Rediscovering Ken Greenhall, by Darrell Schweitzer [Ken Greenhall, *Elizabeth; Hell Hound;* and *Childgrave*]; Some Notes on *Call of Cthulhu* and Other Lovecraftian Video

Games, by Géza A. G. Reilly [*Call of Cthulhu: The Official Video Game*]; Running toward Nothing: B. Catling's Vorrh Trilogy, by Daniel Pietersen [B. Catling, *The Vorrh*; *The Erstwhile*; and *The Cloven*]; The Horror of Mendacity, by Acep Hale [Daniel Powell, *Horror Culture in the New Millennium: Digital Dissonance and Technohorror*]; Marvelous Monsters, by Hank Wagner [Anya Martin, *Sleeping with the Monster*]; Men Kill Women Like Me, by Fiona Maeve Geist [Farah Rose Smith, *Anonyma*]; Meditations on the Agnostic Gothic, by Karen Joan Kohoutek; About the Contributors.

230.   JOHN LANGAN. *Sefira and Other Betrayals*. 2019. 351 pp. hc & tpb.

Contents. Introduction, by Paul Tremblay; Sefira; In Paris, in the Mouth of Kronos; The Third Always Beside You; The Unbearable Proximity of Mr. Dunn's Balloons; Bloom; Renfrew's Course; Bor Urus; At Home in the House of the Devil; Story Notes; Acknowledgments; Publication History.

Notes. Cover illustration by Santiago Caruso. Cover design by Daniel V. Sauer. A long delayed follow-up to Langan's highly successful collection *The Wide, Carnivorous Sky* (item 120), containing both uncollected and unpublished stories. Published simultaneously in paperback and hardcover (500 copies, Covington Group). The hardcover was sent to advance subscribers for the paperback as a reward for their patience. Starred review *in Publishers Weekly*, only the second Hippocampus title to be so honored (after item 39, above). Bram Stoker Award nominee for Superior Achievement in a Fiction Collection. Winner of the This Is Horror Award for short story collection of the year.

231.   BOBBY DERIE. *Weird Talers: Essays on Robert E. Howard and Others*. 2019. 352 pp. tpb.

Contents: Introduction; Howard, Lovecraft, and "The Sin-Eater"; The Shadow out of Spain; The Mirror of E'ch-Pi-El: Robert E. Howard in the Letters of H. P. Lovecraft; Fragments from the Lost Letters of H. P. Lovecraft to Robert E. Howard; Dear Bob; Cordially Yours, Clark Ashton Smith; *Ebony and Crystal*: Robert E. Howard, Clark Ashton Smith, and Fraternal Good Wishes; That Fool Olson; Conan and the Dweller: Robert E. Howard and William Lumley; Conan and Canevin: Robert E. Howard and Henry S. Whitehead; Friend of a Friend: Robert E. Howard and Frank Belknap Long; Weird Talers: Robert E. Howard and Seabury Quinn; Conan and the OAK: Robert E. Howard and Otis Adelbert Kline; A Lost Weird Anthology, 1930–

1933; A Lost Correspondence: Robert E. Howard and Stuart M. Boland; The Two Bobs: Robert E. Howard and Robert H. Barlow; Conan and the Acolyte: Robert E. Howard and F. T. Laney; Fan Mail: Prohibition in "The Souk"; Fan Mail: Robert Bloch vs. Conan; First Fans: Robert E. Howard and Emil Petaja; An Irreparable Loss: Robert E. Howard and *Weird Tales*, 1936; Robert E. Howard and the Amateur Press; Robert E. Howard in Mexico; F. Thurston Torbett and F. Lee Baldwin on Robert E. Howard; Robert E. Howard's Reefer Madness; Dr. Isaac M. Howard, Pellagra, and Homeopathy; Bibliography; Index.

Notes. Cover design by Daniel V. Sauer, incorporating Bobby Derie's photomontage of Robert E. Howard. A volume of essays focusing on Robert E. Howard and his colleagues, many of them having previously appeared on websites but not in print.

232. *Spectral Realms* No. 11 (Summer 2019). EDITED BY S. T. JOSHI. 143 pp.

Contents. POEMS: The Tomb of Wilum Hopfrog Pugmire, by Wade German; The Blackbird's Ghost, by Abigail Wildes; Temptation Entombed, by David Barker; Eternal Lovers, by Carl E. Reed; Gargoyle, by Manuel Arenas; On a Threadbare Photograph of H.P.L. at 66 College St., by Manuel Pérez-Campos; The Witch of Hearts, by Chelsea Arrington; The Legend of Vlad and Juztina, by Tatiana Strange; A Lady and Her Monster, by Christopher Collingwood; The Hill of Bones, by G. O. Clark; Space-Time, by Ron L. Johnson II; The Monsters Within, by Christina Sng; Doctor Fulci's Fantastic Cure for Nightmares, by Liam Garriock; Temple of the Condor, by Ann K. Schwader; Subterranean Hungers, by David C. Kopaska-Merkel; The Great Wheel, by Frank Coffman; The Necromancer's Charm, by Scott J. Couturier; Tomb without Walls, by Ross Balcom; The Final Scrawl, by Pat Calhoun; The Jack-o'-Lantern Hearted, by K. A. Opperman; The Vampire-Need, by Cecelia Hopkins-Drewer; The Duke of Balladry, by Adam Bolivar; Disclosure, by Norbert Góra; Guillotined, by Carl E. Reed; Altar of Yig, by David Barker; Poe, by Randall D. Larson; Haruspex, by Geoffrey A. Landis; The Secret Pool, by Darrell Schweitzer; As One Poet to Another, by G. Sutton Breiding; She Tasted of Gin and Death, by Curtis M. Lawson; Vampire Vigil, by Manuel Arenas; The Thing That Watches While I Write, by Thomas Tyrrell; Plague's Wake, by Ashley Dioses; To a Cat-Daemon: A Litany of Antient Ægypt, by Manuel Pérez-Campos; Methuselah, by Wade German; Cassandra Can't Tell You, by Allan Rozinski; Lair of the Bat People, by Ross Balcom; Reparation, by Christina Sng; In the

Days of the Vertical Ocean, by David C. Kopaska-Merkel; The Underwater Circus, by Kurt Newton; Super-Position, by Ron L. Johnson II; The Absence of Clouds, by G. O. Clark; Divided by Demons, by Mary Krawczak Wilson; Down the Garden Path, by M. F. Webb; The God of Phlegm, by Maxwell Gold; Cruel Eleanora, by Adam Bolivar; Tears of the Raven, by Christopher Collingwood; Graveyard of the Gods, by Scott J. Couturier; Solving for X, by Ann K. Schwader; The Demon Ball, by Tatiana Strange; The Bog Man, by Chelsea Arrington; On Gustave Moreau's Canvas *The Apparition*, by Manuel Pérez-Campos; Black-Tongue Kiss, by Carl E. Reed; Diner of Delights, by Claire Smith; Inquiry Regarding the Dead, by David Barker; Styx, by Christina Sng; The Fairiest, by Oliver Smith; The Separation, by Ian Futter; The Ghost Factory, by F. J. Bergmann; The Baleful Beldam, by Manuel Arenas; Remains, by David C. Kopaska-Merkel; CLASSIC REPRINTS: Fright, by May Sinclair; The Silent House, by Samuel John Alexander; ARTICLES: Clark Ashton Smith and Robert Nelson: Master and Apprentice (Part 3), by Marcos Legaria; REVIEWS: A Guidebook for Witches and Warlocks, by Donald Sidney-Fryer [Frank Coffman, *The Coven's Hornbook and Other Poems*]; Notes on Contributors.

Notes. Cover illustration by Daniel V. Sauer.

233.   DONALD SIDNEY-FRYER. *West of Wherevermore and Other Essays*. 2019. 254 pp. tpb.

Contents. Introduction: "West of Wherevermore"; A Trip to Southeast Asia; A Sentimental Pilgrimage to Mother Egypt; An Interlude in Central America: El Salvador; A Trip to Hawaii and Micronesia; Time-Line Night at Beyond Baroque; Surrealism Is as Surrealism Does; To the Stars and Beyond; A Journey Beyond All Journeys; Enlightenment from the Outer Dark; An Account of Donaldo's Attendance at StokerCon in Providence, R.I.; In the Footsteps of the Masters; Musings Philosophical and Religious; THE MISCELLANEON: POEMS IN VERSE AND PROSE: Apollo-Ganymede; Only Fifty Times Removed; Cet au-delà That Lies Beyond; No Escape from Vehicular Mobility; The Ministers of Chance; The Eden-Paradise That Haunts Our Undersoul; O Brave New World of Faerie Lands Forlorn; No One's Realm; Time Bomb; Some Lordly Helmet; An Achaemenian Munificence; Another Spenserian Stanza-Sonnet Once Again; Moonlight Mood; A Rendezvous in a Newer Carthage; The Black Swan with the Scarlet Bill; Old New Bedford, and Even Older; An Offering as from Afar; An Unknown Isle in 2017?; A Vagrant Vessel Plying Here and There; Return to Paradise Lost; A Victorian Poem in Redwood; An Island Is an Independent Realm; A Futuristic Icon of an Easter Island Head; Some Little Windows on the World; Winter Scene; Kaleidoscopic Odyssey; Change Is as Change Insists; The Miracle of Palm Trees in the Dusk; The Unicorn Looks at the Lady from Afar; Squirrels at Play; An Experiment in Variation; The Uplet and the Cuplet; No More of Majesty; Snowfall; A Fellow Creature on Our Planet; Needments and Oddments; The Elder Daemon. Notes, by Dlanod Yendis; Afterthoughts; Postscriptum: Cape Cod and Canal.

Notes. Cover illustration and design by Daniel V. Sauer. A fascinating collecton of Sidney-Fryer's miscellany, from travel essays to convention reports to recent poetry.

234.   MATT CARDIN. *To Rouse Leviathan.* 2019. 374 pp. tpb.

Contents. PART ONE: DIVINATIONS OF THE DEEP: Preface: Divining the Darkness; An Abhorrence to All Flesh; Notes of a Mad Copyist; The Basement Theater; If It Had Eyes; Judas of the Infinite; PART TWO: DARK AWAKENINGS: Teeth; The Stars Shine without Me; Desert Places; Blackbrain Dwarf; Nightmares, Imported and Domestic (with Mark McLaughlin); The Devil and One Lump; The God of Foulness; PART THREE: APOCRYPHON: Chimeras & Grotesqueries: An Unfinished Fragment of Daemonic Derangement; Prometheus Possessed; The New Pauline Corpus; A Cherished Place at the Center of His Plans (with Mark McLaughlin); Acknowledgments; Publication History.

Notes. Cover illustration, "The Taming of the Leviathan," by Michael Hutter. Cover design by Daniel V. Sauer. First announced in 2012, this long-delayed omnibus of Cardin's highly regarded fiction included a major unpublished novelette (the final collaboration with Mark McLaughlin).

235.   W. H. PUGMIRE. *An Imp of Aether.* 2019. 232 pp. tpb.

Contents. Introduction, by S. T. Joshi; The Hands That Reek and Smoke; The Zanies of Sorrow; Dust to Dust; The House of Idiot Children; Beyond the Realm of Dream; An Implement of Ice; Garden of Shattered Faces; Pickman's Lazarus; Totem Pole; Visions of William Davis Manly; The Boy with the Bloodstained Mouth; Your Seventh Eikon; Heritage of Hunger; Born in Strange Shadow; An Imp of Aether; The Horror on Tempest Hill; Child of Dark Mania; Pale, Trembling Youth; Your Kiss of Filth; Old Time Entombed; The Barrier Between; These Harpies of Carcosa; In Blackness Etched, My Name; This Weave of Witchery; To Move Beneath Autumnal Oaks; The Ghoul's Dilemma; Acknowledgments.

Notes. Cover illustration by Andrea Bonazzi. Cover design by Daniel V. Sauer. A commemorative volume of generally uncollected stories issued some months after Pugmire's untimely passing on March 26, 2019, compiled by Pugmire's literary executor.

236.   DENNIS QUINN, EDITOR. *Lovecraftian Proceedings 3: Select Papers from the Dr. Henry Armitage Memorial Scholarship Symposium: NecronomiCon Providence: 2017.* 2019. 263 pp. tpb.

Contents. Preface: The Dr. Henry Armitage Memorial Scholarship Symposium, by Niels Hobbs; Introduction: Writing Under the Shadow of Dr. Armitage, by Dennis P. Quinn; Lovecraft's Dark Continent: *At the Mountains of Madness* and Antarctic Literature, by Ian Fetters; Alexander Blok and H. P. Lovecraft: On the Mythopoetics of the Supernatural, by Elena Tchougounova-Paulson; At the Mountains of Mars: Viewing the Red Planet through a Lovecraftian Lens, by Edward Guimont; Fascism Eternal Lies: H. P. Lovecraft, by Georges Bataille, and the Destiny of the Fascists, by Ray Huling; Stages of the Spiral: Lovecraft's Descent into the Maelstrom, by Sean Moreland; H. P. Lovecraft and the Dynamics of Detective Fiction, by Heather Poirier; Lovecraft out of Space: Echoes of American Weird Fiction on Brazilian Literature and Cinema, by Lúcio Reis Filho; Red Hand, Red Hook: Machen, Lovecraft, and the Urban Uncanny, by Karen Joan Kohoutek; Naming the Unnamable: Lovecraft's Return of the Text, by Paul Neimann; Correlating the Contents of Lovecraft's Closet, by Fiona Maeve Geist and Sadie Shurberg; Lovecraft Meets the Mummy: Orientalism, Race, and Monstrous Egypt in "Imprisoned with the Pharaohs" and "Out of the Aeons," by Troy Rondinone; The Cosmic Drone of Azathoth: Adapting Literature into Sound, by Nathaniel R. Wallace; Contributors; Appendix: Abstracts of Papers Presented at the Dr. Henry Armitage Memorial Scholarship Symposium NecronomiCon Providence 17–20 August 2017; Dennis P. Quinn, Chair; Index.

Notes. Cover illustration by Pete Von Sholly. The third volume of some of the leading papers at NecronomiCon Providence.

237.   H. P. LOVECRAFT. *Lord of a Visible World: An Autobiography in Letters.* Edited by S. T. Joshi and David E. Schultz. 2019. 377 pp. tpb.

Contents. Introduction; [Biographical Notice]; I. CHILDHOOD AND ADOLESCENCE (1890–1914): Ancestry; Infancy; Youthful Interests; The Loss of His Birthplace; "Blank" Period (1908–13); II. AMATEUR JOURNALISM (1914–1921): A Permanent Amateur; The Providence

Amateur Press Club; The Conservative; Amateur Controversies; Attempted Enlistment; Early Philosophical Views; Aryan Supremacy; Metrical Mechanic; Early Writings: Fiction; Discovery of Lord Dunsany; Dreams; Amatory Phenomena; Illness and Death of Lovecraft's Mother; III. EXPANDING HORIZONS (1921–1924): Romance with Sonia; Travels; Philosophical Development; Literary Development; IV. MARRIAGE AND EXILE (1924–1926): Elopement; Job Prospects; Dieting; The Kalem Club; Robbed!; Clinton Street and Red Hook; Travels; Writings; Jews and Foreigners; Impending Return; V. HOMECOMING (1926–1930): Paradise Regain'd; Reflections on Marriage; Reflections on New England; A Torrent of Fiction Theories of Literature and the Weird; Further Philosophical Ruminations; Travels; Colleagues; VI. THE OLD GENTLEMAN (1931–1937): Weird Fiction: Theory and Practice; Literary and Personal Setbacks; The Move to 66 College Street; Daily Life; Cats!; Travels; Revisionist; Continuing Philosophical Discussions; Literature versus Hackwork; Problems of Politics and Economics; Supporting Hitler; Late Work; Lovecraft as Mentor; The End; APPENDIX: Some Notes on a Nonentity. Glossary of Names; Further Reading; Index.

Notes. Cover art and design by Daniel V. Sauer. A reprint of a volume first published by Ohio University Press (2000), consisting almost exclusively of selections from Lovecraft's letters arranged as an informal autobiography. References and citations have been updated.

238.   *Lovecraft Annual* No. 13 (2019). EDITED BY S. T. JOSHI. 233 pp.

Contents. The Lovecraftian Solar System, by Fred S. Lubnow; "Hungry fer Victuals I Couldn't Raise Nor Buy": Anthropophagy in Lovecraft, by Duncan Norris; The Rings of Cthulhu: Lovecraft, Dürer, Saturn, and Melancholy, by Andrew Paul Wood; "The Cats": An Environmental Ditty, by Cecelia Hopkins-Drewer; Lovecraft's Consolation, by Matthew Beach; "The Inability of the Human Mind": Lovecraft, Zunshine, and Theory of Mind, by Dylan Henderson; H. P. Lovecraft's "Sunset," by H. P. Lovecraft and S. T. Joshi; The Pathos in the Mythos, by Ann McCarthy; "Now Will You Be Good?": Lovecraft, Teetotalism, and Philosophy, by Jan B. W. Pedersen; Lovecraft's Open Boat, by Michael D. Miller; Lovecraft Seeks the Garden of Eratosthenes, by Horace A. Smith; Diabolists and Decadents: H. P. Lovecraft as Purveyor, Indulger, and Appraiser of Puritan Horror Fiction Psychohistory, by Scott Meyer; Aquaman and Lovecraft: An Unlikely Mating, by Duncan Norris; How to Read Lovecraft: A Column, by Steven J. Mariconda; [Review of S. T. Joshi and David E. Schultz, *Ave atque Vale: Reminiscences of H. P. Lovecraft*], by Kenneth W. Faig, Jr.; Briefly Noted.

239.   ARTHUR MACHEN. *Collected Fiction: 1888–1895.* Edited by S. T. Joshi. 2019. 548 pp. tpb.

Contents. Introduction; A Chapter from the Book Called The Ingenious Gentleman Don Quijote de la Mancha Which by Some Mischance Has Not Till Now Been Printed; *The Chronicle of Clemendy*; The Spagyric Quest of Beroaldus Cosmopolita; The Great God Pan; A Remarkable Coincidence; The Autophone; A Double Return; A Wonderful Woman; The Lost Club; An Underground Adventure; Jocelyn's Escape; The Inmost Light; *The Three Impostors; or, The Transmutations:* Prologue; Adventure of the Gold Tiberius; The Encounter of the Pavement; Novel of the Dark Valley; Adventure of the Missing Brother; Novel of the Black Seal; Incident of the Private Bar; The Decorative Imagination; Novel of the Iron Maid; The Recluse of Bayswater; Novel of the White Powder; Strange Occurrence in Clerkenwell; History of the Young Man with Spectacles; Adventure of the Deserted Residence. The Red Hand; The Shining Pyramid; APPENDIX; Folklore and Legends of the North; Preface to "The Great God Pan" (1916); Introduction to *The Three Impostors* (1923); On Re-Reading *The Three Impostors* and the Wonder Story; Bibliography.

Notes. Cover art by Matthew Jaffe. Cover design by Daniel V. Sauer. The first of a three-volume set of Machen's fiction, including novels, novellas, short stories, prose-poems, and sketches; the first time his complete fiction has ever been gathered in a single edition. Joshi has examined the texts of Machen's fiction (manuscripts, magazine and newspaper appearances, book appearances) and established a style sheet for his work. The appendix includes prefaces, introductions, or other work by Machen commenting on his fiction.

240.   ARTHUR MACHEN. *Collected Fiction: 1896–1910.* Edited by S. T. Joshi. 2019. 540 pp. tpb.

Contents. Introduction; *The Hill of Dreams; Ornaments in Jade:* The Rose Garden; The Turanians; The Idealist; Witchcraft; The Ceremony; Psychology; Torture; Midsummer; Nature; The Holy Things. The White People; A Fragment of Life; *The Secret Glory;* APPENDIX: Introduction to *The Hill of Dreams* (1923); Preface to *The Secret Glory* (1922); Epilogue to *The Secret Glory* (1922); Bibliography.

Notes. Cover art by Matthew Jaffe. Cover design by Daniel V. Sauer.

241.   ARTHUR MACHEN. *Collected Fiction: 1911–1937.* Edited by S. T. Joshi. 2019. 557 pp. tpb.

> *Contents.* Introduction; Ten Thousand and One Nights; The Bowmen; The Soldiers' Rest; The Monstrance; The Dazzling Light; The Great Return; The Little Nations; Out of the Earth; The Men from Troy; Munitions of War; The Light That Can Never Be Put Out; The Ghost of Whit-Monday; A New Christmas Carol; Scrooge and the Spirit—of Psycho-analysis; The Terror; The Happy Children; The Islington Mystery; The Gift of Tongues; The Cosy Room; Johnny Double; Awaking: A Children's Story; Opening the Door; The Green Round; The Compliments of the Season; N; The Exalted Omega; The Children of the Pool; The Bright Boy; The Tree of Life; Out of the Picture; Change; The Dover Road; Ritual; APPENDIX: Introduction to *The Angels of Mons*; The Coming of the Terror; Bibliography.

> *Notes.* Cover art by Matthew Jaffe. Cover design by Daniel V. Sauer.

242.   MARK VALENTINE AND TIMOTHY J. JARVIS, EDITORS. *The Secret Ceremonies: Critical Essays on Arthur Machen.* 411 pp. tpb.

> *Contents.* Introduction, by Mark Valentine; I. BIOGRAPHY AND BIBLIOGRAPHY: Arthur Machen: The Evils of Materialism, by S. T. Joshi; Arthur Machen: The Pagan—His Work and His Personality, by Geoffrey H. Wells; Arthur Machen: A Novelist of Ecstasy and Sin, by Vincent Starrett; About My Books, by Arthur Machen; The City, the Vision, and Arthur Machen, by Godfrey Brangham; II AESTHETICISM AND DECADENCE: The Book in Yellow: How Dorian Inspired Lucian, by Roger Dobson; A Yellow Creeper, by Arthur Rickett; Arthur Machen and Decadence: The Flower-Tunicked Priest of New Grub Street, by James Machin; New Arabian Frights: Unholy Trinities and the Masks of Helen, by Roger Dobson; A Glow in the Sky: Some Observations on Machen's Style, by Jon Preece; The Secret and the Secrets: A Look at Machen's *Hieroglyphics,* by John Howard; III. MYSTICISM, MAGIC, AND PAGANISM: Arthur Machen's Panic Fears: Western Esotericism and the Irruption of Negative Epistemology, by Marco Pasi; A Fit Symbol for His Meaning: Arthur Machen and the Inexpressible, by Karen Joan Kohoutek; The Revenge of Vulcan, by G. J. Cooling; Perfume of the Trellised Vine, by Ron Weighell; Of Sacred Groves and Ancient Mysteries: Parallel Themes in the Writings of Arthur Machen and John Buchan, by Peter Bell; Beyond the Veil of Reality: Mysticism in Arthur Machen's "The White People," by Emily Foster; Sanctity Plus Sorcery: The Curious Christianity of Arthur Machen, by Iain Smith; "The Abyss of All Being": "The Great God Pan" and the Death of Metaphysics, by Geoffrey Reiter; Arthur Machen

and King Arthur, Sovereigns of Dream: A Personal Interpretation, by Donald Sidney-Fryer; IV. MYTHS AND WONDERS: The Impossible History: Machen's "A Fragment of Life," by John Howard; Three Great Hoaxes of the War, by Aleister Crowley; The Canning Enigma: Some Observations on Arthur Machen's *The Canning Wonder,* by Jeremy Cantwell; "All Manner of Mysteries": Encounters with the Numinous in *The Cosy Room and Other Stories,* by James Machin; Some Thoughts on "N," by Thomas Kent Miller; "It Is Getting Very Late & Dark": Machen's Last Fiction, by Mark Valentine; Bibliography; Acknowledgments; Index.

Notes. Cover design by Daniel V. Sauer, incorporating a portrait of Arthur Machen. A companion volume to Joshi's edition of Machen's fiction: an extensive collection of criticism, both from Machen's era and from recent years, including several unpublished essays.

243.   H. P. LOVECRAFT. *Letters to Wilfred B. Talman and Helen V. and Genevieve Sully.* Edited by David E. Schultz and S. T. Joshi. 2019. 574 pp. tpb.

Contents. Introduction; LETTERS: To Wilfred B. Talman; To Helen V. Sully; To Genevieve Sully; APPENDIX: H. P. Lovecraft: [Some Backgrounds of Fairyland]; The Pool; *Wilfred Blanch Talman: Cloisonné and Other Verses;* Dream Ships; Death; Haunted Island; Ballade of Creatures Abroad by Night; Izim; The Curse of Alabad and Ghinu and Aratza; A Horror in Profile; Texaco at Home: V—Providence; The Story Teller; Letters to Weird Tales; Bookplates; Lovecraft Revisited; *Rheinhart Kleiner:* To Mistress Katerine Ann Talman; *Genevieve Sully:* Letters to *Weird Tales;* Glossary of Frequently Mentioned Names; Bibliography; Index.

Notes. Cover design by Anastasia Damianakos. First complete publication of Lovecraft's letters to Talman and the Sullys (mother and daughter). Some copies were distributed lacking the text of the title on spine.

244.   D. L. MYERS. *Oracles from the Black Pool.* 2019. 135 pp. tpb.

Content. Origins of the Oracle, by K. A. Opperman; I. THE STREETS OF YOREHAVEN (PLACES): Cold Creek Campground; Along Icicle Creek; The Bone Grove; The Streets of Yorehaven; The Dark Road; Harrow; The Black Road; The Palisade; The Tree and the House; Dark House of Hunger; The Well; Beyond the Veil; II. THE ACOLYTES OF SAMHAIN (AUTUMN): Autumn Moon; The Littlest Werewolf; The Demon Corn; The Death of Twilight; The Acolytes of Samhain; On All Hallow's Eve; III. THE SUMMONS (NATURE): The

Summons; Night Shrikes; *Vul Ravin*; Black Tomb Flowers; The Dark Spaces of the Trees; Haiku One; Dreamclouds; Haiku Two; An Owl Haunts My Dreams; Death's Head; Nightfall; Incense; The Thing on the Mountain; The Cave of Ebon Boughs; The Phosphorescent Fungi; Haiku Three; The Raven's Lament; If All the Seas Were Blood; A Memory of Ocean Lost; IV. THE STAR'S PRISONER (COSMIC HORROR): A Caul of Luminance; After the Light; The Dark Stars; The Star's Prisoner; The Stars Are Black; At the End of Day; V. THE CANKER WITHIN (HORROR)" The Demon Road; The Canker Within; Terror; Jack's A Kidder; VI. THE TEMPLE OF THE RIVER GODDESS (FEMME FATALE); Hazel; Haiku Four; The Temple of the River Goddess; Waterfalls; You Are a Temple in a Moonlit Meadow; To L—; Transcended Vision; Allegory; Ashiel's Garden; Aisha's Revenge; VII. O DARK MUSE (SORCERY AND CREATIVITY); Kylen-Xyr; The Sorcerous Scribe; The Crimson Kist; Word Painting; O Dark Muse; Poetry Is Sorcery; VIII. TRIBUTES: With a Love So Vile, by Ashley Dioses; The Silver Gate, by Adam Bolivar; The Dark Road to Harrow, by K. A. Opperman; Black Oracles, by K. A. Opperman; ILLUSTRATIONS; Harrow; The Palisade; Dark House of Hunger; The Well; Beyond the Veil; The Demon Corn; On All Hallow's Eve; The Summons; Vul Ravin; An Owl Haunts My Dreams; Nightfall; The Thing on the Mountain; The Phosphorescent Fungi; If All the Seas Were Blood; After the Light; The Star's Prisonere; The Canker Within; Jack's a Kidder; Ashiel's Garden; O Dark Muse; Black Oracles.

Notes. Cover and interior illutrations by Daniel V. Sauer. First poetry collection by a leading contemporary weird poet, a member of the Crimson Circle (consisting of K. A. Opperman, Ashley Dioses, Adam Bolivar, and Myers).

245.   H. P. LOVECRAFT. *Letters with Donald and Howard Wandrei and to Emil Petaja.* Edited by S. T. Joshi and David E. Schultz. 2019. 553 pp. tpb.

Contents. Introduction; LETTERS: Of H. P. Lovecraft and Donald Wandrei; Of H. P. Lovecraft and Howard Wandrei; To Emil Petaja; APPENDIX: Donald Wandrei Interviewed; EMIL PETAJA: Dream within a Dream Within; Partings . . .; The Warrior; Asphodel; The Witch's Berceuse; Lost Dream; Famous Fantasy Fiction; The Mist; [Fragmentary Story]. Glossary of Frequently Mentioned Names; Bibliography; Index.

Notes. Cover design by Anastasia Damianakos. A volume that contains Lovecraft's letters to and from Donald Wandrei (first published in the volume *Mysteries of Time and Spirit* in 2002), augmented by letters to and from his brother Howard and Lovecraft's letters to Emil Petaja.

246.   T.E.D. KLEIN. *Providence After Dark* 2019. 591 pp. tpb.

Contents. I. ON LOVECRAFT: Providence After Dark; *The United Amateur*; A Dreamer's Tales; The Festival; The Old Gent; T.E.D. Klein: Master of Ceremonies; II. ON OTHER AUTHORS: Arthur Machen; Ramsey Campbell: An Appreciation; *Slow*; An Afternoon with Aickman; A Haunted House; Frank Belknap Long; Dr. Van Helsing's Handy Guide to Ghost Stories; Introduction to *Dark Love*; Introduction to David Schow's *Seeing Red*; Whiskey, Popcorn, and Gold; *Gaspard de la Nuit*; A Connecticut Yankee; The Ceremonies, 2016 edition: A Note from the Author; A Conversation with T.E.D. Klein; III. THE TWILIGHT ZONE: *Stories from the Twilight Zone*; *Twilight Zone* Magazine; The 13 Most Terrifying Horror Stories; The Book of Hieronymus Bosch; *Twilight Zone: The Movie*; Horrors! An Introduction to Writing Horror Fiction; Standing Behind the Curtains: A Conversation with T.E.D. Klein; IV. ON FILM: They Kill Animals and They Call It Art; Animals in Movies—The Abuse Gets Worse; On Cutting Up Movie Classics; How I Flopped as a Paramount Script Reader; *Annie Hall*; Star Wares; Master of a Lost Art; And Many Happy Returns; T.E.D. Klein Interview; V. ON OTHER TOPICS: Where Do We Go from Here?; Charles Manson, B.M.O.C.; The Joy of Losing; Working for the *Brown Daily Herald*; CrimeBeat; Crime and Punishment; A Higher Standard; A Couple of Letters on . . . Antarctica!; Quotation & Misquotation; Silenced Voices; Three Letters to Brown; Spalding Gone Gray; Lament of an Aging English Instructor; Reassuring Words: An Interview with T.E.D. Klein; VI. REVIEWS: *Legion* by William Peter Blatty; *The Face That Must Die* and *Incarnate* by Ramsey Campbell; *The Suburbs of Hell* by Randolph Stow; More Books; *The Glamour* by Christopher Priest; *Collected Stories* by Ruth Rendell; *The Terrors of Ice and Darkness* by Christoph Ransmayr; *Bring Me Children* by David Martin; A Curate's Egg; *Sci-Fi Entertainment*; A Swedish Podcast.

Notes. Cover photograph by Donna St. Pierre. Cover design by Daniel V. Sauer. An enormous collection of Klein's essays and reviews—a book that was planned years before. It includes not only his essays on supernatural fiction but also on crime (editorials from *Night Beat*, a magazine Klein edited), and also a lengthy interview.

247.   *Dead Reckonings* No. 26 (Fall 2019). EDITED BY ALEX HOUSTOUN AND MICHAEL J. ABOLAFIA. 135 pp.

Contents. A Cultic Gathering, by Darrell Schweitzer; Trio of Terrors, by Greg Gbur [Larry Blamire, *More Tales of the Callamo Mountains*; Orrin Grey, *Guignol and Other Sardonic Tales*; Lucy A. Snyder, *Garden* of *Eldritch Delights*]; The Curated Repast of Subdivisions, by The joey Zone [Ann and Jeff Vandermeer, *The Big Book of Classic Fantasy*]; "The Most Poignant Sensations of My Existence": Visiting the Ladd Observatory at NecronomiCon Providence, by Karen Joan Kohoutek; Two Writers: Lives and Works, by S. T. Joshi [Mike Ashley, *Starlight Man: The Extraordinary Life of Algernon Blackwood*; William F. Nolan. *Writing as Life: Selected Essays of William F. Nolan*, ed. Jason V Brock]; Ramsey's Rant: Volumes of Volumes, by Ramsey Campbell; Sing Your Sadness Deep, Laura Mauro, by Daniel Pietersen [Laura Mauro, *Sing Your Sadness Deep*]; Man as a Mystery, by Donald Sidney-Fryer [Arthur Machen, *Collected Fiction*; Mark Valentine and Timothy J. Jarvis, ed., *The Secret Ceremonies: Critical Essays on Arthur Machen*]; The Unseen, Quiet Dark, by Fiona Maeve Geist [Michael Kelly. *All the Things We Never See*]; Curtains of the Impossible: A Remembrance of Sam Gafford, by Farah Rose Smith; A New Take on the Chambers Mythos, by Acep Hale [Brian Hauser, *Memento Mori: The Fathomless Shadows*]; Ars Necronomica 2019: What Drives the Dark Dreams of That Divine City?, by Michelle Souliere; Delicate, Collectible Screams, by Géza A. G. Reilly [Thomas Ligotti, *A Little White Book of Screams and Whispers*]; "When Blue Meets Yellow in the West": *Stranger Things 3*, by Hank Wagner and Bev Vincent; Train Reading, by Peter Cannon; My NecronomiCon-2019: Wanderings and Wonders, by Elena Tchougounova-Paulson; The Rocky Beginnings of *Weird Tales*, by Darrell Schweitzer [John Locke, *The Thing's Incredible! The Secret Origins of* Weird Tales]; Sam Gafford and Ulthar Press, by S. T. Joshi [Farah Rose Smith, ed. *Machinations and Mesmerism: Tales Inspired by E. T. A. Hoffmann*]; "I No Longer Live in This House": The Liminality of Undeath in the Works of R. Murray Gilchrist, by Daniel Pietersen; Fathoms of Tropes, by Géza A. G. Reilly [Frogwares, *The Sinking City*]; Were We Ever Innocent? Childhood Horrors of Knowledge and Sexuality in Gene Wolfe's Fiction, by Marc Aramini; "We Make Ourselves out of Stories, Y'Know?," by Karen Joan Kohoutek [Eric J. Guignard, *Doorways to the Deadeye*]; Recollections on NecronomiCon 2019, by Edward Guimont; You Know Who the Monster Is, by Michael D. Miller [S. L. Edwards, *Whiskey and Other Unusual Ghosts*]; Loving Horror Films Too Much, by Acep Hale [Jon Kitley, *Discover the Horror: One Man's Quest for Monsters, Maniacs, and the Meaning of It All*]; Haters and Devotees Alike: NecronomiCon 2019, by Geza A. G. Reilly; About the Contributors.

248. ROBERT H. WAUGH. *The Tragic Thread in Science Fiction: Essays on David Lindsay, Olaf Stapledon, Arthur C. Clarke, Mervyn*

Peake, William Gibson, Fritz Leiber, James Tiptree, Jr., and H. P. Lovecraft. 2019. 235 pp. tpb.

Contents. Introduction; The Drum of Arcturus in Lindsay's Strange Music; Lindsay's and Goethe's Celebration of the Pagan World in Lindsay and Goethe; A Speculative Dictionary of *A Voyage to Arcturus;* Stapledon's Music of God: Spirals and Syntheses; Go, Tell It on the Mountain; The Lament of the Midwives in *Childhood's End;* The Lily and the Rose: Polarities in *The City and the Stars;* Titus Alone in the Waste Land; *Neuromancer:* The Fall Is the Case; The Word in the Wilderness: Nehwon, Nowhere, and California; Leiber Covers the Big Gambler Death; Stage Violence, Stage Resurrection in Tiptree and Leiber; The Deeps of Eryx; Works Cited.

Notes. Cover illustration by Robert H. Knox; cover design by Daniel V. Sauer. A series of scintillating essays on key science fiction writers from the 1920s to the present.

249.   *Spectral Realms* No. 12 (Winter 2020). EDITED BY S. T. JOSHI. 141 pp.

Contents. POEMS: Acrostic Sonnet for Wilum Hopfrog Pugmire, by David Barker; Gray, by M. F. Webb; Pilgrim in the Mist, by Wade German; Proem to the Fortress Unvanquishable, by Thomas Tyrrell; Ode to the Great God Pan, by Carl E. Reed; Ghebulax, by Maxwell I. Gold; The Crimson Knight, by Scott J. Couturier; Haematophagy, by Ashley Dioses; Not All of Them Are Ghosts, by Darrell Schweitzer; Poe, on the Morning After, by Don Webb; Homage to *Creepy*, by Manuel Pérez-Campos; Xipe Totec, by Deborah L. Davitt; Necronomicon, by Josh Maybrook; Wretched Raft, by Kieran Dacey Boylan; Satanic Sonata, by Manuel Arenas; Time's Vulture, by Leigh Blackmore; Urban Renewal, by Mike Allen; Graveside Ghost, by Mary Krawczak Wilson; No One Is Safe, by Benjamin Blake; Minoan Messages, by Frank Coffman; Madhouse Getaway, by Manuel Pérez-Campos; Planet Fetish, by Chad Hensley; Jack in Xanadu, by Adam Bolivar; Genesis, by Holly Day; I Want to Taste October, by Ross Balcom; A Tasty Treat, by Adele Gardner; Beyond the Fields, by Andrew J. Wilson; The Tears of Cerberus, by Wade German; A Witch in the House, by Oliver Smith; The Psychopomp, by Cecelia Hopkins-Drewer; The Plague Queen's Song, by Nicole Cushing; I'll Return in Late October, by K. A. Opperman; The Philosophy & Aesthetics of Horror, by Carl E. Reed; Black Wings Return, by Michael D. Miller; Slow the Night Grows Darker, by David Sammons; The Wild Hunt, by Chelsea Arrington; Lines Written in a Providence Churchyard, by David Barker; The God of the Winds, by Christina Sng; Singularity, by Curtis M. Lawson; Dream Hackers, by Maxwell I. Gold; The Bedlam Philharmonic, by Steven Withrow; The House (A Conduit), by Mack W. Mani; The Pack, by Scott J. Couturier; Kiss of Life, by Manuel Arenas; The Last Golem, by Allan Rozinski; A Summoning of Demons, by Michelle Jeffrey; Astral Parasites, by Manuel Pérez-Campos; The Silent Silver Sea, by Leigh Blackmore; Homer Before the Trojan Court, by Darrell Schweitzer; The Witch's Cat, by Deborah L. Davitt; In Arcadia, by Josh Maybrook; My Loveliest Manticore; or, The Queen of the Lamiae, by Wade German; The Conjuring, by Frank Coffman; Wildfires, by Christina Sng; Now and Forever, by Kieran Dacey Boylan; Stela of Selos, by Scott J. Couturier; Southern Gothic; or, Hillbilly Horror, by Carl E. Reed; The Egyptian Splendor, by Ross Balcom; Carrion Dreams, by Maxwell I. Gold; CLASSIC REPRINTS: In a Breton Cemetery, by Ernest Dowson; The Vampire, by Arthur Symons; REVIEWS: A Golgotha of Horror, by S. T. Joshi; Dark Oracles Indeed, by Donald Sidney-Fryer; Notes on Contributors.

Notes. Cover illustration by Albert Joseph Pénot.

250. STEPHEN WOODWORTH. *A Carnival of Chimeras.* 2019. 284 pp. tpb.

Contents. Her; The Hidden Track; Because It Is Bitter; Revival; Scary Monsters; Menagerie of the Maladapted; Street Runes; Prisoners; A Tour of the Catacombs; A Woman Absent; Voodoo; Mr. Casey Is in the House; Transubstantiation; The Colorless People; The Silent Majority; Serial Killers; In the City of Sharp Edges; The Olverung; Acknowledgments.

Notes. Cover illustration by Daniel V. Sauer. A strong collection of fiction (the author's first) by a leading writer of contemporary weird fiction. Several of the stories are powerful and ingenious elaborations of Lovecraftian motifs.

251. S. T. JOSHI, DAVID E. SCHULTZ, AND SCOTT CONNORS. *Clark Ashton Smith: A Comprehensive Bibliography.* 2020. 586 pp. tpb.

Contents. Introduction; I. WORKS BY SMITH IN ENGLISH: A. Books and Pamphlets; Appendix: Ebooks. B. Contributions to Books and Periodicals: i. Fiction; Synopses; ii. Poetry; iii. Translations of Poems; iv. Poems in Prose; v. Nonfiction; vi. Published Letters; vii. Published Artwork; viii. Miscellany; II. WORKS BY SMITH IN TRANSLATION: A. Books and Pamphlets: i. Dutch; ii. Finnish; iii. French; iv. German; v. Greek; vi. Italian; vii. Japanese; viii. Polish; ix. Spanish; x. Turkish; xi. Galician. B. Contributions to Books and Periodicals: i. Fiction; ii.

Poems; iii. Poems in Prose; iv. Nonfiction; v. Published Letters; III. SMITH CRITICISM: A. News Items; B. Encyclopedias; C. Bibliographies; D. Books and Pamphlets about Smith; E. Criticism in Books and Periodicals; F. Book Reviews; G. Special Periodicals and Miscellany; i. Special Periodicals; ii. Miscellany; iii. Media Adaptations; iv. Online Sources; IV. INDEXES: A. Names; B. Titles by Smith; C. Periodicals.

Notes. Cover illustration by Jason Van Hollander. An exhaustive bibliography of writings by and about Smith, and the first work of its kind since Donald Sidney-Fryer's *Emperor of Dreams* (1978). It includes book publications, magazine and newspaper appearances, media adaptations, and Smith criticism in books, magazines, and websites.

252.　MAY SINCLAIR. *If the Dead Knew: The Weird Fiction of May Sinclair.* Edited by S. T. Joshi. 2020. 297 pp. tpb.

Contents. Introduction, by S. T. Joshi; The Intercessor; The Flaw in the Crystal; Fright; The Villa Désirée; The Token; The Victim; Where Their Fire Is Not Quenched; The Nature of the Evidence; If the Dead Knew; The Finding of the Absolute; Jones's Karma; Heaven; The Mahatma's Story; Bibliography.

Notes. Cover illustration by Aeron Alfrey. Cover design and custom title font by Daniel V. Sauer. Complete collection of the weird tales of British writer May Sinclair (1863–1946), known for the delicacy of her character portrayals. The fifth volume in the Classics of Gothic Horror series.

253.　IRVIN S. COBB AND GOUVERNEUR MORRIS. *Back There in the Grass: The Horror Tales of Irvin S. Cobb and Gouverneur Morris.* 2020. 287 pp. tpb.

Contents. Introduction, by S. T. Joshi; IRVIN S. COBB: The Belled Buzzard; Fishhead; The Gallowsmith; Darkness; Snake Doctor; The Second Coming of a First Husband; The Unbroken Chain; Faith, Hope and Charity; GOUVERNEUR MORRIS: The Crocodile; The Footprint; The Execution; The Bride's Dead; Back There in the Grass; Derrick's Return; Bibliography.

Notes. Cover illustration by Aeron Alfrey. Cover design and custom title font by Daniel V. Sauer. Combined edition of the weird tales of Cobb (1876–1944) and Morris (1876–1953), the former best known for "Fishhead," a story that inspired Lovecraft's "The Shadow over Innsmouth." The sixth volume in the Classics of Gothic Horror series.

254. DONALD SIDNEY-FRYER. *A King Called Arthor and Other Morceaux*. 2020. 404 pp. tpb.

Contents. A King Called Arthor; A MEDLEY OF NONFICTION: Introduction to *Etchings in Ivory: Poems in Prose*; Afterword to "As It Is Written"; Emeraude Indeed; Grim News from the Far Future: Introduction to *New Tales of Zothique*; The Phosphor Lamps of Clark Ashton Smith, with Ron Hilger; Captain Volmar and Crew: An Afterword; In Defense of "Little Boys"; James Blish versus Clark Ashton Smith: to Wit, the Young Turk Syndrome; Shadows and Light; Foreword to *Not Quite Atlantis*; Klarkash-Ton, High Priest of Atlantis; Crimson Pages from the Future Perfect Past; Averoigne: An Afterword; Thibaut di Castries, Revenant; Introduction to *Diary of a Sorceress*; H. P. Lovecraft—Beacon and Gateway; A Poetic Original; Letters to "The Lion's Den"; Under the Radar; ARTHUR MACHEN AND KING ARTHUR, SOVEREIGNS OF DREAM; A FINAL LAUREL WREATH OF LYRICS: For Lin Carter; Inspiration; Ayery-Fayery; Pomgarnet Wine; Nor Cleopatra Nor Helen of Troy; No Safe Refuge; The Emperor Steps Down: Uncommon "Comme il faut"; Confessional; A Blessing or a Curse; Nyctalops; A Random Enquiry and Something More; Impermanence and Permanence; Sunset Sail; Adrift; Averonne; In Appreciation of Publius Vergilius Maro; Enigmatic; Mittel Europa in One Single Pile; APPENDIX: CLARK ASHTON SMITH, AS PERCEIVED BY TWO CONTRASTING POETS: Foreword; The Emperor of Dreams, by Donald A. Wandrei; Five Approaches to the Achievements of Clark Ashton Smith, Cosmic Master Artist, by Martin R. Heimstra. Acknowledgments.

Notes. Cover design, based in part on artwork by Gustave Doré, by Daniel V. Sauer, who also contributed a map and key to names. Another volume of miscellany by Sidney-Fryer. The title work is a previously unpublished novella about King Arthur. This is followed by an array of recent essays and reviews, then by some of his new poetry.

255. *Dead Reckonings* No. 27 (Spring 2020). EDITED BY ALEX HOUSTOUN AND MICHAEL J. ABOLAFIA. 97 pp.

Contents. Go Buy *Black Heart Boys' Choir*: A Review and Comparative Reading, by Géza A. G. Reilly [Curtis M. Lawson, *Black Heart Boys' Choir*]; Epistemological Alchemy, by Michael D. Miller [Matt Cardin, *To Rouse Leviathan*]; The Return of the Fanzine, by S. T. Joshi [Obadiah Baird, ed. *The Audient Void*; David Barker, *Half in Light, Half in Shadow*; Graeme Phillips, ed. *Cyäegha*]; Ramsey's Rant: Just a Coincidence, by Ramsey Campbell; The Dark Gnosis of D. L. Myers, by Leigh Blackmore [D. L. Myers, *Oracles from the Black Pool*]; More "Thing," by Darrell Schweitzer [John W. Campbell, Jr., *Frozen Hell,* ed. John Gregory Betancourt]; Polluting Gods: Liminality, Devolution, and the Defamiliarization of Human Identity in Blackwood's "The Wendigo" and Kipling's "The Mark of the Beast", by Michael Abolafia; Unseen Worlds, Waiting to Be Discovered, by Daniel Pietersen [Melissa Edmundson, ed. *Women's Weird: Strange Stories by Women*]; A Trade in Futures, by Daniel Raskin; Dare You Have Fun?, by Fiona Maeve Geist [Nick Mamatas, *Sabbath*]; Dying to Meet You, by Karen Joan Kohoutek [*Playghoul: Special Vampira Issue*]; The Nature of Horror, by S. T. Joshi [Ramsey Campbell, *The Wise Friend*]; Wisdom in Anguish: Sloane Leong's Dysmorphic Space Mechs, by Helen Chazan [Sloane Leong, *With the Blade as Witness*]; Australia's Weird Poet Laureate, by Leigh Blackmore [Kyla Lee Ward, *The Macabre Modern and Other Morbidities*]; An Historical and Environmental Reading of August Derleth's "Ithaqua", by Edward Guimont; Cosmic Horror—with a Dash of Sex, by Gary Fry [S. T. Joshi, *Something from Below*]; Providentially Speaking Again, by Donald Sidney-Fryer [T. E. D. Klein, *Providence After Dark and Other Writings*]; Some of Your Blood: Dracula's Metafictional Mirror, by Philip Challinor; About the Contributors.

256.   CLINT SMITH. *The Skeleton Melodies: A Collection.* 2020. 324 pp. tpb.

Contents. Introduction: The Profane Articulation of Truth, by Adam Golaski; Lisa's Pieces; The Undertow, and They That Dwell Therein; Animalhouse; Fingers Laced, as Though in Prayer; By Goats Be Guided; The Pecking Order; Her Laugh; Knot the Noose; The Rive; The Fall of Tomlinson Hall; or, The Ballad of the Butcher's Cart; Fiending Apophenia; Details That Would Otherwise Be Lost to Shadow; Haunt Me Still; Acknowledgments.

Notes. Cover illustration and design by Daniel V. Sauer. Smith's second collection, following *Ghouljaw and Other Stories* (no. 136). It contains stories published in various venues over the past decade and concludes with a superb novella, "Haunt Me Still," previously unpublished. Starred review in *Publishers Weekly*.

257.   H. P. LOVECRAFT. *Letters to Alfred Galpin and Others.* Edited by S. T. Joshi and David E. Schultz. 2020. 497 pp. tpb.

Contents. Introduction; LETTERS: To Edward H. and E. Sherman Cole; To John T. Dunn; To Alfred Galpin; With Adolphe de Castro; APPENDIX: *Alfred Galpin:* Mystery; Two Loves; Selenaio-Phantasma; Remarks to My Handwriting; Marsh-Mad; The Critic; Stars; Some Tendencies of Modern Poetry; The Spoken Tongue; The World Situation; The United's Policy 1920–1921; Form in Modern Poetry; Picture of a Modern Mood; Nietzsche as a Practical Prophet; To Sam Loveman; The Vivisector; Four Translations from Les Fleurs du mal by Charles Pierre Baudelaire; Mystery; Scattered Remarks upon the Green Cheese Theory; Department of Public Criticism; Intuition in the Philosophy of Bergson; Ennui; A Critic of Poetry; From the French of Pierre de Ronsard ("Amours"—Livre II.); Echoes from Beyond Space; Red . . .; En Route (An American to Paris, 1931); November; *Edward H. Cole:* Some Words for Mr. Lovecraft; *Edith Miniter:* Little Pilgrimages to the Homes of Amateurs; *Adolphe de Castro:* Ambrose Bierce As He Really Was; Let There Be Light!; Glossary of Frequently Mentioned Names; Bibliography; Index.

Notes. Cover design by Anastasia Damianakos. A reprint of *Letters to Alfred Galpin* (no. 13), although omitting the letters to the Gallomo, and augmented by letters to other correspondents. The letters to Edward H. Cole and his infant son are some of the earliest surviving instances of Lovecraft's letters.

258.   *Spectral Realms* No. 13 (Summer 2020). EDITED BY S. T. JOSHI. 140 pp.

Contents. POEMS: King Pest, by Richard L. Tierney; The Protector, by Ian Futter; After Verdun: A Psychomantic Vision, by Manuel Pérez-Campos; Märchen (Fairy Tales), by Carl E. Reed; Nevermore, by Adele Gardner; The Sleeper, by Josh Maybrook; City of Skulls, by Maxwell I. Gold; Among the Petroglyphs, by Ann K. Schwader; The Catacombs, by Tatiana Strange; Illusion of Light, by Ronald Terry; The Hidebehind: A Legend of the North Country, by Frank Coffman; Dream Snatchers, by Ngo Binh Anh Khoa; My Bantam Black Fay, by Manuel Arenas; Doubled Word, by Rahul Gupta; De Quincey Mutations: Our Ladies of Sorrow, by Wade German; Ithaca, Finally, by Darrell Schweitzer; All That I Have Lost, by Christina Sng; Astray, by F. J. Bergmann; Imperishable, by David C. Kopaska-Merkel; Wraith of the Versifier, by David Barker; The Tongueless Dead, by Leigh Blackmore; Sanctuary, by Mary Krawczak Wilson; O Iranon, by Charles Lovecraft; Sweet Discordia Lee, by Oliver Smith; The Harvester, by K. A. Opperman; The Song of Calamity Joe, by Andrey Pissantchev; Jenkin, by Ross Balcom; Amongst the Sargasso, by Scott J. Couturier; Notre Dame Is Burning!, by Lori R. Lopez; The Sweet Dreams of the Dead, by David O'Melia; The Witch-Gallows, by Josh Maybrook; Lord Death, by Ashley Dioses; Our Lady of the Acherontia, by Allan Rozinski; Legion, by Benjamin Blake; Where the New Gods Dwell, by Maxwell I. Gold; Imaginary Friend, by Ngo Binh Anh

Khoa; Lines on Austin Osman Spare's "Arbor Vitae", by Manuel Pérez-Campos; In the Forest, Where Wild Things Live, by Claire Smith; Melinoë, by Wade German; Hell-Flower, by Manuel Arenas; Haunted, by Ronald Terry; He Who Waits, by Frank Coffman; Splenetic IV: After Baudelaire, by Rahul Gupta; The Graves, by Steven Withrow; A Conspiracy Penetrated, by Carl E. Reed; Frozen Voices, by Leigh Blackmore; Calling All Witches, by Adele Gardner; To the Wolves, by Scott J. Couturier; Red Land, Black Pharaoh, by Ann K. Schwader; Ouroboros, by Frank Coffman; The Draining Chair, by Thomas Tyrrell; Retrieval, by F. J. Bergmann; The Rider of the Pegasi, by C. d. G. Nightingale; Testament of Doom: A Paean to Clark Ashton Smith, by Manuel Pérez-Campos; The Passive Vampire, by Wade German; The Pores of Earth, by Charles Lovecraft; Moribond, by Manuel Arenas; The Variant, by Maxwell I. Gold; To Gaelle Lacroix, Lone Survivor of the Trufort Massacre, by Steven Withrow; Dr. Ripper, I Presume?, by Carl E. Reed; Red Tresses, by Scott C. Couturier; CLASSIC REPRINTS: Strife, by R. H. Barlow; It Will Be Thus, by Arthur Goodenough; REVIEWS: The Sun Sings Loud and Clear, by Donald Sidney-Fryer; Terror and Poignancy, by S. T. Joshi; A Queen of Dark Poetry, by Sunni Brock; NOTES ON CONTRIBUTORS.

259. H. P. LOVECRAFT. *Letters to Family and Family Friends, Volume 1: 1911–1925.* Edited by S. T. Joshi and David E. Schultz. 2020. 529 pp.

  Contents. Introduction; LETTERS: To Sarah Susan Lovecraft; To Lillian D. Clark and Annie E. P. Gamwell (1921–25).

  Notes. Cover illustration by David C. Verba. The first of an immense two-volume edition, this one containing the relatively few letters to Lovecraft's mother and the first few years of an enormous quantity of letters to his two aunts. The letters from 1924–25 provide incredible insights into the smallest details of his daily life in New York, his relations to his wife, Sonia, and other discussions rarely found in his correspondence to friends or colleagues.

260. H. P. LOVECRAFT. *Letters to Family and Family Friends, Volume 2: 1926–1936.* Edited by S. T. Joshi and David E. Schultz. 2020. 572 pp.

  Contents. LETTERS: To Lillian D. Clark and Annie E. P. Gamwell (1926–36); To Nelson Rogers; To Bertha Rausch; To Mayte Sutton; To Marian F. Bonner; APPENDIX: Letters by Whipple V. Phillips to H. P. Lovecraft; GLOSSARY OF FREQUENTLY MENTIONED NAMES; BIBLIOGRAPHY; INDEX.

Notes. Cover illustration by David C. Verba. The volume picks up with additional letters to his aunts, chronicling his return to Providence in April 1926 and then proceeding with detailed accounts of his travels of the later 1920s and early 1930s. The volume concludes with letters to family friends as well as some letters from his grandfather to Lovecraft in 1893–94.

261.   *Lovecraft Annual* No. 14 (2020). EDITED BY S. T. JOSHI. 252 pp.

Contents. National Defense, by H. P. Lovecraft and R. H. Barlow; National Defense, by E. D. Barlow; Atmosphere and the Qualitative Analysis of "The Colour out of Space," by Steven J. Mariconda; H. P. Lovecraft's First Appearance in Print, by Richard Bleiler; Missing the Punchline: The Subversive Nature of H. P. Lovecraft's Occult Detective, by Dylan Henderson; Yuletide Horror: "Festival" and "The Messenger," by Cecelia Hopkins-Drewer; The Doomed Lovecrafts of Rochester, by Will Murray; How to Read Lovecraft: A Column by Steven J. Mariconda; John Osborne Austin's Seven Club Tales: Did They Inspire Lovecraft?, by Ken Faig, Jr.; The "Extreme Fantasy" of Delirious New York, by Andrew Gipe-Lazarou; An Arctic Mystery: The Lovecraftian North Pole, by Edward Guimont; Textual Sources and Corrigenda Minora to "A Living Heritage: Roman Architecture in Today's America," by César Guarde-Paz; On Hawthorne's Unwitting "Children": The Strange Case of H. P. Lovecraft, by Simone Turco; Zeitgeist and Untoten: Lovecraft and the Walking Dead, by Duncan Norris; REVIEWS: [Review of H. P. Lovecraft, *Letters with Donald and Howard Wandrei and to Emil Petaja*], by D. H. Olson; [Review of Oobmab, *The Flock of Ba-Hui and Other Stories*], by S. T. Joshi; [Review of H. P. Lovecraft, *Letters to Alfred Galpin and Others*], by Martin Andersson; [Review of H. P. Lovecraft, *Letters to Wilfred B. Talman and to Helen V. and Genevieve Sully*], by Leigh Blackmore; Briefly Noted.

262.   MARK SAMUELS. *The Age of Decayed Futurity: The Best of Mark Samuels.* 2020. 267 pp. tpb.

Contents. Introduction, by Michael Dirda; Mannequins in Aspects of Terror; The White Hands; Apartment 205; Vrolyck; Ghorla; Cesare Thodol: Some Lines Written on a Wall; Sentinels; A Gentleman from Mexico; The Black Mould; Thyxxolqu; Regina vs. Zoskia; The Age of Decayed Futurity; My World Has No Memories; Outside Interference; The Crimson Fog; Court of Midnight; In the Complex; Acknowledgments.

Notes. Cover design and illustration by Aeron Alfrey. A selection of complex, richly textured weird fiction, often focusing on the horrors of technology. Starred review in *Publishers Weekly*; named by *Rue Morgue* magazine as the best single-author collection of 2020.

263.   LEAH BODINE DRAKE. *The Song of the Sun: Collected Writings.* Edited by David E. Schultz. 2020. 767 pp. hc & tpb.

Contents. Introduction; Photographs; COLLECTED POEMS: *A Dream of Samarkand (1919–1934)*: On a Chinese Screen; I. Lady Writing a Letter; II. Moon Festival; III. The Deserted Courtyard; IV. By the River; V. A Lady of the Emperor's Palace; VI. One Intoxicated; Mombāsa; To a Lost Sweetheart; Song at Sunrise; Words After Wisdom; The Ballad of Fair Elspeth; Gazelles in a Zoo; Apple; The Land of the Japanese Prints; Burma: Moulmein Bazaar; The Country Lover; Belle and Beau; The Sailorman (1690); A Dream of Samarkand; Our Lady's Song; The Pixy Fair; Turn of Year; The Croon of the Mer-Mother; Jilly and the Elf; The Saints of Four-Mile-Water; The Haunted Hour; Mad Jenny; Little Things; "There Are Fairies"; The Little Piper; Peddler's Pack; "My Help Cometh from the Hills"; *Descent of Angels (1935–1936)*: In the Shadows; The Man Who Married a Swan-Maiden; High Renaissance; India: In the Garden of Spices; He Dreams of Barbary; The Assyrian Lion; A Sigh in Spring; The Fairies in Autumn; The Giant's Garden; Unhappy Ending; *Winter Harvests*: Frozen Heart; Owl's Cry; "Peace on Earth"; Winter Harvest. Explanation; Figures in a Nightmare; The Witch Walks in Her Garden; Descent of Angels; Terror by Night; Old Wives' Tale; *A Hornbook for Witches*: I. The Covenant; II. The Besom; III. The Coven; IV. The Hell-Broth; V. The Magic Circle; VI. The Conjuration; VII. The Pentagram; VIII. The Spells; IX. Magician's Hat; X. Witch's Wheel; XI. The Familiar; XII. Enchanted Sleep; The Nixie's Pool. The Wind and the Leaves; All-Saints' Eve; Witches on the Heath; Curious Story; The Girl in the Glass; Goat-Song; *Fantasy in a Forest (1937–1941)*: The Path through the Marsh; Tiger; Crocodile; Japan: The Persimmon Gatherers; The Old Khan and His Falcon; 'Round and 'Round; Midsummer Night; Ducks and Pigs; Puss-in-Boots and the Three Mice; The Journey of the Queen of Sheba; Serpent-Ring; The Seven Sons of the King of Thule; Conversation in an Oak-Tree; The Last Faun; The Naughty Fairy; The Three Green Ladies of Greenwich; Born under Capricorn; The Bittern; The Centaurs; Rabbit-Dance; The Old Granny's Story; Sea-Shell; The Stranger; "What Are Little Girls Made Of?"; The Tenants; Bad Company; "Run with the Fox"; Encounter in Broceliande; A Star Came Out; The Daughter of the Grand Turk Loses Her Ball; "Apples and Apricots, Peaches and

Plums"; The Steps in the Field; Mouse Heaven; Protective Colouring; They Run Again; The Wood-Wife; House Accursed; The Minotaur; Rhymes without Reason; or, History Made Difficult; *From* Nonsensical Rhymes; I Met a Lion; Fantasy in a Forest; Full Moon, 1940; The Girl on the Saw-Backed Mountain; Lost Heritage; King Gog and King Magog; Gold from a Kettle; Drake of Devon; Griffon's Gold; On a Night of Stars; Man in Winter; The Hen-Wife's Chickens; *Honey from the Lion (1942–1948):* Vestal; The Singer from the Waste; The Fruit Uneaten; Gage to a Lover; A Vase from Araby; The Window on the Stair; The Phoenix Egg; Changeling; Retrogression; Bread of Solitude; Music for Sun and Moon; Enchanted Honey; Luna; Ballad of the Seal-Woman's Daughter; Fairy Cider; King Solomon; Turning Point; Nativities; The Comet; Bird's-Eye View; December Stars; Cold Orchard; Bats; The Unclimbed Hill; The House in the Hollow; The Black Peacock; Snowy Night; Cinder-Jewels; Birds in a Barn; A Country Grave; No Refuge; Earth: Atomic Age; Daphne; To an Atheist; Cold Comfort; The Beaches Beyond Oblivion; Ballad of the Jabberwock; To One Who Fears Poetry Is Useless; Design for a Tapestry: 14th Century; To Elinor Wylie; Legend; Beyond Eden; Heard on the Roof at Midnight; Help Wanted; A Likely Story!; Leonardo Before His Canvas; Dark Memory; Snow Crystals; The Vision; Minor Poet; Old Daphne; Wild Geese in Spring; Moment at Sunset; Poplar-Wind; The Fur Coat; Honey from the Lion; The Heads on Easter Island; The Return; Song against Smallness; Willow-Women; Mad Woman's Song; Song of the Sun; The Old World of Green; Currier and Ives Prints; The False Messiah; The Unknown Land; The Green Door; After the Green Star Dies; "Like Breath upon a Glass"; The Pool; *Precarious Ground (1949–1952):* The Windows of Chartres; The Lariat: 6000 B.C.; Gifts for Christ; The Darkened Glass; Atavism; Dirge for a Doomed Planet; To Certain Poetry Critics; The Undine; Sunset Apocalypse; Kingfisher Lake; The Revenant; Cave Paintings, Altamira; The Unploughed Field; We Come Out of the Forest, Fearing Stars; The Vision of Jenghiz-Khan; Precarious Ground; Love Song; The Mermaid; Cobra; Six Merry Farmers; The Wind in the Chimney; Out!; Bookworm; A Warning to Skeptics; The Final Green; The Foam-Born; Red Ghosts in Kentucky; *An Unlikely Noah's Ark:* Wyvern; Satyr; Centaur; Pooka; Minotaur; Werewolf; Fury; Cockatrice; Chimaera; Spirit-Fox; Salamander; Ghoul; Roc; Sphinx. Overheard in Baghdad; Atlantis; The Four; The Birth of Beauty; *We Move on Turning Stone (1953–1956):* Powers of the Air; The Web; Fool's Paradise; The Enchanted Swans; Gipsies; Solar; Cat Mummy; The Jannigogs; The Middle Ages: Two Views; Semele; Childhood Summers; Railroad Tracks; The Web of Living; Air; Flemish Artists; Through-Train; The

Unicorn Wounded; Incoming Tide; Drone; We Move on Turning Stone; The Gods of the Dana; Ark; Rock and Bramble; Fairy-Tale: Twentieth Century; The Lazy Prince; The Storks; Old Man on the Seashore; Zanzibar; The Woods Grow Darker; The Crows; The Rain on the Stone; The Weeds and the Wilderness; The Well; Under Funereal Lilies; The Good-Advisors; The Crying of the Grass; Noon Light; High Wire; The Word of Willow; The Harvest; The Fawn; Moment in Paradise; Comment on Man; A Memory; The Forerunner; The Nail; Multiple Clay; The Hand; The Prisoner; *The Face in the Water (1957–1964):* The Rider; The Robin; The Hellenic World; "In the Night I Awoke"; "Brightness Falls from the Air"; Alone; "I Dreamed That You Took My Arm." . . .; Uncle Jay; Folk-Tale; The Tale of Tannhauser; Lullaby After Death; With Her Death; To Mother; Ariadne on Naxos; A Voice; The Convent Bell; "Only a Little Dust"; That Summer; Lying Awake; What the Devil Said; The Cry; [Untitled]; The Spray; On the Night-Wind; The Growing Tree; The Wasp in the Window; The Witches; A Meeting on a Northern Moor; Tarascon; Little Song; Orchids; The Snake; In the Night; The Terrible Meek; The Morning; All-Hallows; Royal; Circe; The Presence; The Face in the Water; The Eve of St. Tib; At Alise Sainte-Reine; Fairy Tale; Ask the Trees; A Back-Country Road in God's Country; The Gossip; Okio's Geese; *Alternate Readings and Unfinished Poems:* Evening in Late Summer; Unicorn; Coming Back to the House; Nativities; Gothic; Cold Orchard; Unlikely Story; Poplar Wind; Landscape with Horses: 6000 B.C.; Dirge for a Doomed Planet; Reincarnation; This Side of Oblivion; The Under-Seas; The Under-Seas; The Cytherean; Air; Adam's Hand; With Every Death; That Summer; From a destroyed early poem; "Hunter"; Adam the First Poet; From a poem to Mother; The Five Angels; A Charm for the New Year; [Untitled]; Coral Reef at Calico Key; Switzerland; in the woods of the Vaud; FICTION: Time and the Sphinx; Whisper Water; Foxy's Hollow; Mop-Head; NONFICTION: Frederic Prokosch; [Untitled judge's report]; Gremlins; Whimsy and Whamsy; The Devil and Miss Barker; Abracadabra; Miscellaneous Reviews; [On "We Come out of the Forest . . ."]; New Voices in Poetry; The New Poetry; Books and Pictures Which Influenced My Poems; Magic Casements; A Poem Should Have; To Be a Poet; Life in These United States; [*for* The Living Voice]: What Poetry Means to Me; The Web; Precarious Ground; Old Man on the Sea Shore: Morning; The Undine; The Birth of Beauty; Final Green. Foreword [to *The Various Light*]; LETTERS: *Published Letters:* To the *Chicago Sunday Tribune*; To *Hearst's International*; To *Photoplay,* "Brickbats & Bouquets"; To *Weird Tales*; Letter to *Sight and Sound*; Letter to *American Mercury*; *Unpublished Letters:* To August Derleth; To Anthony Boucher; To William Rose Benét; To Joseph Payne Brennan; To Grace and Fletcher Stewart; With Lawrence S. Thompson; To the Stuart Art Gallery; APPENDIX: [Announcement of Award]; Leah Bodine Drake Writes Volume of "Macabre" Poems; Possible Earnings on *A Hornbook for Witches*; A Hornbook for Witches [Jacket Blurb]; The Lineaments of Faerie; [From *The International Who's Who in Poetry*]; [From *The Supplement to Who's Who*, March–May 1959]; [Death Announcement]. Bibliography; Index of Titles of Poems; Index of First Lines of Poems.

Notes. Cover illustration by Cornelia Bodine Drake, the poet's mother. Interior illustrations (fifteen) by Jason C. Eckhardt. Published simultaneously in paperback and limited hardcover (200 copies, Covington Group). A towering landmark of scholarship by Schultz, who spent years examining Drake's manuscripts and early publications. Drake (1904–1964) is best known for the rare poetry volume *A Hornbook for Witches* (1950), but she published one more volume of poetry and left behind hundreds of uncollected and unpublished poems, which are gathered here for the first time. The book also contains her small body of short fiction, reviews and essays (mostly on contemporary poetry), and a generous selection of letters. The lengthy introduction by Schultz provides a detailed account of Drake's peripatetic life as well as an assessment of her literary work.

264.　*Penumbra* No. 1 (2020). EDITED BY S. T. JOSHI. 316 pp.

Contents. Editorial, by S. T. Joshi; FICTION: If Destiny Still Reigns, by Mark Samuels; The Truth about Vampires, by Curtis M. Lawson; Las Llorasangres, by Michael Parker; Static, by Belicia Rhea; The Slug, by Jon Bockes; Counter-Current, by Michael Aronovitz; The Crazy Mountains, by Dylan Henderson; The Hell of Mirrors, by Manuel Arenas; Door Skin, by Belicia Rhea; CLASSIC REPRINT: The Caves of Death, by Gertrude Atherton; NONFICTION: Icy Bleakness and Killing Sadness: The Desolating Impact of Thomas Ligotti's "The Bungalow House," by Matt Cardin; The Cosmic Scale of Elfland, by Michael D. Miller; The Idea of the North in the Fiction of Simon Strantzas, by James Goho; I Walked with a Zombie: The Tragicomic World of the Firefly Clan, by Jason V Brock; "The Terror of Solitude": The Supernatural Fiction of Edith Wharton, by John C. Tibbetts; Finding Sherlock Holmes in Weird Fiction, by Nancy Holder; Confessions, by Stefan Grabinski; "The Weird Dominions of the Infinite": Edgar Allan Poe and the Scientific Gothic, by Sorina Higgins; The Psychic Sleuth Who Survived, by Lee Weinstein; The Resurgence of a Fallen Angel: Echoes of *The Ghost Pirates* in "The Mainz Psalter," by Hubert

Van Calenbergh; Monstrous Tourism: Petromodernity in China Miéville's "Covehithe," by Rhonda Knight; John Collier: A Weird Fantasist in Jester's Motley, by Darrell Schweitzer; POETRY: Mormo, by Wade German; To Live at the Edge of a Black Hole, by John Shirley; Et in Arcadia Jack, by Adam Bolivar; The Mysteries of the Worm, by Darrell Schweitzer; *Delirium Vivens*, by Nicole Cushing; The Fantastic Flame, by Leigh Blackmore. NOTES ON CONTRIBUTORS.

Notes. Cover art by George Cotronis; cover design by Daniel V. Sauer. The first installment of a proposed annual magazine or anthology of weird fiction, criticism, and poetry. This volume contains fiction by both veterans and novices, along with articles on a wide array of weird writers from Poe to Simon Strantzas, and poetry by well-known contemporary poets.

265. CHARLES HOFFMAN AND MARC CERASINI. *Robert E. Howard: A Closer Look.* 2020. 300 pp. tpb.

Contents: Introduction; I. Howard's Life, Career, and Legacy; II. Bran Mak Morn; III. Solomon Kane; IV. King Kull; V. Conan; VI. Other Fantasies; VII. Horror Stories; VIII. Other Prose and Poetry; IX. Conclusion; Works Cited; Bibliography; Index.

Notes. Cover illustration by Rick McCollum. An exhaustive revision and expansion of a volume first published as part of the Starmont Reader's Guides series in 1987. The authors, who are among the leading authorities on Howard, supply a broad overview of his life and then examine the various story cycles focusing around superheroes (Conan, King Kull, Solomon Kane, etc.); they also discuss his horror tales and poetry.

266. BENJAMIN BLAKE. *Tenebrae in Aeternum: A Collection of Stygian Verse.* 2020. 138 pp. tpb.

Contents. Introduction, by S. T. Joshi; A Note on the Text; Overture; The Gates of Hell Stand Open Once More; Crematorium; A Prayer to Brother Bacchus; Goetic Demons in Popular Culture; Burning Coffins; I Am One with the Dead Trees & Razorblade Winters; Est Scientia Dei; Like Knives; Sycamores; The Nightmare Card; Funeral Attire; Stolen Hearse; Anatomy of a Teenage Prostitute; Carnal House; Mayflowers; Jaguar; Valentine for a Vixen; Ever So Faint; The Isle; Pioneer Cemetery; Dago Red; And Jesus Wept . . .; Glossolalia; St. Catherine's; Executing the Vivian Girls; Scissors; Esoteric Symbolism; The Charlotte Wheel; Letter-Wrench; Dead Bird; Pulsator; Circle of Salt; Uncertain Death; Visage; A Sunken Star; Theatre of War;

The Grand Chancellor; Dead Night; It, Too, Will Fade; Elderflower; Lychgate; A Hole in the Ground; The Sound of Reality Breaking; Exposure; Baphomet with a Broken Horn; Weepers; Bedlam; Mr. Scarley; Captivated; Vampirism; Test Strip; Fire Cleanses All; A City, a Tomb; Hades; Campanile; An Older Hell; Cornicello; Recidivation; Bróðorlufu; Swamp Thing; Death Omens; Phantasm; Lucifuge; The Forsaken; An Attic, Sealed Like a Tomb; Paper Skeletons; Like Flowers for the Dead; Somewhere, Something; Lucia; Gravemarker; Phantom Breeze; Chimerical; The Oaks Are Turning Red; Dog Rose; Lake of Remembrance; Draped Urn; Succubus; No Light; Soft Focus; Meretricious; Cypress, Cedar, and Pine; Viaticum; Swarm; God's Half Acre; The Seasons Stutter; Meet Me in the Abyss; Black Lake Wolf; Maple Street Serenade; The Killings Stopped; Winchester; Pride of the Hometown; Spent Shells; The Lost Art of Getting Lost; Autumn Harvest/Samhain; A Modern Life Cut Short; Kill Me; The Otherside of Suicide; Sexton; With Gnarled Hands; The Patron Saint of the Sepulchre; Only a Lifetime to Go; Under a Blood-Red Sky, I Weep; What Happens When the Fire Keeper Fails?; Slashing Wrists with Stained-Glass; Black Adepts; Son of Serpents; Perdition; Doom Painting; Catherine Wheel; For Hope, Despair; Necrology; The Missing Tower; Strange, the Way the Sentences Seem to Scatter Like Boneyard Leaves in the October Wind; Threnody.

Notes. Cover photograph of Lola Zaza Crowley. A scintillating volume of poetry, mostly free verse, that draws upon familiar weird topics in an innovative fashion, with an emphasis on the "eternal feminine." A follow-up to Blake's earlier volume, *Standing on the Threshold of Madness* (2017).

267.   H. P. LOVECRAFT. *Letters to Rheinhart Kleiner and Others.* Edited by S. T. Joshi and David E. Schultz. 2020. 544 pp.

Contents. INTRODUCTION; LETTERS: To Rheinhart Kleiner; To Arthur Harris; To James Larkin Pearson; To Winifred V. Jackson; To Arthur Leeds; To Paul J. Campbell; APPENDIX: *Poems by Rheinhart Kleiner:* Alas!; Dream Days; or, Metrical Musings; Another Endless Day; Motes; At Providence in 1918; Brooklyn, My Brooklyn; Epistle to Mr. and Mrs. Lovecraft; The Four of Us!; After a Decade; H. P. L.; *Essays by Rheinhart Kleiner:* A Note on Howard P. Lovecraft's Verse; The Kleicomolo; After a Decade and the Kalem Club; Howard Phillips Lovecraft; Lovecraft in Brooklyn; Some Lovecraft Memories; *Rheinhart Kleiner vs. H. P. Lovecraft:* To Mary of the Movies; To Charlie of the Comics; To a Movie Star; To Mistress Sophia Simple, Queen of the Cinema; Grace; Ruth; John Oldham: 1653–1683; John Oldham:

A Defence; Ethel: Cashier in a Broad Street Buffet; Cindy: Scrub-Lady in a State Street Skyscraper; On Collaboration; *Poems by H. P. Lovecraft Addressed to Rheinhart Kleiner:* The Bookstall; Content; To Mr. Kleiner, on Receiving from Him the Poetical Works of Addison, Gay, and Somerville; R. Kleiner, Laureatus, in Heliconem; To Rheinhart Kleiner, Esq., Upon His Town Fables and Elegies; [On Rheinhart Kleiner Being Hit by an Automobile]; *Arthur Harris:* The Birth of British Amateur Journalism; Charles Dickens; *James Larkin Pearson:* You Jes' as Well Laugh as to Cry; Fifty Acres; Contemplations; When Inspiration Fails; The Poetry fer Me; The River and the Sea; The Lives of Men; The Grave-Tree; Israel; The Secret of Attainment; *Winifred Virginia Jackson:* Song of the North Wind; Galileo and Swammerdam; April; In Morven's Mead; The Night Wind Bared My Heart; Insomnia; The Pool; The Vagrant; On Shore; April Shadows; Who Will Fare With Me?; The Cobbler in the Moon; Finality; The Tricksy Tune; Eyes; Deafness; Hoofin' It; The Purchase; Have You Met My Buddy?; That I Might Be in the Cool Blue Wind; *Arthur Leeds:* The Man Who Shunned the Light; *Paul J. Campbell:* Ideals of the Amateur; A Representative Official Organ; Adventures in Amateur Journalism; The Alumni and the United Amateur Press Association; Going to a Funeral; The Joke Was On the White Man; The Good Will of a Dog; This Ain't Love; Founding the Fraternity of the Wooden Leg; *W. Paul Cook:* The United Amateur Press Association—An Historical Survey: 1895–1912; An Historical Survey: 1915 (by Paul J. Campbell); GLOSSARY OF FREQUENTLY MENTIONED NAMES; BIBLIOGRAPHY; INDEX.

Notes. Cover design by Anastasia Damianakos. A reprint of *Letters to Alfred Galpin* (no. 25), although omitting the letters to the Kleicomolo, and augmented by letters to other correspondents.

268.   CLARK ASHTON SMITH AND AUGUST DERLETH. *Eccentric, Impractical Devils: The Letters of August Derleth and Clark Ashton Smith.* Edited by David E. Schultz and S. T. Joshi. 2019. 601 pp. tpb.

Contents. Introduction; ECCENTRIC, IMPRACTICAL DEVILS [letters]; August Derleth and Carol Smith: Extracts from Letters; APPENDIX: Letter from *Revue des Deux Mondes*; Local Boy Makes Good; More Anent Auburn Poet; Auburn Artist-Poet Utilizes Native Rock in Sculptures; Ms. Enclosures Smith Sent to Derleth [WHS]; Other Mss. Sent to Derleth [WHS]; Lists of Carvings by Smith: Checklist: The Carvings of Clark Ashton Smith; Other Checklists. From *The Poets Sing Frontiers*, by August Derleth; The New Books: Things That Bump, by August

Derleth; Prose Reviews, by Lilith Lorraine; Smith's Earnings on Arkham House Books. Glossary of Frequently Mentioned Names; BIBLIOGRAPHY; INDEX.

Notes. Cover illustration and design by Jason Van Hollander. First publication of the complete extant joint correspondence of Smith and Derleth, extending from 1930 to Smith's death in 1961. The letters provide fascinating glimpses into each author's literary production, the founding and operation of Arkham House, the work of H. P. Lovecraft, and other subjects. A small number of copies were distributed with the order of names in the subtitle reversed.

269.   ARTHUR MACHEN. *Autobiographical Writings.* Edited by S. T. Joshi 2020. 481 pp. tpb.

Contents. INTRODUCTION; FAR OFF THINGS; THINGS NEAR AND FAR; THE LONDON ADVENTURE; OR, THE ART OF WANDERING; SUPPLEMENTARY ESSAYS: Strange Roads; With the Gods in Spring; Sixty Years Since; A Lament for London's Lost Inns; One Night When I Was Frightened; The Ready Reporter; The Treasure of the Humble; My Murderer; PRECIOUS BALMS: [Preface]; *The Great God Pan* and *The Three Impostors*; *Hieroglyphics*; *The House of Souls*; *The Hill of Dreams*; *The Secret Glory*; *Far Off Things* and *Things Near and Far*; *Dog and Duck*; The Other Side; APPENDIX: Eleusinia; Beneath the Barley: A Note on the Origins of *Eleusinia*; Introductory Letter to "Confessions of a Literary Man"; BIBLIOGRAPHY; INDEX.

Notes. Cover design by Daniel V. Sauer, incorporating a photograph of Machen. An omnibus of Machen's autobiographies, *Far Off Things* (1922), *Things Near and Far* (1923), and *The London Adventure* (1924), along with other autobiographical essays, the volume *Precious Balms* (1924; a collection of the reviews—many of them unfavorable—that Machen received over a lifetime), and the early poem *Eleusinia* (1881).

270.   *Dead Reckonings* No. 28 (Fall 2020). EDITED BY ALEX HOUSTOUN AND MICHAEL J. ABOLAFIA. 118 pp.

Contents. An Up-and-Comer, by Darrell Schweitzer [Stephen Woodworth, *A Carnival of Chimeras*]; *Lovecraft Country*: A Bumpy But Enjoyable Ride, by Greg Gbur; A Weird Tarot Deck, by Michael D. Miller [Richard Gavin, *Grotesquerie*]; Legerdemain at The Last, by The joey Zone [Ann and Jeff VanderMeer, *The Big Book of Modern Fantasy*]; *Dark*'s Gothic Use of Time Travel, by Karen Joan Kohoutek; Other Worlds, Other Voices, by Daniel Pietersen [Melissa Edmundson, ed., *Women's Weird 2. More Strange Stories by Women, 1891–1937*]; Ramsey's Rant: The Urge To Splurge, by Ramsey Campbell; Sharpening a Dulled Blade: A Conversation with Jason Carney, Editor of *Whetstone*, by Alex Houstoun; "A Monstrous Rhapsody on Otherness," by Jerome Winter [James Goho, *Caitlín R. Kiernan: A Critical Study of Her Dark Fiction*]; Ambiguous to a Fault, by Géza A. G. Reilly [Michael Griffin, *Armageddon House*]; A Trade in Futures, by Dan Raskin; Starlight in One's Hand, by The joey Zone [Leah Bodine Drake, *The Song of The Sun: Collected Writings*]; Nodens in the Nutmeg State, by Edward Guimont [Sam Gafford, *The House of Nodens*]; Sandalwood and Jade: The Weird and Fantastic Verse of Lin Carter, by Leigh Blackmore; June Ruins Everything, by June Pulliam [Short Reviews of Streaming Horror Film and Television for the Covid Era]; *Devil's Night* Investigated: An Interview with Curtis M. Lawson, by Géza A. G. Reilly; The Light That Never Warms, by Michael D. Miller [*The Lighthouse*, dir. Robert Eggers]; About the Contributors.

271.   AMBROSE BIERCE. *Collected Fiction, Volume 1: Tales of Psychological and Supernatural Horror.* Edited by S. T. Joshi. 2020. 375 pp. tpb.

Contents. INTRODUCTION; The Discomfited Demon; The Haunted Valley; The Night-Doings at "Deadman's"; The Famous Gilson Bequest; A Psychological Shipwreck; A Holy Terror; An Inhabitant of Carcosa; The Man out of the Nose; Bodies of the Dead; Bodies of the Dead; Hither from Hades; Behind the Veil; Whither?; One of Twins; Two Haunted Houses; The Suitable Surroundings; A Watcher by the Dead; The Man and the Snake; The Realm of the Unreal; The Middle Toe of the Right Foot; Haïta the Shepherd; A Lady from Redhorse; The Boarded Window; The Secret of Macarger's Gulch; The Thing at Nolan; A Baby Tramp; The Death of Halpin Frayser; An Adventure at Brownville, with Ina Lillian Peterson; The Applicant; John Bartine's Watch; The Damned Thing; A Jug of Sirup; The Eyes of the Panther; Moxon's Master; At Old Man Eckert's; A Diagnosis of Death; A Vine on a House; A Man with Two Lives; A Wireless Message; An Arrest; One Summer Night; John Mortonson's Funeral, with Leigh Bierce; The Moonlit Road; Beyond the Wall; The Stranger; An Untitled Tale; APPENDIX A: VARIANT TEXTS: Bodies of the Dead; Present at a Hanging; A Fruitless Assignment; The Isle of Pines; A Cold Greeting; The Difficulty of Crossing a Field; An Unfinished Race; Charles Ashmore's Trail; The Spook House; A Doppelganger; APPENDIX B: BIERCE ON HIS FICTION: Preface to Bubbles Like Us; Preface to Can Such Things Be?; [Prefatory Note to "The Ways of Ghosts"]; BIBLIOGRAPHY.

Notes. Cover design by Kevin Slaughter, based on a drawing of Bierce from *Wasp* (13 May 1893) by P. M. Boeringer. The first of a three-volume series of Bierce's collected fiction, largely derived (but without the scholarly apparatus) from *The Short Fiction of Ambrose Bierce: A Comprehensive Edition* (University of Tennessee Press, 2006; 3 vols.). In that edition the stories were arranged chronologically; here the stories are arranged thematically.

272.   AMBROSE BIERCE. *Collected Fiction, Volume 2: Tales of the Civil War and Tales of the Grotesque.* Edited by S. T. Joshi. 2020. 406 pp. tpb.

Contents. INTRODUCTION; I. TALES OF THE CIVIL WAR: George Thurston; Jupiter Doke, Brigadier-General; Killed at Resaca; One of the Missing; A Son of the Gods; A Tough Tussle; Chickamauga; One Officer, One Man; A Horseman in the Sky; The Coup de Grâce; The Affair at Coulter's Notch; The Major's Tale; The Story of a Conscience; An Occurrence at Owl Creek Bridge; Parker Adderson, Philosopher; The Mocking-Bird; One Kind of Officer; An Affair of Outposts; A Baffled Ambuscade; Two Military Executions; The Other Lodgers; A Resumed Identity; Three and One Are One; II. TALES OF THE GROTESQUE: Dr. Deadwood, I Presume; The Magician's Little Joke; Nut-Cracking; Sundered Hearts; A Fowl Witch; A Tale of Spanish Vengeance; Juniper; Four Jacks and a Knave; Seafaring; No Charge for Attendance; Feodora; A Tale of the Bosphorus; The Grateful Bear; The Early History of Bath; Converting a Prodigal; The Civil Service in Florida; Mrs. Dennison's Head; Pernicketty's Fright; Following the Sea; Tony Rollo's Conclusion; "The Following Dorg"; Maumee's Mission; Snaking; Maud's Papa; Jim Beckwourth's Pond; How to Saw Bears; Jo Dornan and the Ram; How I Came to Like Dogs; Mr. Jim Beckwourth's Adventure; A Providential Intimation; The Baptism of Dobsho; Perry Chumly's Eclipse; Stringing a Bear; Curried Cow; The Captain of the *Camel*; Boarding a Bear; The Following Bear; A Cargo of Cat; An Imperfect Conflagration; My Credentials; A Revolt of the Gods; A Bottomless Grave; Hades in Trouble; My Favorite Murder; The City of the Gone Away; His Waterloo; Burbank's Crime; Oil of Dog; The Widower Turmore; The Hypnotist; APPENDIX: Preface to *Tales of Soldiers and Civilians*; Preface to *In the Midst of Life*; BIBLIOGRAPHY.

Notes. Cover design by Kevin Slaughter, based on a drawing of Bierce from *Wasp* (13 May 1893) by P. M. Boeringer. The second of a three-volume set of Bierce's collected fiction.

273.   AMBROSE BIERCE. *Collected Fiction, Volume 3: Tall Tales and Satirical Sketches; Political Fantasies and Future Histories.* Edited by S. T. Joshi. 2020. 366 pp. tpb.

Contents. INTRODUCTION. I. TALL TALES AND SATIRICAL SKETCHES: The New Bedder; Samuel Baxter, M.D.; Jeph Benedick's Grandmother; The Sanctity of an Oath; A Remarkable Adventure; The Dempsters; Authenticating a Ghost; Banking at Mexican Hill; To Fiji and Return; Concerning Balloons; Two Stories about Johnson; A Champion of the Sex; Why I Am Not Editing "The Stinger"; Corrupting the Press; The Evolution of a Story; Mr. Barcle's Mill; Little Larry; My Muse; Confessions of a Sad Dog; The Wreck of the Orion; The Late John Sweetbosh, Esq.; Largo al Gapperino; The Race at Left Bower; A Literary Riot; A Shipwreckollection; Perry Chumly's Eclipse; Mr. Masthead, Journalist; Mr. Swiddler's Flip-Flap; The Lion at Bay; The Little Story; The Failure of Hope & Wandel; The Miraculous Guest; A Representative Inquest; Storm and Sunshine; An Upper Class Misdemeanant; A Holiday Experience; The Man Overboard; Sam Baxter's Eel; "A Bad Woman"; That Dog; "By Her Own Hand"; Infernia; A Mirage in Arizona; The History of Windbag the Sailor; "The Bubble Reputation"; A Story at the Club; The A. L. C. B.; The Alternative Proposal; II. POLITICAL FANTASIES AND FUTURE HISTORIES; Letters from a Hdkhoite; The Aborigines of Oakland; A Scientific Dream; Across the Continent; John Smith, Liberator; For the Ahkoond; The Wizard of Bumbassa; The Great Strike of 1895; Annals of the Future Historian; The Maid of Podunk; The Extinction of the Smugwumps; Industrial Discontent in Ancient America; The Future Historian and His Fatigue; A Chronicle of the Time to Be; Rise and Fall of the Aëroplane; The Dispersal; An Ancient Hunter; A Leaf Blown In from Days to Be; Ashes of the Beacon; The Land Beyond the Blow; Thither; Sons of the Fair Star; An Interview with Gnarmag-Zote; The Tamtonians; Marooned on Ug; The Dog in Ganegwag; A Conflagration in Ghargaroo; An Execution in Batrugia; The Jumjum of Gokeetle-guk; The Kingdom of Tortirra; Hither; APPENDIX: The *Jeannette* and the *Corwin.* BIBLIOGRAPHY.

Notes. Cover design by Kevin Slaughter, based on a drawing of Bierce from *Wasp* (13 May 1893) by P. M. Boeringer. The third of a three-volume set of Bierce's collected fiction.

274.   CLARK ASHTON SMITH. *The Averoigne Chronicles: The Complete Averoigne Stories of Clark Ashton Smith*. Edited by Ron Hilger. 2020. 284 pp. tpb.

Contents. Introduction; A Note on the Text; Averoigne; A Night In Malnéant; The Nevermore-to-be; The Maker of Gargoyles; The Broken Lute; The Holiness of Azédarac; In Cocaigne; The Colossus of Ylourgne; Necromancy; The Enchantress of Sylaire; Amithaine; The Beast of Averoigne; Song of the Necromancer; Mother of Toads; The Witch with Eyes of Amber; A Rendezvous in Averoigne; The Dark Château; The Mandrakes; Canticle; The Satyr; Cambion; The Disinterment of Venus; "O Golden-Tongued Romance"; The End of the Story; To Klarkash-Ton, Lord of Averoigne; Averoigne: An Afterword, by Donald Sidney-Fryer; Acknowledgments.

Notes. Cover and interior art by David Ho.

275.   DERRICK HUSSEY, S. T. JOSHI, AND DAVID E. SCHULTZ. *Twenty Years of Hippocampus Press: 2000–2020*. 2020. 230 pp. tpb.

Contents. Foreword, by Derrick Hussey; My Years with Hippocampus Press, by S. T. Joshi; Publications of Hippocampus Press: 2000–2020; Index of Authors, Editors, and Artists.

Notes. Cover illustration and design by Daniel V. Sauer. An expanded version of item 174.

Index of Titles

Index of Authors, Editors, and Artists

Numbers refer to item, not to page.

Hodgson, William Hope 116, 123n, 146n
Hoffman, Charles 34, 265
Hogg, James 116
Holder, Nancy 264
Holland-Toll, Linda J. 3
Holmes, Daniel 172
Holmes, Oliver Wendell 116
Hölzing, Roland 92
Homer 116
Hood, Thomas 116
Hopkins-Drewer, Cecelia 220, 232, 238, 249, 261. *See also* Drewer, Cecelia
Horace 116, 129
Housman, A. E. 116
Houstoun, Alex 92, 195, 210, 215, 226, 229, 247, 255, 270
Howard, John 242
Howard, Robert E. 34n, 68, 91, 116, 204, 265
Hughes, Martin 41
Hughes, Rhys 147
Hughes, William 97
Hugo, Victor 37n, 116
Huling, Ray 236
Hussey, Derrick 86, 174, 275

Hutter, Michael 234

Ibarbarou, Juana de 37n
Indick, Ben P. 40, 45, 52, 59, 64
Ivaska, Gaile 20

Jaffe, Matthew 239, 240, 241
Jackson, Jennifer Ruth 187
Jackson, Joseph Henry 85
Jackson, Winifred Virginia 204
Jacobs, W. W. 218
Jaffe, Matthew 163
James, M. R. 41n, 97, 123n
Jamneck, Lynne 110
Jarvis, Timothy J. 242

Jeffrey, Michelle 222, 249
joey Zone, The 226, 247, 270
Johnson, Clay F. 189
Johnson, Erik T. 219
Johnson, George Clayton 155
Johnson, Hal 219
Johnson, Jonathan 79, 133, 151
Johnson, Ron L., II 232
Jones, Haydon 46
Jordan, Stephen J. 4
Joshi, S. T. 1, 2, 3, 4, 5, 7, 8, 9, 10, 11, 13, 14, 15, 16, 17, 18, 19, 20, 21, 22, 23, 25, 26, 28, 29, 30, 32, 33, 34, 36, 37, 38, 40, 41, 44, 45, 46, 48, 50, 52, 54, 56, 57, 58, 59, 61, 64, 65, 66, 67, 68, 71, 72, 75, 78, 79, 80, 81, 82, 85, 86, 87, 88, 89, 90, 91, 92, 95, 101, 102, 103, 110, 112, 113, 114, 116, 117, 118, 119, 121, 123, 124, 129, 130, 131, 133, 134, 136, 137, 139, 140, 141, 144, 145, 146, 149, 151, 154, 155, 159, 162, 164, 165, 166, 167, 168, 169, 170, 171, 174, 176, 177, 180, 181, 182, 186, 187, 188, 189, 191, 192, 195, 199, 200, 202, 204, 205, 206, 210, 211, 212, 213, 214, 215, 216, 217, 218, 220, 222, 223, 224, 225, 226, 228, 229, 232, 235, 237, 238, 239, 240, 241, 242, 243, 245, 247, 249, 251, 252, 253, 255, 257, 258, 259, 260, 261, 264, 266, 267, 268, 269, 271, 272, 273, 275

Keats, John 116
Keil, Paul Livingston 85
Kelly, Michael 154
Kent, Josh 152

221

HIPPOCAMPUS PRESS derives its name from H. P. Lovecraft's term of address (used thrice), in unpublished parts of letters to Frank Belknap Long, of which the following (from 6 April 1923) is representative: "be a nice little amethystine hippocampus, write your Old Grandpa, and prepare to visit Providentia's sequester'd shades when the sun is warm and genial."

www.ingramcontent.com/pod-product-compliance
Lightning Source LLC
Chambersburg PA
CBHW060741050426
42449CB00008B/1283